Mastering OpenCV
Third Edition

A comprehensive guide to building computer vision and image processing applications with C++

Roy Shilkrot
David Millán Escrivá

BIRMINGHAM - MUMBAI

Mastering OpenCV 4
Third Edition

Commissioning Editor: Aaron Lazar
Acquisition Editor: Shahnish Khan
Content Development Editor: Zeeyan Pinheiro
Technical Editor: Ketan Kamble
Copy Editor: Safis Editing
Project Coordinator: Vaidehi Sawant
Proofreader: Safis Editing
Indexer: Pratik Shirodkar
Graphics: Alishon Mendonsa
Production Coordinator: Jisha Chirayil

First published: December 2012
Second edition: April 2017
Third edition: December 2018

Production reference: 1221218

Published by Packt Publishing Ltd.
Livery Place
35 Livery Street
Birmingham
B3 2PB, UK.

ISBN 978-1-78953-357-6

www.packtpub.com

To my dearest wife, Inbal, and my daughters, Roni and Noam, for being both my wings and my anchor, and for their incredible ability to know which one of the two I need at any given moment. Thank you, I love you. To my family, Asia, Baruch, Liraz, and Orit, for your endless loving support.

– Roy Shilkrot

To my wife, Izaskun, my daughter, Eider, and my son, Pau, for their unlimited patience and support at all times. They have changed my life and made it awesome every day. Love you all. I would like to thank the OpenCV team and community, for this wonderful library, and my coauthors and Packt, for supporting and helping me complete this book.

- David Millán Escrivá

`mapt.io`

Mapt is an online digital library that gives you full access to over 5,000 books and videos, as well as industry leading tools to help you plan your personal development and advance your career. For more information, please visit our website.

Why subscribe?

- Spend less time learning and more time coding with practical eBooks and videos from over 4,000 industry professionals

- Improve your learning with Skill Plans built especially for you

- Get a free eBook or video every month

- Mapt is fully searchable

- Copy and paste, print, and bookmark content

Packt.com

Did you know that Packt offers eBook versions of every book published, with PDF and ePub files available? You can upgrade to the eBook version at `www.packt.com` and as a print book customer, you are entitled to a discount on the eBook copy. Get in touch with us at `customercare@packtpub.com` for more details.

At `www.packt.com`, you can also read a collection of free technical articles, sign up for a range of free newsletters, and receive exclusive discounts and offers on Packt books and eBooks.

Contributors

About the authors

Roy Shilkrot is an assistant professor of computer science at Stony Brook University, where he leads the Human Interaction group. Dr. Shilkrot's research is in computer vision, human-computer interfaces, and the cross-over between these two domains, funded by US federal, New York State, and industry grants. Dr. Shilkrot graduated from the **Massachusetts Institute of Technology (MIT)** with a PhD, and has authored more than 25 peer-reviewed papers published at premier computer science conferences, such as CHI and SIGGRAPH, as well as in leading academic journals such as ACM **Transaction on Graphics (TOG)** and ACM **Transactions on Computer-Human Interaction (ToCHI)**. Dr. Shilkrot is also a co-inventor of several patented technologies, a co-author of a number of books, serves on the scientific advisory board of numerous start-up companies, and has over 10 years of experience as an engineer and an entrepreneur.

David Millán Escrivá was eight years old when he wrote his first program on an 8086 PC in Basic, which enabled the 2D plotting of basic equations. In 2005, he finished his studies in IT through the Universitat Politécnica de Valenci with honors in human-computer interaction supported by computer vision with OpenCV (v0.96). He had a final project based on this subject and published it on HCI Spanish congress. He has worked with Blender, an open source, 3D software project, and worked on his first commercial movie, *Plumiferos - Aventuras voladoras*, as a computer graphics software developer. David now has more than 10 years of experience in IT, with experience in computer vision, computer graphics, and pattern recognition, working with different projects and start-ups, applying his knowledge of computer vision, optical character recognition, and augmented reality. He is the author of the *DamilesBlog* blog, where he publishes research articles and tutorials about OpenCV, computer vision in general, and optical character recognition algorithms.

About the reviewers

Arun Ponnusamy works as a senior computer vision engineer at a start-up (OIC Apps) in India. He is a lifelong learner, passionate about image processing, computer vision and machine learning. He is an engineering graduate from PSG College of Technology, Coimbatore. He started his career at MulticoreWare Inc., where he spent most of his time on image processing, OpenCV, software optimization, and GPU computing.

Arun loves to understand computer vision concepts clearly and explain them in an intuitive way on his blog. He has created an open source Python library for computer vision named `cvlib`, which is aimed at simplicity and user-friendliness. He is currently researching object detection, generative networks, and reinforcement learning.

> *I would like to thank acquisition editor Shahnish Khan and project coordinator Vaidehi Sawant for providing me the opportunity to help improve the content of this book and for all the encouraging words.*

Marc Amberg is an experienced machine learning and computer vision engineer with a proven history of working in the IT and service industries. He is skilled in Python, C/C++, OpenGL, 3D reconstruction, and Java. He is a strong engineering professional with a master's degree in computer science (image, vision, and interactions) from Université des Sciences et Technologies de Lille (Lille I).

Vikas Gupta is a computer vision researcher with a master's degree in this domain from India's premier institute: Indian Institute of Science. His research interests are in the field of machine perception, scene understanding, deep learning and robotics.

He has been working in this field in various roles including lecturer, software engineer and data scientist. He is passionate about teaching and sharing knowledge. He has spent 3 years teaching computer vision, embedded systems, and robotics to undergraduate students, and over 3 years working on various projects involving deep learning and computer vision. He has also co-authored a computer vision course at LearnOpenCV.

Packt is searching for authors like you

If you're interested in becoming an author for Packt, please visit `authors.packtpub.com` and apply today. We have worked with thousands of developers and tech professionals, just like you, to help them share their insight with the global tech community. You can make a general application, apply for a specific hot topic that we are recruiting an author for, or submit your own idea.

Table of Contents

Preface

Mastering OpenCV, now in its third edition, is a book series targeting computer vision engineers in their first steps in using OpenCV as a tool. Keeping the mathematical formulations to a solid but bare minimum, the book delivers complete projects from ideation to running code, targeting current hot topics in computer vision including face recognition, landmark detection and pose estimation, number recognition with deep convolutional networks, structure from motion and scene reconstruction for augmented reality, and mobile phone computer vision in native and web environments. This book brings together the vast knowledge of the authors in implementing computer vision products and projects, both in academia and in industry, in a comfortable package. It takes readers through an explanation of the API functionality, while providing insights into design choices in a complete computer vision project, and elevates beyond the basics of computer vision to implement solutions for complex image recognition projects.

Who this book is for

This book is targeted at novice computer vision engineers looking to get started with OpenCV, mostly in a C++ environment, with a hands-on approach as opposed to a traditional ground-up knowledge construction. It provides concrete use case examples of the OpenCV API with regard to current common computer vision tasks, while encouraging copy-paste-run and trying to keep the mathematical fundamentals to the bare minimum.

Computer vision engineers nowadays have a wide range of tools and packages to choose from, including OpenCV, dlib, Matlab packages, SimpleCV, XPCV, and scikit-image. None provide better coverage and cross-platform functionality than OpenCV. However, getting started with OpenCV may seem daunting, with many thousands of functions in the official modules' API alone, excluding contributed modules. While many documenting projects exist, beyond OpenCV's own extensive tutorial offerings, most do not cater for an engineer looking to go from start to finish on a project.

What this book covers

This book covers much of the functionality in OpenCV, including many contributed modules, either directly by means of a dedicated chapter, or indirectly through the code and text of a chapter. It also provides an opportunity to use OpenCV on the web, on an iOS and Android device, as well as in a Python Jupyter Notebook. Each chapter approaches a different problem and provides a complete, buildable, and runnable code example of how to achieve it, alongside a walkthrough of the solution and its theoretical context.

The book is structured to offer readers the following:

- Working OpenCV code samples for contemporary, non-trivial computer vision problems
- Best practices in engineering and maintaining OpenCV projects
- Pragmatic, algorithmic design approaches for complex computer vision tasks
- Familiarity with OpenCV's most up-to-date API (v4.0.0) hands-on by example

The following chapters are covered in this book:

Chapter 1, *Cartoonifier and Skin Color Analysis on the RaspberryPi*, demonstrates how to write some image processing filters for desktops and for small embedded systems such as Raspberry Pi.

Chapter 2, *Explore Structure from Motion with the SfM Module*, demonstrates how to use the SfM module to reconstruct a scene to a sparse point cloud, including camera poses, and also obtain a dense point cloud using multi-view stereo.

Chapter 3, *Face Landmark and Pose with the Face Module*, explains the process of face landmark (also known as facemark) detection using the face module.

Chapter 4, *Number Plate Recognition with Deep Convolutional Networks*, introduces image segmentation and feature extraction, pattern recognition basics, and two important pattern recognition algorithms, the **Support Vector Machine (SVM)** and **deep neural network (DNN)**.

Chapter 5, *Face Detection and Recognition with the DNN Module*, demonstrates different techniques for detecting faces on the images, ranging from more classic algorithms using cascade classifiers with Haar features through to newer techniques employing deep learning.

Chapter 6, *Introduction to Web Computer Vision with OpenCV.js*, demonstrates a new way to develop computer vision algorithms for the web using OpenCV.js, a compiled version of OpenCV for JavaScript.

Chapter 7, *Android Camera Calibration and AR Using the ArUco Module*, shows how to implement an **augmented reality** (**AR**) application in the Android ecosystem, using OpenCV's ArUco module, Android's Camera2 APIs, and the JMonkeyEngine 3D game engine.

Chapter 8, *iOS Panoramas with the Stitching Module*, shows how to build a panoramic image stitching application on the iPhone using OpenCV's precompiled library for iOS.

Chapter 9, *Finding the Best OpenCV Algorithm for the Job*, discusses a number of methods to follow when considering options within OpenCV.

Chapter 10, *Avoiding Common Pitfalls in OpenCV*, reviews the historic development of OpenCV, and the gradual increase in the framework and algorithmic offering, alongside the development of computer vision at large.

To get the most out of this book

The book assumes that readers have a firm grasp of programming concepts and software engineering skills, building and running software from scratch in C++. The book also features code in JavaScript, Python, Java, and Swift. Engineers looking to dive deeper into those sections will benefit from programming language knowledge beyond C++.

Readers of this book should be able to obtain an installation of OpenCV in its various flavors. Some chapters will require a Python, others an Android, installation. Obtaining these and installing them is discussed thoroughly in the accompanying code and in the text.

Download the example code files

You can download the example code files for this book from your account at www.packt.com. If you purchased this book elsewhere, you can visit www.packt.com/support and register to have the files emailed directly to you.

You can download the code files by following these steps:

1. Log in or register at www.packt.com.
2. Select the **SUPPORT** tab.
3. Click on **Code Downloads & Errata**.
4. Enter the name of the book in the **Search** box and follow the onscreen instructions.

Once the file is downloaded, please make sure that you unzip or extract the folder using the latest version of:

- WinRAR/7-Zip for Windows
- Zipeg/iZip/UnRarX for Mac
- 7-Zip/PeaZip for Linux

The code bundle for the book is also hosted on GitHub at `https://github.com/PacktPublishing/Mastering-OpenCV-4-Third-Edition`. In case there's an update to the code, it will be updated on the existing GitHub repository.

We also have other code bundles from our rich catalog of books and videos available at `https://github.com/PacktPublishing/`. Check them out!

Download the color images

We also provide a PDF file that has color images of the screenshots/diagrams used in this book. You can download it here: `http://www.packtpub.com/sites/default/files/downloads/9781789533576_ColorImages.pdf`.

Conventions used

There are a number of text conventions used throughout this book.

`CodeInText`: Indicates code words in text, database table names, folder names, filenames, file extensions, pathnames, dummy URLs, user input, and Twitter handles. Here is an example: "To see the remaining space on your SD card, run `df -h | head -2`."

A block of code is set as follows:

```
Mat bigImg;
  resize(smallImg, bigImg, size, 0,0, INTER_LINEAR);
  dst.setTo(0);
  bigImg.copyTo(dst, mask);
```

When we wish to draw your attention to a particular part of a code block, the relevant lines or items are set in bold:

```
Mat bigImg;
  resize(smallImg, bigImg, size, 0,0, INTER_LINEAR);
  dst.setTo(0);
  bigImg.copyTo(dst, mask);
```

Any command-line input or output is written as follows:

```
sudo apt-get purge -y wolfram-engine
```

Bold: Indicates a new term, an important word, or words that you see on screen. For example, words in menus or dialog boxes appear in the text like this. Here is an example: "Navigate to **Media | Open Network Stream**."

Warnings or important notes appear like this.

Tips and tricks appear like this.

Get in touch

Feedback from our readers is always welcome.

General feedback: If you have questions about any aspect of this book, mention the book title in the subject of your message and email us at customercare@packtpub.com.

Errata: Although we have taken every care to ensure the accuracy of our content, mistakes do happen. If you have found a mistake in this book, we would be grateful if you would report this to us. Please visit www.packt.com/submit-errata, selecting your book, clicking on the Errata Submission Form link, and entering the details.

Piracy: If you come across any illegal copies of our works in any form on the internet, we would be grateful if you would provide us with the location address or website name. Please contact us at copyright@packt.com with a link to the material.

If you are interested in becoming an author: If there is a topic that you have expertise in, and you are interested in either writing or contributing to a book, please visit authors.packtpub.com.

Reviews

Please leave a review. Once you have read and used this book, why not leave a review on the site that you purchased it from? Potential readers can then see and use your unbiased opinion to make purchase decisions, we at Packt can understand what you think about our products, and our authors can see your feedback on their book. Thank you!

For more information about Packt, please visit `packt.com`.

Cartoonifier and Skin Color Analysis on the RaspberryPi

1

This chapter will show how to write some image processing filters for desktops and for small embedded systems such as Raspberry Pi. First, we develop for the desktop (in C/C++) and then port the project to Raspberry Pi, since this is the recommended scenario when developing for embedded devices. This chapter will cover the following topics:

- How to convert a real-life image to a sketch drawing
- How to convert to a painting and overlay the sketch to produce a cartoon
- A scary evil mode to create bad characters instead of good characters
- A basic skin detector and skin color changer, to give someone green alien skin
- Finally, how to create an embedded system based on our desktop application

Note that an **embedded system** is basically a computer motherboard placed inside a product or device, designed to perform specific tasks, and **Raspberry Pi** is a very low-cost and popular motherboard for building an embedded system:

The preceding picture shows what you could make after this chapter: a battery-powered Raspberry Pi plus screen you could wear to Comic Con, turning everyone into a cartoon!

We want to make the real-world camera frames automatically look like they are from a cartoon. The basic idea is to fill the flat parts with some color and then draw thick lines on the strong edges. In other words, the flat areas should become much more flat and the edges should become much more distinct. We will detect edges, smooth the flat areas, and draw enhanced edges back on top, to produce a cartoon or comic book effect.

When developing an embedded computer vision system, it is a good idea to build a fully working desktop version first before porting it to an embedded system, since it is much easier to develop and debug a desktop program than an embedded system! So, this chapter will begin with a complete Cartoonifier desktop program that you can create using your favorite IDE (for example, Visual Studio, XCode, Eclipse, or QtCreator). After it is working properly on your desktop, the last section shows how to create an embedded system based on the desktop version. Many embedded projects require some custom code for the embedded system, such as to use different inputs and outputs, or use some platform-specific code optimizations. However, for this chapter, we will actually be running identical code on the embedded system and the desktop, so we only need to create one project.

The application uses an **OpenCV** GUI window, initializes the camera, and with each camera frame it calls the `cartoonifyImage()` function, containing most of the code in this chapter. It then displays the processed image in the GUI window. This chapter will explain how to create the desktop application from scratch using a USB webcam and the embedded system based on the desktop application, using the Raspberry Pi Camera Module. So, first you will create a desktop project in your favorite IDE, with a `main.cpp` file to hold the GUI code given in the following sections, such as the main loop, webcam functionality, and keyboard input, and you will create a `cartoon.cpp` file with the image processing operations with most of this chapter's code in a function called `cartoonifyImage()`.

Accessing the webcam

To access a computer's webcam or camera device, you can simply call the `open()` function on a `cv::VideoCapture` object (OpenCV's method of accessing your camera device), and pass 0 as the default camera ID number. Some computers have multiple cameras attached, or they do not work with a default camera of 0, so it is common practice to allow the user to pass the desired camera number as a command-line argument, in case they want to try camera 1, 2, or -1, for example. We will also try to set the camera resolution to 640 x 480 using `cv::VideoCapture::set()` to run faster on high-resolution cameras.

Depending on your camera model, driver, or system, OpenCV might not change the properties of your camera. It is not important for this project, so don't worry if it does not work with your webcam.

You can put this code in the main() function of your main.cpp file:

```
auto cameraNumber = 0;
if (argc> 1)
cameraNumber = atoi(argv[1]);

// Get access to the camera.
cv::VideoCapture camera;
camera.open(cameraNumber);
if (!camera.isOpened()) {
    std::cerr<<"ERROR: Could not access the camera or video!"<< std::endl;
    exit(1);
}

// Try to set the camera resolution.
camera.set(cv::CV_CAP_PROP_FRAME_WIDTH, 640);
camera.set(cv::CV_CAP_PROP_FRAME_HEIGHT, 480);
```

After the webcam has been initialized, you can grab the current camera image as a cv::Mat object (OpenCV's image container). You can grab each camera frame by using the C++ streaming operator from your cv::VideoCapture object in a cv::Mat object, just like if you were getting input from a console.

 OpenCV makes it very easy to capture frames from a video file (such as an AVI or MP4 file) or network stream instead of a webcam. Instead of passing an integer such as camera.open(0), pass a string such as camera.open("my_video.avi") and then grab frames just like it was a webcam. The source code provided with this book has an initCamera() function that opens a webcam, video file, or network stream.

Main camera processing loop for a desktop app

If you want to display a GUI window on the screen using OpenCV, you call the cv::namedWindow() function and then the cv::imshow() function for each image, but you must also call cv::waitKey() once per frame, otherwise your windows will not update at all! Calling cv::waitKey(0) waits forever until the user hits a key in the window, but a positive number such as waitKey(20) or higher will wait for at least that many milliseconds.

Put this main loop in the main.cpp file, as the basis of your real-time camera app:

```cpp
while (true) {
    // Grab the next camera frame.
    cv::Mat cameraFrame;
    camera >> cameraFrame;
    if (cameraFrame.empty()) {
        std::cerr<<"ERROR: Couldn't grab a camera frame."<<
        std::endl;
        exit(1);
    }
    // Create a blank output image, that we will draw onto.
    cv::Mat displayedFrame(cameraFrame.size(), cv::CV_8UC3);

    // Run the cartoonifier filter on the camera frame.
    cartoonifyImage(cameraFrame, displayedFrame);

    // Display the processed image onto the screen.
    imshow("Cartoonifier", displayedFrame);

    // IMPORTANT: Wait for atleast 20 milliseconds,
    // so that the image can be displayed on the screen!
    // Also checks if a key was pressed in the GUI window.
    // Note that it should be a "char" to support Linux.
    auto keypress = cv::waitKey(20); // Needed to see anything!
    if (keypress == 27) { // Escape Key
        // Quit the program!
        break;
    }
}//end while
```

Generating a black and white sketch

To obtain a sketch (black and white drawing) of the camera frame, we will use an edge detection filter, whereas to obtain a color painting, we will use an edge preserving filter (bilateral filter) to further smooth the flat regions while keeping edges intact. By overlaying the sketch drawing on top of the color painting, we obtain a cartoon effect, as shown earlier in the screenshot of the final app.

There are many different edge detection filters, such as Sobel, Scharr, and Laplacian filters, or a Canny edge detector. We will use a Laplacian edge filter since it produces edges that look most similar to hand sketches compared to Sobel or Scharr, and is quite consistent compared to a Canny edge detector, which produces very clean line drawings but is affected more by random noise in the camera frames, and therefore the line drawings would often change drastically between frames.

Nevertheless, we still need to reduce the noise in the image before we use a Laplacian edge filter. We will use a median filter because it is good at removing noise while keeping edges sharp, but is not as slow as a bilateral filter. Since Laplacian filters use grayscale images, we must convert from OpenCV's default BGR format to grayscale. In your empty `cartoon.cpp` file, put this code at the top so you can access OpenCV and STD C++ templates without typing `cv::` and `std::` everywhere:

```cpp
// Include OpenCV's C++ Interface
#include <opencv2/opencv.hpp>

using namespace cv;
using namespace std;
```

Put this and all remaining code in a `cartoonifyImage()` function in your `cartoon.cpp` file:

```cpp
Mat gray;
cvtColor(srcColor, gray, CV_BGR2GRAY);
const int MEDIAN_BLUR_FILTER_SIZE = 7;
medianBlur(gray, gray, MEDIAN_BLUR_FILTER_SIZE);
Mat edges;
const int LAPLACIAN_FILTER_SIZE = 5;
Laplacian(gray, edges, CV_8U, LAPLACIAN_FILTER_SIZE);
```

The Laplacian filter produces edges with varying brightness, so to make the edges look more like a sketch, we apply a binary threshold to make the edges either white or black:

```cpp
Mat mask;
const int EDGES_THRESHOLD = 80;
threshold(edges, mask, EDGES_THRESHOLD, 255, THRESH_BINARY_INV);
```

In the following diagram, you see the original image (to the left) and the generated edge mask (to the right), which looks similar to a sketch drawing. After we generate a color painting (explained later), we also put this edge mask on top to have black line drawings:

Generating a color painting and a cartoon

A strong bilateral filter smooths flat regions while keeping edges sharp, and therefore is great as an automatic cartoonifier or painting filter, except that it is extremely slow (that is, measured in seconds or even minutes, rather than milliseconds!). Therefore, we will use some tricks to obtain a nice cartoonifier, while still running at an acceptable speed. The most important trick we can use is that we can perform bilateral filtering at a lower resolution and it will still have a similar effect as a full resolution, but run much faster. Let's reduce the total number of pixels by four (for example, half width and half height):

```
Size size = srcColor.size();
Size smallSize;
smallSize.width = size.width/2;
smallSize.height = size.height/2;
Mat smallImg = Mat(smallSize, CV_8UC3);
resize(srcColor, smallImg, smallSize, 0,0, INTER_LINEAR);
```

Rather than applying a large bilateral filter, we will apply many small bilateral filters, to produce a strong cartoon effect in less time. We will truncate the filter (refer to the following diagram) so that instead of performing a whole filter (for example, a filter size of 21 x 21, when the bell curve is 21 pixels wide), it just uses the minimum filter size needed for a convincing result (for example, with a filter size of just 9 x 9 even if the bell curve is 21 pixels wide). This truncated filter will apply the major part of the filter (gray area) without wasting time on the minor part of the filter (white area under the curve), so it will run several times faster:

Therefore, we have four parameters that control the bilateral filter: color strength, positional strength, size, and repetition count. We need a temp Mat since the bilateralFilter() function can't overwrite its input (referred to as **in-place processing**), but we can apply one filter storing a temp Mat and another filter storing back the input:

```
Mat tmp = Mat(smallSize, CV_8UC3);
auto repetitions = 7; // Repetitions for strong cartoon effect.
for (auto i=0; i<repetitions; i++) {
    auto ksize = 9; // Filter size. Has large effect on speed.
    double sigmaColor = 9; // Filter color strength.
    double sigmaSpace = 7; // Spatial strength. Affects speed.
    bilateralFilter(smallImg, tmp, ksize, sigmaColor, sigmaSpace);
    bilateralFilter(tmp, smallImg, ksize, sigmaColor, sigmaSpace);
}
```

Remember that this was applied to the shrunken image, so we need to expand the image back to the original size. Then, we can overlay the edge mask that we found earlier. To overlay the edge mask sketch onto the bilateral filter painting (left-hand side of the following image), we can start with a black background and copy the painting pixels that aren't edges in the sketch mask:

```
Mat bigImg;
resize(smallImg, bigImg, size, 0,0, INTER_LINEAR);
dst.setTo(0);
bigImg.copyTo(dst, mask);
```

The result is a cartoon version of the original photo, as shown on the right-hand side of the following image, where the *sketch* mask is overlaid on the painting:

Generating an evil mode using edge filters

Cartoons and comics always have both good and bad characters. With the right combination of edge filters, a scary image can be generated from the most innocent looking people! The trick is to use a small edge filter that will find many edges all over the image, then merge the edges using a small median filter.

We will perform this on a grayscale image with some noise reduction, so the preceding code for converting the original image to grayscale and applying a 7 x 7 median filter should still be used (the first image in the following diagram shows the output of the grayscale median blur). Instead of following it with a Laplacian filter and Binary threshold, we can get a scarier look if we apply a 3 x 3 Scharr gradient filter along *x* and *y* (second image in the diagram), then a binary threshold with a very low cutoff (third image in the diagram), and a 3 x 3 median blur, producing the final *evil* mask (fourth image in the diagram):

```
Mat gray;
cvtColor(srcColor, gray, CV_BGR2GRAY);
const int MEDIAN_BLUR_FILTER_SIZE = 7;
medianBlur(gray, gray, MEDIAN_BLUR_FILTER_SIZE);
Mat edges, edges2;
Scharr(srcGray, edges, CV_8U, 1, 0);
Scharr(srcGray, edges2, CV_8U, 1, 0, -1);
edges += edges2;
// Combine the x & y edges together.
const int EVIL_EDGE_THRESHOLD = 12
threshold(edges, mask, EVIL_EDGE_THRESHOLD, 255,
THRESH_BINARY_INV);
medianBlur(mask, mask, 3)
```

The following diagram shows the evil effect applied in the fourth image:

Now that we have an *evil* mask, we can overlay this mask onto the *cartoonified* painting image as we did with the regular *sketch* edge mask. The final result is shown on the right-hand side of the following diagram:

Generating an alien mode using skin detection

Now that we have a *sketch* mode, a *cartoon* mode (*painting* + *sketch* mask), and an *evil* mode (*painting* + *evil* mask), for fun, let's try something more complex: an *alien* mode, by detecting the skin regions of the face and then changing the skin color to green.

Skin detection algorithm

There are many different techniques used for detecting skin regions, from simple color thresholds using **RGB** (short for **Red-Green-Blue**) or **HSV** (short for **Hue-Saturation-Brightness**) values, or color histogram calculation and re-projection, to complex machine learning algorithms of mixture models that need camera calibration in the **CIELab** color space, offline training with many sample faces, and so on. But even the complex methods don't necessarily work robustly across various camera and lighting conditions and skin types. Since we want our skin detection to run on an embedded device, without any calibration or training, and we are just using skin detection for a fun image filter; it is sufficient for us to use a simple skin detection method. However, the color responses from the tiny camera sensor in the Raspberry Pi Camera Module tend to vary significantly, and we want to support skin detection for people of any skin color but without any calibration, so we need something more robust than simple color thresholds.

For example, a simple HSV skin detector can treat any pixel as skin if its hue color is fairly red, saturation is fairly high but not extremely high, and its brightness is not too dark or extremely bright. But cameras in mobile phones or Raspberry Pi Camera Modules often have bad white balancing; therefore, a person's skin might look slightly blue instead of red, for instance, and this would be a major problem for simple HSV thresholding.

A more robust solution is to perform face detection with a Haar or LBP cascade classifier (shown in Chapter 5, *Face Detection and Recognition with the DNN Module*), then look at the range of colors for the pixels in the middle of the detected face, since you know that those pixels should be skin pixels of the actual person. You could then scan the whole image or nearby region for pixels of a similar color as the center of the face. This has the advantage that it is very likely to find at least some of the true skin region of any detected person, no matter what their skin color is or even if their skin appears somewhat blueish or reddish in the camera image.

Unfortunately, face detection using cascade classifiers is quite slow on current embedded devices, so that method might be less ideal for some real-time embedded applications. On the other hand, we can take advantage of the fact that for mobile apps and some embedded systems, it can be expected that the user will be facing the camera directly from a very close distance, so it can be reasonable to ask the user to place their face at a specific location and distance, rather than try to detect the location and size of their face. This is the basis of many mobile phone apps, where the app asks the user to place their face at a certain position or perhaps to manually drag points on the screen to show where the corners of their face are in a photo. So, let's simply draw the outline of a face in the center of the screen, and ask the user to move their face to the position and size shown.

Showing the user where to put their face

When the *alien* mode is first started, we will draw the face outline on top of the camera frame so the user knows where to put their face. We will draw a big ellipse covering 70% of the image height, with a fixed aspect ratio of 0.72, so that the face will not become too skinny or fat depending on the aspect ratio of the camera:

```
// Draw the color face onto a black background.
Mat faceOutline = Mat::zeros(size, CV_8UC3);
Scalar color = CV_RGB(255,255,0); // Yellow.
auto thickness = 4;

// Use 70% of the screen height as the face height.
auto sw = size.width;
auto sh = size.height;
int faceH = sh/2 * 70/100; // "faceH" is radius of the ellipse.

// Scale the width to be the same nice shape for any screen width.
int faceW = faceH * 72/100;
// Draw the face outline.
ellipse(faceOutline, Point(sw/2, sh/2), Size(faceW, faceH),
0, 0, 360, color, thickness, CV_AA);
```

To make it more obvious that it is a face, let's also draw two eye outlines. Rather than drawing an eye as an ellipse, we can give it a bit more realism (refer to the following image) by drawing a truncated ellipse for the top of the eye and a truncated ellipse for the bottom of the eye, because we can specify the start and end angles when drawing with the `ellipse()` function:

```
// Draw the eye outlines, as 2 arcs per eye.
int eyeW = faceW * 23/100;
int eyeH = faceH * 11/100;
int eyeX = faceW * 48/100;
int eyeY = faceH * 13/100;
Size eyeSize = Size(eyeW, eyeH);

// Set the angle and shift for the eye half ellipses.
auto eyeA = 15; // angle in degrees.
auto eyeYshift = 11;

// Draw the top of the right eye.
ellipse(faceOutline, Point(sw/2 - eyeX, sh/2 -eyeY),
eyeSize, 0, 180+eyeA, 360-eyeA, color, thickness, CV_AA);

// Draw the bottom of the right eye.
ellipse(faceOutline, Point(sw/2 - eyeX, sh/2 - eyeY-eyeYshift),
eyeSize, 0, 0+eyeA, 180-eyeA, color, thickness, CV_AA);
```

```
// Draw the top of the left eye.
ellipse(faceOutline, Point(sw/2 + eyeX, sh/2 - eyeY),
eyeSize, 0, 180+eyeA, 360-eyeA, color, thickness, CV_AA);

// Draw the bottom of the left eye.
ellipse(faceOutline, Point(sw/2 + eyeX, sh/2 - eyeY-eyeYshift),
eyeSize, 0, 0+eyeA, 180-eyeA, color, thickness, CV_AA);
```

We can do the same to draw the bottom lip of the mouth:

```
// Draw the bottom lip of the mouth.
int mouthY = faceH * 48/100;
int mouthW = faceW * 45/100;
int mouthH = faceH * 6/100;
ellipse(faceOutline, Point(sw/2, sh/2 + mouthY), Size(mouthW,
mouthH), 0, 0, 180, color, thickness, CV_AA);
```

To make it even more obvious that the user should put their face where shown, let's write a message on the screen!

```
// Draw anti-aliased text.
int fontFace = FONT_HERSHEY_COMPLEX;
float fontScale = 1.0f;
int fontThickness = 2;
char *szMsg = "Put your face here";
putText(faceOutline, szMsg, Point(sw * 23/100, sh * 10/100),
fontFace, fontScale, color, fontThickness, CV_AA);
```

Now that we have the face outline drawn, we can overlay it onto the displayed image by using alpha blending to combine the cartoonified image with this drawn outline:

```
addWeighted(dst, 1.0, faceOutline, 0.7, 0, dst, CV_8UC3);
```

This results in the outline in the following image, showing the user where to put their face, so we don't have to detect the face location:

Implementation of the skin color changer

Rather than detecting the skin color and then the region with that skin color, we can use OpenCV's `floodFill()` function, which is similar to the bucket fill tool in most image editing software. We know that the regions in the middle of the screen should be skin pixels (since we asked the user to put their face in the middle), so to change the whole face to have green skin, we can just apply a green flood fill on the center pixel, which will always color some parts of the face green. In reality, the color, saturation, and brightness are likely to be different in different parts of the face, so a flood fill will rarely cover all the skin pixels of a face unless the threshold is so low that it also covers unwanted pixels outside of the face. So instead of applying a single flood fill in the center of the image, let's apply a flood fill on six different points around the face that should be skin pixels.

A nice feature of OpenCV's `floodFill()` is that it can draw the flood fill in an external image rather than modify the input image. So, this feature can give us a mask image for adjusting the color of the skin pixels without necessarily changing the brightness or saturation, producing a more realistic image than if all the skin pixels became an identical green pixel (losing significant face detail).

Skin color changing does not work so well in the RGB color space, because you want to allow brightness to vary in the face but not allow skin color to vary much, and RGB does not separate brightness from the color. One solution is to use the HSV color space since it separates the brightness from the color (hue) as well as the colorfulness (Saturation). Unfortunately, HSV wraps the hue value around red, and since the skin is mostly red, it means that you need to work both with *hue < 10%* and *hue > 90%* since these are both red. So, instead we will use the **Y'CrCb** color space (the variant of YUV that is in OpenCV), since it separates brightness from color and only has a single range of values for typical skin color rather than two. Note that most cameras, images, and videos actually use some type of YUV as their color space before conversion to RGB, so in many cases you can get a YUV image free without converting it yourself.

Since we want our alien mode to look like a cartoon, we will apply the alien filter after the image has already been cartoonified. In other words, we have access to the shrunken color image produced by the bilateral filter, and access to the full-sized edge mask. Skin detection often works better at low resolutions, since it is the equivalent of analyzing the average value of each high-resolution pixel's neighbors (or the low-frequency signal instead of the high-frequency noisy signal). So, let's work at the same shrunken scale as the bilateral filter (half-width and half-height). Let's convert the painting image to YUV:

```
Mat yuv = Mat(smallSize, CV_8UC3);
  cvtColor(smallImg, yuv, CV_BGR2YCrCb);
```

We also need to shrink the edge mask so it is on the same scale as the painting image. There is a complication with OpenCV's `floodFill()` function, when storing to a separate mask image, in that the mask should have a one-pixel border around the whole image, so if the input image is *W x H* pixels in size, then the separate mask image should be *(W+2) x (H+2)* pixels in size. But the `floodFill()` function also allows us to initialize the mask with edges that the flood fill algorithm will ensure it does not cross. Let's use this feature, in the hope that it helps prevent the flood fill from extending outside of the face. So, we need to provide two mask images: one is the edge mask of *W x H* in size, and the other image is the exact same edge mask but *(W+2) x (H+2)* in size because it should include a border around the image. It is possible to have multiple `cv::Mat` objects (or headers) referencing the same data, or even to have a `cv::Mat` object that references a sub-region of another `cv::Mat` image. So, instead of allocating two separate images and copying the edge mask pixels across, let's allocate a single mask image including the border, and create an extra `cv::Mat` header of *W x H* (which just references the region of interest in the flood fill mask without the border). In other words, there is just one array of pixels of size *(W+2) x (H+2)* but two `cv::Mat` objects, where one is referencing the whole *(W+2) x (H+2)* image and the other is referencing the *W x H* region in the middle of that image:

```
auto sw = smallSize.width;
auto sh = smallSize.height;
Mat mask, maskPlusBorder;
maskPlusBorder = Mat::zeros(sh+2, sw+2, CV_8UC1);
mask = maskPlusBorder(Rect(1,1,sw,sh));
// mask is now in maskPlusBorder.
resize(edges, mask, smallSize); // Put edges in both of them.
```

The edge mask (shown on the left of the following diagram) is full of both strong and weak edges, but we only want strong edges, so we will apply a binary threshold (resulting in the middle image in the following diagram). To join some gaps between edges, we will then combine the morphological operators `dilate()` and `erode()` to remove some gaps (also referred to as the close operator), resulting in the image on the right:

```
const int EDGES_THRESHOLD = 80;
threshold(mask, mask, EDGES_THRESHOLD, 255, THRESH_BINARY);
dilate(mask, mask, Mat());
erode(mask, mask, Mat());
```

We can see the result of applying thresholding and morphological operation in the following image, first image is the input edge map, second the thresholding filter, and last image is the dilate and erode morphological filters:

As mentioned earlier, we want to apply flood fills in numerous points around the face, to make sure we include the various colors and shades of the whole face. Let's choose six points around the nose, cheeks, and forehead, as shown on the left-hand side of the following screenshot. Note that these values are dependent on the face outline being drawn earlier:

```
auto const NUM_SKIN_POINTS = 6;
Point skinPts[NUM_SKIN_POINTS];
skinPts[0] = Point(sw/2, sh/2 - sh/6);
skinPts[1] = Point(sw/2 - sw/11, sh/2 - sh/6);
skinPts[2] = Point(sw/2 + sw/11, sh/2 - sh/6);
skinPts[3] = Point(sw/2, sh/2 + sh/16);
skinPts[4] = Point(sw/2 - sw/9, sh/2 + sh/16);
skinPts[5] = Point(sw/2 + sw/9, sh/2 + sh/16);
```

Now, we just need to find some good lower and upper bounds for the flood fill. Remember that this is being performed in the Y'CrCb color space, so we basically decide how much the brightness can vary, how much the red component can vary, and how much the blue component can vary. We want to allow the brightness to vary a lot, to include shadows as well as highlights and reflections, but we don't want the colors to vary much at all:

```
const int LOWER_Y = 60;
const int UPPER_Y = 80;
const int LOWER_Cr = 25;
const int UPPER_Cr = 15;
const int LOWER_Cb = 20;
const int UPPER_Cb = 15;
Scalar lowerDiff = Scalar(LOWER_Y, LOWER_Cr, LOWER_Cb);
Scalar upperDiff = Scalar(UPPER_Y, UPPER_Cr, UPPER_Cb);
```

We will use the `floodFill()` function with its default flags, except that we want to store to an external mask, so we must specify `FLOODFILL_MASK_ONLY`:

```
const int CONNECTED_COMPONENTS = 4; // To fill diagonally, use 8.
const int flags = CONNECTED_COMPONENTS | FLOODFILL_FIXED_RANGE
| FLOODFILL_MASK_ONLY;
Mat edgeMask = mask.clone(); // Keep a copy of the edge mask.
// "maskPlusBorder" is initialized with edges to block floodFill().
for (int i = 0; i < NUM_SKIN_POINTS; i++) {
  floodFill(yuv, maskPlusBorder, skinPts[i], Scalar(), NULL,
  lowerDiff, upperDiff, flags);
}
```

The following image on the left-hand side shows the six flood fill locations (shown as circles), and the right-hand side of the image shows the external mask that is generated, where the skin is shown as gray and edges are shown as white. Note that the right-hand image was modified for this book so that skin pixels (of value 1) are clearly visible:

The `mask` image (shown on the right-hand side of the preceding image) now contains the following:

- Pixels of value 255 for the edge pixels
- Pixels of value 1 for the skin regions
- Pixels of value 0 for the rest

Meanwhile, `edgeMask` just contains edge pixels (as value 255). So to get just the skin pixels, we can remove the edges from it:

```
mask -= edgeMask;
```

The `mask` variable now just contains 1s for skin pixels and 0s for non-skin pixels. To change the skin color and brightness of the original image, we can use the `cv::add()` function with the skin mask to increase the green component in the original BGR image:

```
auto Red = 0;
```

```
auto Green = 70;
auto Blue = 0;
add(smallImgBGR, CV_RGB(Red, Green, Blue), smallImgBGR, mask);
```

The following diagram shows the original image on the left and the final alien cartoon image on the right, where at least six parts of the face will now be green!

Notice that we have made the skin look green but also brighter (to look like an alien that glows in the dark). If you want to just change the skin color without making it brighter, you can use other color changing methods, such as adding 70 to green while subtracting 70 from red and blue, or convert to the HSV color space using cvtColor(src, dst, "CV_BGR2HSV_FULL") and adjust the hue and saturation.

Reducing the random pepper noise from the sketch image

Most of the tiny cameras in smartphones, Raspberry Pi Camera Modules, and some webcams have significant image noise. This is normally acceptable, but it has a big effect on our 5 x 5 Laplacian edge filter. The edge mask (shown as the sketch mode) will often have thousands of small blobs of black pixels called **pepper noise**, made of several black pixels next to each other on a white background. We are already using a median filter, which is usually strong enough to remove pepper noise, but in our case it may not be strong enough. Our edge mask is mostly a pure white background (value of 255) with some black edges (value of 0) and the dots of noise (also value of 0). We could use a standard closing morphological operator, but it will remove a lot of edges. So instead, we will apply a custom filter that removes small black regions that are surrounded completely by white pixels. This will remove a lot of noise while having little effect on actual edges.

We will scan the image for black pixels, and at each black pixel, we'll check the border of the 5 x 5 square around it to see if all the 5 x 5 border pixels are white. If they are all white, then we know we have a small island of black noise, so then we fill the whole block with white pixels to remove the black island. For simplicity in our 5 x 5 filter, we will ignore the two border pixels around the image and leave them as they are.

The following diagram shows the original image from an Android tablet on the left side, with a sketch mode in the center, showing small black dots of pepper noise and the result of our pepper noise removal shown on the right-hand side, where the skin looks cleaner:

The following code can be named the removePepperNoise() function to edit the image in place for simplicity:

```
void removePepperNoise(Mat &mask)
{
    for (int y=2; y<mask.rows-2; y++) {
    // Get access to each of the 5 rows near this pixel.
    uchar *pUp2 = mask.ptr(y-2);
    uchar *pUp1 = mask.ptr(y-1);
    uchar *pThis = mask.ptr(y);
    uchar *pDown1 = mask.ptr(y+1);
    uchar *pDown2 = mask.ptr(y+2);

    // Skip the first (and last) 2 pixels on each row.
    pThis += 2;
    pUp1 += 2;
    pUp2 += 2;
    pDown1 += 2;
    pDown2 += 2;
    for (auto x=2; x<mask.cols-2; x++) {
        uchar value = *pThis; // Get pixel value (0 or 255).
        // Check if it's a black pixel surrounded bywhite
```

```
        // pixels (ie: whether it is an "island" of black).
        if (value == 0) {
            bool above, left, below, right, surroundings;
            above = *(pUp2 - 2) && *(pUp2 - 1) && *(pUp2) && *(pUp2 + 1)
                && *(pUp2 + 2);
            left = *(pUp1 - 2) && *(pThis - 2) && *(pDown1 - 2);
            below = *(pDown2 - 2) && *(pDown2 - 1) && (pDown2) &&
                (pDown2 + 1) && *(pDown2 + 2);
            right = *(pUp1 + 2) && *(pThis + 2) && *(pDown1 + 2);
            surroundings = above && left && below && right;
            if (surroundings == true) {
                // Fill the whole 5x5 block as white. Since we
                // knowthe 5x5 borders are already white, we just
                // need tofill the 3x3 inner region.
                *(pUp1 - 1) = 255;
                *(pUp1 + 0) = 255;
                *(pUp1 + 1) = 255;
                *(pThis - 1) = 255;
                *(pThis + 0) = 255;
                *(pThis + 1) = 255;
                *(pDown1 - 1) = 255;
                *(pDown1 + 0) = 255;
                *(pDown1 + 1) = 255;
                // Since we just covered the whole 5x5 block with
                // white, we know the next 2 pixels won't be
                // black,so skip the next 2 pixels on the right.
                pThis += 2;
                pUp1 += 2;
                pUp2 += 2;
                pDown1 += 2;
                pDown2 += 2;
            }
        }
        // Move to the next pixel on the right.
        pThis++;
        pUp1++;
        pUp2++;
        pDown1++;
        pDown2++;
        }
    }
}
```

That's all! Run the app in the different modes until you are ready to port it to the embedded device!

Porting from desktop to an embedded device

Now that the program works on the desktop, we can make an embedded system from it. The details given here are specific to Raspberry Pi, but similar steps apply when developing for other embedded Linux systems such as BeagleBone, ODROID, Olimex, Jetson, and so on.

There are several different options for running our code on an embedded system, each with some advantages and disadvantages in different scenarios.

There are two common methods for compiling the code for an embedded device:

- Copy the source code from the desktop onto the device and compile it directly on board the device. This is often referred to as **native compilation** since we are compiling our code natively on the same system that it will eventually run on.
- Compile all the code on the desktop but using special methods to generate code for the device, and then you copy the final executable program onto the device. This is often referred to as **cross-compilation** since you need a special compiler that knows how to generate code for other types of CPUs.

Cross-compilation is often significantly harder to configure than native compilation, especially if you are using many shared libraries, but since your desktop is usually a lot faster than your embedded device, cross-compilation is often much faster at compiling large projects. If you expect to be compiling your project hundreds of times, in order to work on it for months, and your device is quite slow compared to your desktops, such as the Raspberry Pi 1 or Raspberry Pi Zero, which are very slow compared to a desktop, then cross-compilation is a good idea. But in most cases, especially for small, simple projects, you should just stick with native compilation since it is easier.

Note that all the libraries used by your project will also need to be compiled for the device, so you will need to compile OpenCV for your device. Natively compiling OpenCV on a Raspberry Pi 1 can take hours, whereas cross-compiling OpenCV on a desktop might take just 15 minutes. But you usually only need to compile OpenCV once and then you'll have it for all your projects, so it is still worth sticking with native compilation of your project (including the native compilation of OpenCV) in most cases.

There are also several options for how to run the code on an embedded system:

- Use the same input and output methods you used on the desktop, such as the same video files, USB webcam, or keyboard as input, and display text or graphics on an HDMI monitor in the same way you were doing on the desktop.
- Use special devices for input and output. For example, instead of sitting at a desk using a USB webcam and keyboard as input and displaying the output on a desktop monitor, you could use the special Raspberry Pi Camera Module for video input, use custom GPIO push buttons or sensors for input, and use a 7-inch MIPI DSI screen or GPIO LED lights as the output, and then by powering it all with a common **portable USB charger**, you can be wearing the whole computer platform in your backpack or attaching it on your bicycle!
- Another option is to stream data in or out of the embedded device to other computers, or even use one device to stream out the camera data and one device to use that data. For example, you can use the GStreamer framework to configure the Raspberry Pi to stream H.264 compressed video from its camera module to the Ethernet network or through Wi-Fi, so that a powerful PC or server rack on the local network or the Amazon AWS cloud computing services can process the video stream somewhere else. This method allows a small and cheap camera device to be used in a complex project requiring large processing resources located somewhere else.

If you do wish to perform computer vision on board the device, be aware that some low-cost embedded devices such as Raspberry Pi 1, Raspberry Pi Zero, and BeagleBone Black have significantly less computing power than desktops or even cheap netbooks or smartphones, perhaps 10-50 times slower than your desktop, so depending on your application you might need a powerful embedded device or stream video to a separate computer, as mentioned previously. If you don't need much computing power (for example, you only need to process one frame every 2 seconds, or you only need to use 160 x 120 image resolution), then a Raspberry Pi Zero running some computer vision on board might be fast enough for your requirements. But many computer vision systems need far more computing power, and so if you want to perform computer vision on board the device, you will often want to use a much faster device with a CPU in the range of 2 GHz, such as a Raspberry Pi 3, ODROID-XU4, or Jetson TK1.

Equipment setup to develop code for an embedded device

Let's begin by keeping it as simple as possible, by using a USB keyboard and mouse and an HDMI monitor just like our desktop system, compiling the code natively on the device, and running our code on the device. Our first step will be to copy the code onto the device, install the build tools, and compile OpenCV and our source code on the embedded system.

Many embedded devices such as Raspberry Pi have an HDMI port and at least one USB port. Therefore, the easiest way to start using an embedded device is to plug in an HDMI monitor and USB keyboard and mouse for the device, to configure settings and see the output, while doing the code development and testing using your desktop machine. If you have a spare HDMI monitor, plug that into the device, but if you don't have a spare HDMI monitor, you might consider buying a small HDMI screen just for your embedded device.

Also, if you don't have a spare USB keyboard and mouse, you might consider buying a wireless keyboard and mouse that has a single USB wireless dongle, so you only use up a single USB port for both the keyboard and mouse. Many embedded devices use a 5V power supply, but they usually need more power (electrical current) than a desktop or laptop will provide in its USB port. So, you should obtain either a separate 5V USB charger (at least 1.5 amps, ideally 2.5 amps) or a portable USB battery charger that can provide at least 1.5 amps of output current. Your device might only use 0.5 amps most of the time, but there will be occasional times when it needs over 1 amp, so it's important to use a power supply that is rated for at least 1.5 amps or more, otherwise your device will occasionally reboot, or some hardware could behave strangely at important times, or the filesystem could become corrupt and you lose your files! A 1 amp supply might be good enough if you don't use cameras or accessories, but 2.0-2.5 amps is safer.

For example, the following photographs show a convenient setup containing a Raspberry Pi 3, a good quality 8 GB micro-SD card for $10 (http://ebay.to/2ayp6Bo), a 5-inch HDMI resistive touchscreen for $30-$45 (http://bit.ly/2aHQO2G), a wireless USB keyboard and mouse for $30 (http://ebay.to/2aN2oXi), a **5V 2.5 A** power supply for $5 (https://amzn.to/2UafanD), a USB webcam such as the very fast **PS3 Eye** for just $5 (http://ebay.to/2aVWCUS), a Raspberry Pi Camera Module v1 or v2 for $15-$30 (http://bit.ly/2aF9PxD), and an Ethernet cable for $2 (http://ebay.to/2aznnjd), connecting the Raspberry Pi to the same LAN network as your development PC or laptop. Notice that this HDMI screen is designed specifically for the Raspberry Pi, since the screen plugs directly into the Raspberry Pi below it, and has an HDMI male-to-male adapter (shown in the right-hand photo) for the Raspberry Pi so you don't need an HDMI cable, whereas other screens may require an HDMI cable (https://amzn.to/2Rvet6H), or MIPI DSI or SPI cable.

Also note that some screens and touch panels need configuration before they will work, whereas most HDMI screens should work without any configuration:

Notice the black USB webcam (on the far left of the LCD), the Raspberry Pi Camera Module (green and black board sitting on the top-left corner of the LCD), Raspberry Pi board (underneath the LCD), HDMI adapter (connecting the LCD to the Raspberry Pi underneath it), a blue Ethernet cable (plugged into a router), a small USB wireless keyboard and mouse dongle, and a micro-USB power cable (plugged into a **5V 2.5A** power supply).

Configuring a new Raspberry Pi

The following steps are specific to Raspberry Pi, so if you are using a different embedded device or you want a different type of setup, search the web about how to set up your board. To set up an Raspberry Pi 1, 2, or 3 (including their variants such as Raspberry Pi Zero, Raspberry Pi 2B, 3B, and so on, and Raspberry Pi 1A+ if you plug in a USB Ethernet dongle), follow these steps:

1. Get a fairly new, good quality micro-SD card of at least 8 GB. If you use a cheap micro-SD card or an old micro-SD card that you already used many times before and it has degraded in quality, it might not be reliable enough to boot the Raspberry Pi, so if you have trouble booting the Raspberry Pi, you should try a good quality Class 10 micro-SD card (such as SanDisk Ultra or better) that says it handles at least 45 Mbps or can handle 4K video.

2. Download and burn the latest **Raspbian IMG** (not NOOBS) to the micro-SD card. Note that burning an IMG is different to simply copying the file to SD. Visit `https://www.raspberrypi.org/documentation/installation/installing-images/` and follow the instructions for your desktop's OS to burn Raspbian to a micro-SD card. Be aware that you will lose any files that were previously on the card.

3. Plug a USB keyboard, mouse, and HDMI display into the Raspberry Pi, so you can easily run some commands and see the output.

4. Plug the Raspberry Pi into a 5V USB power supply with at least 1.5 A, ideally 2.5 A or higher. Computer USB ports aren't powerful enough.

5. You should see many pages of text scrolling while it is booting up Raspbian Linux, then it should be ready after 1 or 2 minutes.

6. If, after booting, it's just showing a black console screen with some text (such as if you downloaded **Raspbian Lite**), you are at the text-only login prompt. Log in by typing `pi` as the username and then hit *Enter*. Then, type `raspberry` as the password and hit *Enter* again.

7. Or if it booted to the graphical display, click on the black **Terminal** icon at the top to open a shell (Command Prompt).

8. Initialize some settings in your Raspberry Pi:
   - Type `sudo raspi-config` and hit *Enter* (see the following screenshot).
   - First, run **Expand Filesystem** and then finish and reboot your device, so the Raspberry Pi can use the whole micro-SD card.
   - If you use a normal (US) keyboard, not a British keyboard, in **Internationalization Options**, change to **Generic 104-key keyboard**, **Other**, **English (US)**, and then for the **AltGr** and similar questions, just hit *Enter* unless you are using a special keyboard.
   - In **Enable Camera**, enable the Raspberry Pi Camera Module.
   - In **Overclock Options**, set to Raspberry Pi 2 or similar to the device runs faster (but generates more heat).
   - In **Advanced Options**, enable the SSH server.
   - In **Advanced Options**, if you are using Raspberry Pi 2 or 3, change **Memory Split** to 256 MB so the GPU has plenty of RAM for video processing. For Raspberry Pi 1 or Zero, use 64 MB or the default.
   - Finish, then reboot the device.

9. (Optional): Delete Wolfram to save 600 MB of space on your SD card:

```
sudo apt-get purge -y wolfram-engine
```

It can be reinstalled using `sudo apt-get install wolfram-engine`.

To see the remaining space on your SD card, run `df -h | head -2`:

10. Assuming you plugged the Raspberry Pi into your internet router, it should already have internet access. So, update your Raspberry Pi to the latest Raspberry Pi firmware, software locations, OS, and software. **Warning**: many Raspberry Pi tutorials say you should run `sudo rpi-update`; however, in recent years, it's no longer a good idea to run `rpi-update` since it can give you an unstable system or firmware. The following instructions will update your Raspberry Pi to have stable software and firmware (note that these commands might take up to one hour):

```
sudo apt-get -y update
sudo apt-get -y upgrade
sudo apt-get -y dist-upgrade
sudo reboot
```

11. Find the IP address of the device:

```
hostname -I
```

12. Try accessing the device from your desktop. For example, assume the device's IP address is `192.168.2.101`. Enter this on a Linux desktop:

```
ssh-X pi@192.168.2.101
```

Or, do this on a Windows desktop:
    1. Download, install, and run PuTTY
    2. Then in PuTTY, connect to the IP address (192.168.2.101), as the user `pi` with the password `raspberry`

13. Optionally, if you want your Command Prompt to be a different color than the commands and show the error value after each command, use this:

```
nano ~/.bashrc
```

14. Add this line to the bottom:

```
PS1="[e[0;44m]u@h: w ($?) $[e[0m] "
```

15. Save the file (hit *Ctrl* + *X*, then hit *Y*, and then hit *Enter*).
16. Start using the new settings:

```
source ~/.bashrc
```

17. To prevent the screensaver/screen blank power saving feature in Raspbian from turning off your screen on idle, use this:

```
sudo nano /etc/lightdm/lightdm.conf
```

18. And follow these steps:
    1. Look for the line that says `#xserver-command=X` (jump to line `87` by pressing *Alt* + *G* and then typing `87` and hitting *Enter*).
    2. Change it to `xserver-command=X -s 0 dpms`.
    3. Save the file (hit *Ctrl* + *X*, then hit *Y*, then hit *Enter*).

19. Finally, reboot the Raspberry Pi:

```
sudo reboot
```

You should be ready to start developing on the device now!

Installing OpenCV on an embedded device

There is a very easy way to install OpenCV and all its dependencies on a Debian-based embedded device such as Raspberry Pi:

```
sudo apt-get install libopencv-dev
```

However, that might install an old version of OpenCV from one or two years ago.

To install the latest version of OpenCV on an embedded device such as Raspberry Pi, we need to build OpenCV from the source code. First, we install a compiler and build system, then libraries for OpenCV to use, and finally OpenCV itself. Note that the steps for compiling OpenCV from source on Linux are the same whether you are compiling for desktop or for embedded systems. A Linux script, install_opencv_from_source.sh, is provided with this book; it is recommended you copy the file onto your Raspberry Pi (for example, with a USB flash stick) and run the script to download, build, and install OpenCV, including potential multi-core CPU and **ARM NEON SIMD** optimizations (depending on hardware support):

```
chmod +x install_opencv_from_source.sh
 ./install_opencv_from_source.sh
```

 The script will stop if there is an error, for example, if you don't have internet access or a dependency package conflicts with something else you already installed. If the script stops with an error, try using info on the web to solve that error, then run the script again. The script will quickly check all the previous steps and then continue from where it finished last time. Note that it will take between 20 minutes and 12 hours depending on your hardware and software!

It's highly recommended to build and run a few OpenCV samples every time you install OpenCV, so when you have problems building your own code, at least you will know whether the problem is the OpenCV installation or a problem with your code.

Let's try to build the simple edge sample program. If we try the same Linux command to build it from OpenCV 2, we get a build error:

```
cd ~/opencv-4.*/samples/cpp
 g++ edge.cpp -lopencv_core -lopencv_imgproc -lopencv_highgui
 -o edge
 /usr/bin/ld: /tmp/ccDqLWSz.o: undefined reference to symbol
'_ZN2cv6imreadERKNS_6StringEi'
 /usr/local/lib/libopencv_imgcodecs.so.4..: error adding symbols: DSO
missing from command line
 collect2: error: ld returned 1 exit status
```

The second to last line of that error message tells us that a library was missing from the command line, so we simply need to add `-lopencv_imgcodecs` in our command next to the other OpenCV libraries we linked to. Now, you know how to fix the problem anytime you are compiling an OpenCV 3 program and you see that error message. So, let's do it correctly:

```
cd ~/opencv-4.*/samples/cpp
g++ edge.cpp -lopencv_core -lopencv_imgproc -lopencv_highgui
-lopencv_imgcodecs -o edge
```

It worked! So, now you can run the program:

```
./edge
```

Hit *Ctrl* + *C* on your keyboard to quit the program. Note that the `edge` program might crash if you try running the command in an SSH Terminal and you don't redirect the window to display on the device's LCD screen. So, if you are using SSH to remotely run the program, add `DISPLAY=:0` before your command:

```
DISPLAY=:0 ./edge
```

You should also plug a USB webcam into the device and test that it works:

```
g++ starter_video.cpp -lopencv_core -lopencv_imgproc
-lopencv_highgui -lopencv_imgcodecs -lopencv_videoio \
-o starter_video
DISPLAY=:0 ./starter_video 0
```

Note: if you don't have a USB webcam, you can test using a video file:

```
DISPLAY=:0 ./starter_video ../data/768x576.avi
```

Now that OpenCV is successfully installed on your device, you can run the Cartoonifier applications we developed earlier. Copy the `Cartoonifier` folder onto the device (for example, by using a USB flash stick, or using `scp` to copy files over the network). Then, build the code just like you did for the desktop:

```
cd ~/Cartoonifier
export OpenCV_DIR="~/opencv-3.1.0/build"
mkdir build
cd build
cmake -D OpenCV_DIR=$OpenCV_DIR ..
make
```

And run it:

```
DISPLAY=:0 ./Cartoonifier
```

And if all is fine, we will see a window with our application running as follows:

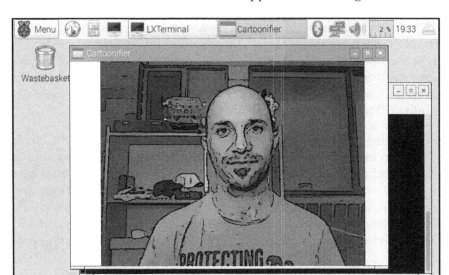

Using the Raspberry Pi Camera Module

While using a USB webcam on Raspberry Pi has the convenience of supporting identical behavior and code on the desktop as on an embedded device, you might consider using one of the official Raspberry Pi Camera Modules (referred to as the **Raspberry Pi Cams**). They have some advantages and disadvantages over USB webcams.

The Raspberry Pi Cams use the special MIPI CSI camera format, designed for smartphone cameras to use less power. They have a smaller physical size, faster bandwidth, higher resolutions, higher frame rates, and reduced latency compared to USB. Most USB 2.0 webcams can only deliver 640 x 480 or 1280 x 720 30 FPS video since USB 2.0 is too slow for anything higher (except for some expensive USB webcams that perform onboard video compression) and USB 3.0 is still too expensive. However, smartphone cameras (including the Raspberry Pi Cams) can often deliver 1920 x 1080 30 FPS or even Ultra HD/4K resolutions. The Raspberry Pi Cam v1 can, in fact, deliver upto 2592 x 1944 15 FPS or 1920 x 1080 30 FPS video even on a $5 Raspberry Pi Zero, thanks to the use of MIPI CSI for the camera and compatible video processing ISP and GPU hardware inside the Raspberry Pi. The Raspberry Pi Cams also support 640 x 480 in 90 FPS mode (such as for slow-motion capture), and this is quite useful for real-time computer vision so you can see very small movements in each frame, rather than large movements that are harder to analyze.

However, the Raspberry Pi Cam is a plain circuit board that is *highly sensitive* to electrical interference, static electricity, or physical damage (simply touching the small, flat orange cable with your finger can cause video interference or even permanently damage your camera!). The big flat white cable is far less sensitive but it is still very sensitive to electrical noise or physical damage. The Raspberry Pi Cam comes with a very short 15 cm cable. It's possible to buy third-party cables on eBay with lengths between 5 cm and 1 m, but cables 50 cm or longer are less reliable, whereas USB webcams can use 2 m to 5 m cables and can be plugged into USB hubs or active extension cables for longer distances.

There are currently several different Raspberry Pi Cam models, notably the NoIR version that doesn't have an internal infrared filter; therefore, a NoIR camera can easily see in the dark (if you have an invisible infrared light source), or see infrared lasers or signals far clearer than regular cameras that include an infrared filter inside them. There are also two different versions of Raspberry Pi Cam: Raspberry Pi Cam v1.3 and Raspberry Pi Cam v2.1, where v2.1 uses a wider angle lens with a Sony 8 megapixel sensor instead of a 5 megapixel **OmniVision** sensor, has better support for motion in low lighting conditions, and adds support for 3240 x 2464 video at 15 FPS and potentially up to 120 FPS video at 720p. However, USB webcams come in thousands of different shapes and versions, making it easy to find specialized webcams such as waterproof or industrial-grade webcams, rather than requiring you to create your own custom housing for a Raspberry Pi Cam.

IP cameras are also another option for a camera interface that can allow 1080p or higher resolution videos with Raspberry Pi, and IP cameras support not just very long cables, but potentially even work anywhere in the world using the internet. But IP cameras aren't quite as easy to interface with OpenCV as USB webcams or Raspberry Pi Cams.

In the past, Raspberry Pi Cams and the official drivers weren't directly compatible with OpenCV; you often used custom drivers and modified your code in order to grab frames from Raspberry Pi Cams, but it's now possible to access a Raspberry Pi Cam in OpenCV in the exact same way as a USB webcam! Thanks to recent improvements in the v4l2 drivers, once you load the v4l2 driver, the Raspberry Pi Cam will appear as a `/dev/video0` or `/dev/video1` file like a regular USB webcam. So, traditional OpenCV webcam code such as `cv::VideoCapture(0)` will be able to use it just like a webcam.

Installing the Raspberry Pi Camera Module driver

First, let's temporarily load the v4l2 driver for the Raspberry Pi Cam to make sure our camera is plugged in correctly:

```
sudo modprobe bcm2835-v4l2
```

If the command failed (if it printed an error message to the console, it froze, or the command returned a number besides 0), then perhaps your camera is not plugged in correctly. Shut down and then unplug power from your Raspberry Pi and try attaching the flat white cable again, looking at photos on the web to make sure it's plugged in the correct way around. If it is the correct way around, it's possible the cable wasn't fully inserted before you closed the locking tab on the Raspberry Pi. Also, check whether you forgot to click **Enable Camera** when configuring your Raspberry Pi earlier, using the sudoraspi-config command.

If the command worked (if the command returned 0 and no error was printed to the console), then we can make sure the v4l2 driver for the Raspberry Pi Cam is always loaded on bootup by adding it to the bottom of the /etc/modules file:

```
sudo nano /etc/modules
# Load the Raspberry Pi Camera Module v4l2 driver on bootup:
bcm2835-v4l2
```

After you save the file and reboot your Raspberry Pi, you should be able to run ls /dev/video* to see a list of cameras available on your Raspberry Pi. If the Raspberry Pi Cam is the only camera plugged into your board, you should see it as the default camera (/dev/video0), or if you also have a USB webcam plugged in, then it will be either /dev/video0 or /dev/video1.

Let's test the Raspberry Pi Cam using the starter_video sample program we compiled earlier:

```
cd ~/opencv-4.*/samples/cpp
 DISPLAY=:0 ./starter_video 0
```

If it's showing the wrong camera, try DISPLAY=:0 ./starter_video 1.

Now that we know the Raspberry Pi Cam is working in OpenCV, let's try Cartoonifier:

```
cd ~/Cartoonifier
 DISPLAY=:0 ./Cartoonifier 0
```

Or, use DISPLAY=:0 ./Cartoonifier 1 for the other camera.

Making Cartoonifier run in fullscreen

In embedded systems, you often want your application to be fullscreen and hide the Linux GUI and menu. OpenCV offers an easy method to set the fullscreen window property, but make sure you created the window using the NORMAL flag:

```
// Create a fullscreen GUI window for display on the screen.
namedWindow(windowName, WINDOW_NORMAL);
setWindowProperty(windowName, PROP_FULLSCREEN, CV_WINDOW_FULLSCREEN);
```

Hiding the mouse cursor

You might notice the mouse cursor is shown on top of your window even though you don't want to use a mouse in your embedded system. To hide the mouse cursor, you can use the xdotool command to move it to the bottom-right corner pixel, so it's not noticeable, but is still available if you want to occasionally plug in your mouse to debug the device. Install xdotool and create a short Linux script to run it with Cartoonifier:

```
sudo apt-get install -y xdotool
cd ~/Cartoonifier/build
```

After installing xdotool, now is the time to create the script, create a new file with your favorite editor with the name runCartoonifier.sh and the following content:

```
#!/bin/sh
# Move the mouse cursor to the screen's bottom-right pixel.
xdotoolmousemove 3000 3000
# Run Cartoonifier with any arguments given.
/home/pi/Cartoonifier/build/Cartoonifier "$@"
```

Finally, make your script executable:

```
chmod +x runCartoonifier.sh
```

Try running your script to make sure it works:

```
DISPLAY=:0 ./runCartoonifier.sh
```

Running Cartoonifier automatically after bootup

Often, when you build an embedded device, you want your application to be executed automatically after the device has booted up, rather than requiring the user to manually run your application. To automatically run our application after the device has fully booted up and logged in to the graphical desktop, create an `autostart` folder with a file in it with these contents, including the full path to your script or application:

```
mkdir ~/.config/autostart
 nano ~/.config/autostart/Cartoonifier.desktop
 [Desktop Entry]
 Type=Application
 Exec=/home/pi/Cartoonifier/build/runCartoonifier.sh
 X-GNOME-Autostart-enabled=true
```

Now, whenever you turn the device on or reboot it, Cartoonifier will begin running!

Speed comparison of Cartoonifier on desktop versus embedded

You will notice that the code runs much slower on Raspberry Pi than on your desktop! By far the two easiest ways to run it faster are to use a faster device or use a smaller camera resolution. The following table shows some frame rates, **frames per seconds (FPS)**, for both the *sketch* and *paint* modes of Cartoonifier on a desktop, Raspberry Pi 1, Raspberry Pi 2, Raspberry Pi 3, and Jetson TK1. Note that the speeds don't have any custom optimizations and only run on a single CPU core, and the timings include the time for rendering images to the screen. The USB webcam used is the fast PS3 Eye webcam running at 640 x 480 since it is the fastest low-cost webcam on the market.

It's worth mentioning that Cartoonifier is only using a single CPU core, but all the devices listed have four CPU cores except for Raspberry Pi 1, which has a single core, and many x86 computers have hyperthreading to give roughly eight CPU cores. So, if you wrote your code to efficiently make use of multiple CPU cores (or GPU), the speeds might be 1.5 to 3 times faster than the single-threaded figures shown:

Computer	Sketch mode	Paint mode
Intel Core i7 PC	20 FPS	2.7 FPS
Jetson TK1ARM CPU	16 FPS	2.3 FPS
Raspberry Pi 3	4.3 FPS	0.32 FPS (3 seconds/frame)
Raspberry Pi 2	3.2 FPS	0.28 FPS (4 seconds/frame)
Raspberry Pi Zero	2.5 FPS	0.21 FPS (5 seconds/frame)
Raspberry Pi 1	1.9 FPS	0.12 FPS (8 seconds/frame)

Notice that Raspberry Pi is extremely slow at running the code, especially the *paint* mode, so we will try simply changing the camera and the resolution of the camera.

Changing the camera and camera resolution

The following table shows how the speed of the *sketch* mode compares on Raspberry Pi 2 using different types of cameras and different camera resolutions:

Hardware	640 x 480 resolution	320 x 240 resolution
Raspberry Pi 2 with Raspberry Pi Cam	3.8 FPS	12.9 FPS
Raspberry Pi 2 with PS3 Eye webcam	3.2 FPS	11.7 FPS
Raspberry Pi 2 with unbranded webcam	1.8 FPS	7.4 FPS

As you can see, when using the Raspberry Pi Cam in 320 x 240, it seems we have a good enough solution to have some fun, even if it's not in the 20-30 FPS range that we would prefer.

Power draw of Cartoonifier running on desktop versus embedded system

We've seen that various embedded devices are slower than desktops, from the Raspberry Pi 1 being roughly 20 times slower than a desktop, up to Jetson TK1 being roughly 1.5 times slower than a desktop. But for some tasks, low speed is acceptable if it means there will also be significantly lower battery draw, allowing for small batteries or low year-round electricity costs for a server, or low heat generation.

Raspberry Pi has different models even for the same processor, such as Raspberry Pi 1B, Zero, and 1A+, which all run at similar speeds but have significantly different power draws. MIPI CSI cameras such as the Raspberry Pi Cam also use less electricity than webcams. The following table shows how much electrical power is used by different hardware running the same Cartoonifier code. Power measurements of Raspberry Pi were performed as shown in the following photo using a simple USB current monitor (for example, J7-T Safety Tester (http://bit.ly/2aSZa6H) for $5) and a DMM multimeter for the other devices:

Idle power measures power when the computer is running but no major applications are being used, whereas **Cartoonifier power** measures power when Cartoonifier is running. **Efficiency** is Cartoonifier power/Cartoonifier speed in a 640 x 480 *sketch* mode:

Hardware	Idle power	Cartoonifier power	Efficiency
Raspberry Pi Zero with PS3 Eye	1.2 Watts	1.8 Watts	1.4 Frames per Watt
Raspberry Pi 1A+ with PS3 Eye	**1.1 Watts**	**1.5 Watts**	1.1 Frames per Watt
Raspberry Pi 1B with PS3 Eye	2.4 Watts	3.2 Watts	0.5 Frames per Watt
Raspberry Pi 2B with PS3 Eye	1.8 Watts	2.2 Watts	1.4 Frames per Watt
Raspberry Pi 3B with PS3 Eye	2.0 Watts	2.5 Watts	1.7 Frames per Watt
Jetson TK1 with PS3 Eye	2.8 Watts	4.3 Watts	**3.7 Frames per Watt**
Core i7 laptop with PS3 Eye	14.0 Watts	39.0 Watts	0.5 Frames per Watt

We can see that Raspberry Pi 1A+ uses the least power, but the most power efficient options are Jetson TK1 and Raspberry Pi 3B. Interestingly, the original Raspberry Pi (Raspberry Pi 1B) has roughly the same efficiency as an x86 laptop. All later Raspberry Pis are significantly more power efficient than the original (Raspberry Pi 1B).

Disclaimer: The author is a former employee of NVIDIA, which produced the Jetson TK1, but the results and conclusions are believed to be authentic.

Let's also look at the power draw of different cameras that work with Raspberry Pi:

Hardware	Idle power	Cartoonifier power	Efficiency
Raspberry Pi Zero with PS3 Eye	1.2 Watts	1.8 Watts	1.4 Frames per Watt
Raspberry Pi Zero with Raspberry Pi Cam v1.3	0.6 Watts	1.5 Watts	2.1 Frames per Watt
Raspberry Pi Zero with Raspberry Pi Cam v2.1	**0.55 Watts**	**1.3 Watts**	**2.4 Frames per Watt**

We see that Raspberry Pi Cam v2.1 is slightly more power efficient than Raspberry Pi Cam v1.3 and significantly more power efficient than a USB webcam.

Streaming video from Raspberry Pi to a powerful computer

Thanks to the hardware-accelerated video encoders in all modern ARM devices, including Raspberry Pi, a valid alternative to performing computer vision on board an embedded device is to use the device to just capture video and stream it across a network in real time to a PC or server rack. All Raspberry Pi models contain the same video encoder hardware, so an Raspberry Pi 1A+ or Raspberry Pi Zero with a Pi Cam is quite a good option for a low-cost, low-power portable video streaming server. Raspberry Pi 3 adds Wi-Fi for additional portable functionality.

There are numerous ways live camera video can be streamed from a Raspberry Pi, such as using the official Raspberry Pi V4L2 camera driver to allow the Raspberry Pi Cam to appear like a webcam, then using GStreamer, liveMedia, netcat, or VLC to stream the video across a network. However, these methods often introduce one or two seconds of latency and often require customizing the OpenCV client code or learning how to use GStreamer efficiently. So instead, the following section will show how to perform both the camera capture and network streaming using an alternative camera driver named **UV4L**:

1. Install UV4L on the Raspberry Pi by following the instructions at http://www.linux-projects.org/uv4l/installation/:

```
curl http://www.linux-projects.org/listing/uv4l_repo/lrkey.asc
sudo apt-key add -
sudo su
echo "# UV4L camera streaming repo:">> /etc/apt/sources.list
echo "deb http://www.linux-projects.org/listing/uv4l_repo/raspbian/jessie main">>
/etc/apt/sources.list
exit
```

```
sudo apt-get update
sudo apt-get install uv4l uv4l-raspicam uv4l-server
```

2. Run the UV4L streaming server manually (on the Raspberry Pi) to check that it works:

```
sudo killall uv4l
 sudo LD_PRELOAD=/usr/lib/uv4l/uv4lext/armv6l/libuv4lext.so
uv4l -v7 -f --sched-rr --mem-lock --auto-video_nr
--driverraspicam --encoding mjpeg
--width 640 --height 480 --framerate15
```

3. Test the camera's network stream from your desktop, following these steps to check all is working fine:
    - Install VLC Media Player.
    - Navigate to **Media | Open Network Stream** and enter http://192.168.2.111:8080/stream/video.mjpeg.
    - Adjust the URL to the IP address of your Raspberry Pi. Run hostname -I on Raspberry Pi to find its IP address.

4. Run the UV4L server automatically on bootup:

```
sudo apt-get install uv4l-raspicam-extras
```

5. Edit any UV4L server settings you want in uv4l-raspicam.conf, such as resolution and frame rate to customize the streaming:

```
sudo nano /etc/uv4l/uv4l-raspicam.conf
 drop-bad-frames = yes
 nopreview = yes
 width = 640
 height = 480
 framerate = 24
```

You will need to reboot to make all changes take effect.

6. Tell OpenCV to use our network stream as if it was a webcam. As long as your installation of OpenCV can use FFMPEG internally, OpenCV will be able to grab frames from an MJPEG network stream just like a webcam:

```
./Cartoonifier http://192.168.2.101:8080/stream/video.mjpeg
```

Your Raspberry Pi is now using UV4L to stream the live 640 x 480 24 FPS video to a PC that is running Cartoonifier in *sketch* mode, achieving roughly 19 FPS (with 0.4 seconds of latency). Notice this is almost the same speed as using the PS3 Eye webcam directly on the PC (20 FPS)!

Note that when you are streaming the video to OpenCV, it won't be able to set the camera resolution; you need to adjust the UV4L server settings to change the camera resolution. Also note that instead of streaming MJPEG, we could have streamed H.264 video, which uses a lower bandwidth, but some computer vision algorithms don't handle video compression such as H.264 very well, so MJPEG will cause fewer algorithm problems than H.264.

 If you have both the official Raspberry Pi V4L2 driver and the UV4L driver installed, they will both be available as cameras 0 and 1 (devices `/dev/video0` and `/dev/video1`), but you can only use one camera driver at a time.

Customizing your embedded system!

Now that you have created a whole embedded Cartoonifier system, and you know the basics of how it works and which parts do what, you should customize it! Make the video full screen, change the GUI, change the application behavior and workflow, change the Cartoonifier filter constants or the skin detector algorithm, replace the Cartoonifier code with your own project ideas, or stream the video to the cloud and process it there!

You can improve the skin detection algorithm in many ways, such as using a more complex skin detection algorithm (for example, using trained Gaussian models from many recent CVPR or ICCV conference papers at http://www.cvpapers.com), or add face detection (see the *Face detection* section of Chapter 5, *Face Detection and Recognition with the DNN Module*) to the skin detector, so it detects where the user's face is, rather than asking the user to put their face in the center of the screen. Be aware that face detection may take many seconds on some devices or high-resolution cameras, so they may be limited in their current real-time uses. But embedded system platforms are getting faster every year, so this may be less of a problem over time.

The most significant way to speed up embedded computer vision applications is to reduce the camera resolution absolutely as much as possible (for example, 0.5 megapixels instead of 5 megapixels), allocate and free images as rarely as possible, and perform image format conversions as rarely as possible. In some cases, there might be some optimized image processing or math libraries, or an optimized version of OpenCV from the CPU vendor of your device (for example, Broadcom, NVIDIA Tegra, Texas Instruments OMAP, or Samsung Exynos), or for your CPU family (for example, ARM Cortex-A9).

Summary

This chapter has shown several different types of image processing filters that can be used to generate various cartoon effects, from a plain sketch mode that looks like a pencil drawing, a paint mode that looks like a color painting, to a cartoon mode that overlays the *sketch* mode on top of the paint mode to appear like a cartoon. It also shows that other fun effects can be obtained, such as the evil mode, which greatly enhanced noisy edges and the alien mode, which changed the skin of a face to appear bright green.

There are many commercial smartphone apps that add similar fun effects on the user's face, such as cartoon filters and skin color changes. There are also professional tools using similar concepts, such as skin-smoothing video post-processing tools that attempt to beautify women's faces by smoothing their skin while keeping the edges and non-skin regions sharp, in order to make their faces appear younger.

This chapter shows how to port the application from a desktop to an embedded system by following the recommended guidelines of developing a working desktop version first, and then porting it to an embedded system and creating a user interface that is suitable for the embedded application. The image processing code is shared between the two projects so that the reader can modify the cartoon filters for the desktop application, and easily see those modifications in the embedded system as well.

Remember that this book includes an OpenCV installation script for Linux and full source code for all projects discussed.

In the next chapter, we are going to learn how to use **multiple view stereo** (**MVS**) and **structure from motion** (**SfM**) for 3D reconstruction, and how to export the final result in OpenMVG format.

2
Explore Structure from Motion with the SfM Module

Structure from motion (SfM) is the process of recovering both the positions of cameras looking at a scene, and the sparse geometry of the scene. The motion between the cameras imposes geometric constraints that can help us recover the *structure* of objects, hence why the process is called SfM. Since OpenCV v3.0+, a contributed (`"contrib"`) module called `sfm` was added, which assists in performing end-to-end SfM processing from multiple images. In this chapter, we will learn how to use the SfM module to reconstruct a scene to a sparse point cloud, including camera poses. Later, we will also *densify* the point cloud, adding many more points to it to make it dense by using an open **Multi-View Stereo (MVS)** package called OpenMVS. SfM is used for high-quality three-dimensional scanning, visual odometry for autonomous navigation, aerial photo mapping, and many more applications, making it one of the most fundamental pursuits within computer vision. Computer vision engineers are expected to be familiar with the core concepts of SfM, and the topic is regularly taught in computer vision courses.

The following topics will be covered in this chapter:

- Core concepts of SfM: **Multi-View Geometry (MVG)**, three-dimensional reconstruction, and **Multi-View Stereo (MVS)**
- Implementing a SfM pipeline using the OpenCV SfM modules
- Visualizing the reconstruction results
- Exporting the reconstruction to OpenMVG and densifying the sparse cloud into a full reconstruction

Technical requirements

These technologies and installations are required to build and run the code in this chapter:

- OpenCV 4 (compiled with the `sfm contrib` module)
- Eigen v3.3+ (required by the `sfm` module)
- Ceres solver v2+ (required by the `sfm` module)
- CMake 3.12+
- Boost v1.66+
- OpenMVS
- CGAL v4.12+ (required by OpenMVS)

The build instructions for the components listed, as well as the code to implement the concepts in this chapter, will be provided in the accompanying code repository. Using OpenMVS is optional, and we may stop after getting the sparse reconstruction. However, the full MVS reconstruction is much more impressive and useful; for instance, for 3D printing replicas.

Any set of photos with sufficient overlap may be sufficient for 3D reconstruction. For example, we may use a set of photos I took of the Crazy Horse memorial head in South Dakota that is bundled with this chapter code. The requirement is that the images should be taken with sufficient movement between them, but enough to have significant overlap to allow for a strong pair-wise match.

In the following example from the Crazy Horse memorial dataset, we can notice a slight change in view angle between the images, with a very strong overlap. Notice how we can also see a great variation below the statue where people are walking about; this will not interfere with the 3D reconstruction of the stone face:

The code files for this book can be downloaded from `https://github.com/PacktPublishing/Mastering-OpenCV-4-Third-Edition`.

Core concepts of SfM

Before we delve into the implementation of a SfM pipeline, let's revisit some key concepts that are an essential part of the process. The foremost class of theoretical topics in SfM is **epipolar geometry (EG)**, the geometry of multiple views or MVG, which builds upon knowledge of **image formation** and **camera calibration**; however, we will only brush over these basic subjects. After we cover a few basics in EG, we will shortly discuss **stereo reconstruction** and look over subjects such as **depth from disparity** and **triangulation**. Other crucial topics in SfM, such as **Robust Feature Matching**, are more mechanical than theoretical, and we will cover them as we advance in coding the system. We intentionally leave out some very interesting topics, such as **camera resectioning**, **PnP algorithms**, and **reconstruction factorization**, since these are handled by the underlying `sfm` module and we need not invoke them, although functions to perform them do exist in OpenCV.

All of these subjects were a source of an incredible amount of research and literature over the last four decades and serve as topics for thousands of academic papers, patents, and other publications. Hartley and Zisserman's *Multiple View Geometry* is by far the most prominent resource for SfM and MVG mathematics and algorithms, although an incredible secondary asset is Szeliski's *Computer Vision: Algorithms and Applications*, which explains SfM in great detail, focusing on Richard Szeliski's seminal contributions to the field. For a tertiary source of explanation, I recommend grabbing a copy of Prince's *Computer Vision: Models, Learning, and Inference*, which features beautiful figures, diagrams, and meticulous mathematical derivation.

Calibrated cameras and epipolar geometry

Our images begin with a projection. The 3D world they see through the lens is *flattened* down on the 2D sensor inside the camera, essentially losing all depth information. How can we then go back from 2D images to 3D structures? The answer, in many cases with standard intensity cameras, is MVG. Intuitively, if we can see (in 2D) an object from at least two views, we can estimate its distance from the cameras. We do that constantly as humans, with our two eyes. Our human depth perception comes from multiple (two) views, but not just that. In fact, human visual perception, as it pertains to sensing depth and 3D structure, is very complex and has to do with the muscles and sensors of the eyes, not just the *images* on our retinas and their processing in the brain. The human visual sense and its magical traits are well beyond the scope of this chapter; however, in more than one way, SfM (and all of computer vision!) is inspired by the human sense of vision.

Back to our cameras. In standard SfM, we utilize the **pinhole camera model**, which is a simplification of the entire optical, mechanical, electrical, and software process that goes on in real cameras. The pinhole model describes how real-world objects turn into pixels and involve some parameters that we call **intrinsic parameters**, since they describe the intrinsic features of the camera:

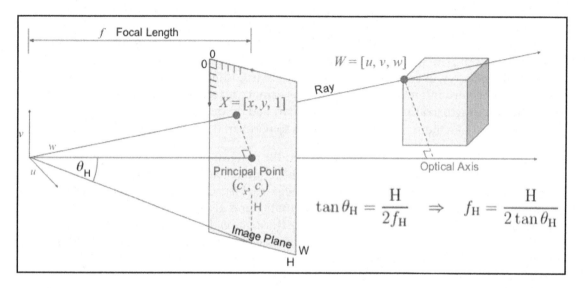

Using the pinhole model, we find the 2D positions of a 3D point on the image plane by applying a projection. Note how the 3D point w and the camera origin form a right-angled triangle, where the adjacent side equals w. The image point x shares the same angle with adjacent f, which is the distance from the origin to the image plane. This distance is called the **focal length**, but that name can be deceiving since the image plane is not actually the focal plane; we converge the two for simplicity. The elementary geometry of overlapping right-angled triangles will tell us that $x = u \cdot f/w$; however, since we deal with images, we must account for the **Principle Point** (c_x, c_y) and arrive at $x = u \cdot f/w + c_x$. If we do the same for the y axis, this follows:

$$
s \begin{bmatrix} x \\ y \\ 1 \end{bmatrix} = \begin{bmatrix} f_W & 0 & c_x \\ 0 & f_H & c_y \\ 0 & 0 & 1 \end{bmatrix} \begin{bmatrix} u \\ v \\ w \end{bmatrix}
$$

The 3 x 3 matrix is called the **intrinsic parameters matrix**, usually denoted as K; however, a number of things seem off about this equation and require explanation. First, we're missing the division by w, where did it go? Second, what is that mysterious s that came about on the LHS of the equation? The answer is **homogeneous coordinates**, meaning we add a 1 at the end of the vector. This useful notation allows us to linearize these operations and perform the division later. At the end of the matrix multiplication step, which we might do for thousands of points at once, we divide the result by the last entry in the vector, which happens to be exactly the w we're looking for. As for s, this is an unknown arbitrary scale factor we must keep in mind, which comes from a perspective in our projection. Imagine we had a toy car very close to the camera, and next to it a real-sized car 10 meters away from the camera; in the image, they would appear to be the same size. In other words, we could move the 3D point W anywhere along the ray going out from the camera and still get the same X coordinate in the image. That is the curse of perspective projection: we lose the depth information, which we mentioned at the beginning of this chapter.

One more thing we must consider is the pose of our camera in the world. Not all cameras are placed at the origin point $(0, 0, 0)$, especially if we have a system with many cameras. We conveniently place one camera at the origin, but the rest will have a rotation and translation (rigid transform) component with respect to themselves. We, therefore, add another matrix to the projection equation:

$$s \begin{bmatrix} x \\ y \\ 1 \end{bmatrix} = \begin{bmatrix} f_W & 0 & c_x \\ 0 & f_H & c_y \\ 0 & 0 & 1 \end{bmatrix} \begin{bmatrix} r_1 & r_2 & r_3 & t_x \\ r_4 & r_5 & r_6 & t_y \\ r_7 & r_8 & r_9 & t_z \end{bmatrix} \begin{bmatrix} u \\ v \\ w \\ 1 \end{bmatrix}$$

The new 3 x 4 matrix is usually called the **extrinsic parameters matrix** and carries 3 x 3 rotation and 3 x 1 translation components. Notice we use the same homogeneous coordinates trick to help incorporate the translation into the calculation by adding 1 at the end of $\vec{W}$. We will often see this entire equation written as $sX = K[R|t]W$ in the literature:

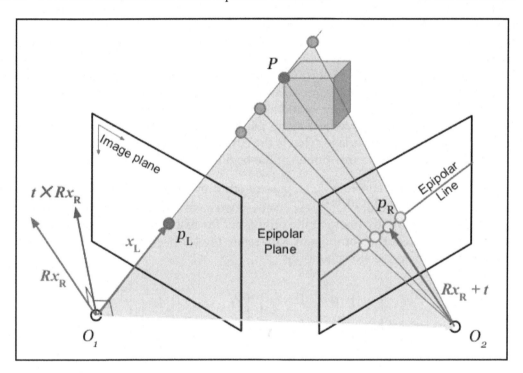

Consider two cameras looking at the same object point. As we just discussed, we can slide the *real* location of the 3D point along the axis from the camera and still observe the same 2D point, thus losing the depth information. Intuitively, two viewing angles should be enough to find the real 3D positions, as the rays from both viewpoints converge at it. Indeed, as we slide the point on the ray, in the other camera looking from a different angle, this position changes. In fact, any point in camera **L** (left) will correspond to a *line* in camera **R** (right), called the **epipolar line** (sometimes known as **epiline**), which lies on the **epipolar plane** constructed by the two cameras' optical centers and the 3D point. This can be used as a geometric constraint between the two views that can help us find a relationship.

We already know that between the two cameras, there's a rigid transform $[R|t]$. If we want to represent x_R, a point in camera **R**, in the coordinate frame of camera **L**, we can write . If we take the cross product $t \times Rx_R$, we will receive a vector *perpendicular* to the epipolar plane. Therefore, it follows that $x_L \cdot t \times Rx_R = 0$ since x_L lies *on* the epipolar plane and a dot product would yield 0. We take the skew symmetric form for the cross product and we can write $x_L^T [t]_\times Rx_R = 0$, then combine this into a single matrix $x_L^T E x_R = 0$. We call E the **essential matrix**. The essential matrix gives us an **epipolar constraint** over all pairs of points between camera L and camera R that converge at a real 3D point. If a pair of points (from **L** and **R**) fails to satisfy this constraint, it is most likely not a valid pairing. We can also estimate the essential matrix using a number of point pairings since they simply construct a homogeneous system of linear equations. The solution can be easily obtained with an eigenvalue or **singular value decomposition (SVD)**.

So far in our geometry, we assumed our cameras were normalized, essentially meaning $K = I$, the identity matrix. However, in real-life images with particular pixel sizes and focal lengths, we must account for the real intrinsic. To that end, we can apply the inverse of on both sides: $(K^{-1}x_L)^T E K^{-1} x_R = x_L^T K^{-T} E K^{-1} x_R = x_L^T F x_R = 0$. This new matrix we end up with is called the **fundamental matrix**, which can be estimated right from enough pairings of pixel coordinate points. We can then get the essential matrix if we know K; however, the fundamental matrix may serve as a good epipolar constraint all on its own.

Stereo reconstruction and SfM

In SfM, we would like to recover both the poses of cameras and the position of 3D feature points. We have just seen how simple 2D pair matches of points can help us estimate the essential matrix and thus encode the rigid geometric relationship between views: $[R|t]$. The essential matrix can be decomposed into R and t by way of SVD, and having found R and t, we proceed with finding the 3D points and fulfilling the SfM task for the two images.

We have seen the geometric relationship between two 2D views and the 3D world; however, we are yet to see how to recover 3D shape from the 2D views. One insight we had is that given two views of the same point, we can cross the two rays from the optic center of the cameras and the 2D points on the image plane, and they will converge on the 3D point. This is the basic idea of **triangulation.** One simple way to go about solving for the 3D point is to write the projection equation and equate, since the 3D point (W) is common, $x_L = P_L W, x_R = P_R W$, where the P matrices are the $K[R|t]$ projection matrices. The equations can be worked into a homogeneous system of linear equations and can be solved, for example, by SVD. This is known as the **direct linear method** for triangulation; however, it is severely sub-optimal since it makes no direct minimization of a meaningful error functor. Several other methods have been suggested, including looking at the closest point between the rays, which generally do not directly intersect, known as the **mid-point method**.

After getting a baseline 3D reconstruction from two views, we can proceed with adding more views. This is usually done in a different method, employing a match between existing 3D and incoming 2D points. The class of algorithms is called **Point-n-Perspective (PnP)**, which we will not discuss here. Another method is to perform pairwise stereo reconstruction, as we've seen already, and calculate the scaling factor, since each image pair reconstructed may result in a different scale, as discussed earlier.

Another interesting method for recovering depth information is to further utilize the epipolar lines. We know that a point in image **L** will lie on a line in image **R**, and we can also calculate the line precisely using E. The task is, therefore, to find the right point on the epipolar line in image **R** that best matches the point in image L. This line matching method may be called **stereo depth reconstruction**, and since we can recover the depth information for almost every pixel in the image, it is most times a **dense** reconstruction. In practice, the epipolar lines are first **rectified** to be completely horizontal, mimicking a **pure horizontal translation** between the images. This reduces the problem of matching only on the x axis:

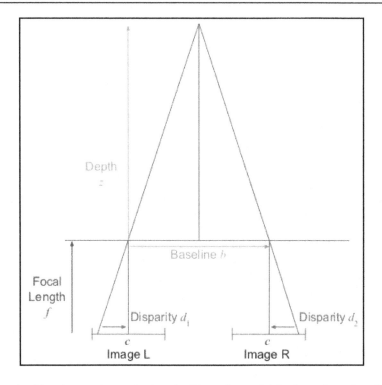

The major appeal of horizontal translation is **disparity**, which describes the distance an interest point travels horizontally between the two images. In the preceding diagram, we can notice that due to right overlapping triangles: $\frac{B}{z} = \frac{d}{f}$, which leads to $d = \frac{B \cdot f}{z}$. The baseline B (horizontal motion), and the focal length f are constant with respect to the particular 3D point and its distance from the camera. Therefore, the insight is that the **disparity is inversely proportional to depth**. The smaller the disparity, the farther the point is from the camera. When we look at the horizon from a moving train's window, the faraway mountains move very slowly, while the close by trees move very fast. This effect is also known as **parallax**. Using disparity for 3D reconstruction is at the base of all stereo algorithms.

Another topic of wide research is MVS, which utilizes the epipolar constraint to find matching points from multiple views at once. Scanning the epilines in multiple images all at once can impose further constraints on the matching features. Only when a match that satisfies all the constraints is found is it considered. When we recover multiple camera positions, we could employ MVS to get a dense reconstruction, which is what we will do later in this chapter.

Implementing SfM in OpenCV

OpenCV has an abundance of tools to implement a full-fledged SfM pipeline from first principles. However, such a task is very demanding and beyond the scope of this chapter. The former edition of this book presented just a small taste of what building such a system will entail, but luckily now we have at our disposal a tried and tested technique integrated right into OpenCV's API. Although the sfm module allows us to get away with simply providing a non-parametric function with a list of images to crunch and receive a fully reconstructed scene with a sparse point cloud and camera poses, we will not take that route. Instead, we will see in this section some useful methods that will allow us to have much more control over the reconstruction and exemplify some of the topics we discussed in the last section, as well as be more robust to noise.

This section will begin with the very basics of SfM: **matching images** using key points and feature descriptors. We will then advance to finding **tracks**, and multiple views of similar features through the image set, using a match graph. We proceed with **3D reconstruction**, **3D visualization**, and finally MVS with OpenMVS.

Image feature matching

SfM, as presented in the last section, relies on the understanding of the geometric relationship between images as it pertains to the visible objects in them. We saw that we can calculate the exact motion between two images with sufficient information on how the objects in the images move. The essential or fundamental matrices, which can be estimated linearly from image features, can be decomposed to the rotation and translation elements that define a **3D rigid transform**. Thereafter, this transform can help us triangulate the 3D position of the objects, from the 3D-2D projection equations or from a dense stereo matching over the rectified epilines. It all begins with image feature matching, so we will see how to obtain robust and noise-free matching.

OpenCV has an extensive offering of 2D feature **detectors** (also called **extractors**) and **descriptors**. Features are designed to be invariant to image deformations so they can be matched through translation, rotation, scaling, and other more complicated transformations (affine, projective) of the objects in the scene. One of the latest additions to OpenCV's APIs is the AKAZE feature extractor and detector, which presents a very good compromise between speed of calculation and robustness to transformation. AKAZE was shown to outperform other prominent features, such as **ORB** (short for **Oriented BRIEF**) and **SURF** (short for **Speeded Up Robust Features**).

The following snippet will extract an AKAZE key point, calculate AKAZE features for each of the images we collect in imagesFilenames, and save them in the keypoints and descriptors arrays respectively:

```
auto detector = AKAZE::create();
auto extractor = AKAZE::create();

for (const auto& i : imagesFilenames) {
    Mat grayscale;
    cvtColor(images[i], grayscale, COLOR_BGR2GRAY);
    detector->detect(grayscale, keypoints[i]);
    extractor->compute(grayscale, keypoints[i], descriptors[i]);

    CV_LOG_INFO(TAG, "Found " + to_string(keypoints[i].size()) + "
    keypoints in " + i);
}
```

Note we also convert the images to grayscale; however, this step may be omitted and the results will not suffer.

Here's a visualization of the detected features in two adjacent images. Notice how many of them repeat; this is known as feature **repeatability**, which is one of the most desired functions in a good feature extractor:

Next up is matching the features between every pair of images. OpenCV provides an excellent feature matching suite. AKAZE feature descriptors are *binary*, meaning they cannot be regarded as binary-encoded numbers when matched; they must be compared on the bit level with bit-wise operators. OpenCV offers a **Hamming distance** metric for binary feature matchers, which essentially count the number of incorrect matches between the two-bit sequences:

```
vector<DMatch> matchWithRatioTest(const DescriptorMatcher& matcher,
                                  const Mat& desc1,
                                  const Mat& desc2)
{
    // Raw match
    vector< vector<DMatch> > nnMatch;
```

```
matcher.knnMatch(desc1, desc2, nnMatch, 2);

// Ratio test filter
vector<DMatch> ratioMatched;
for (size_t i = 0; i < nnMatch.size(); i++) {
    const DMatch first = nnMatch[i][0];
    const float dist1 = nnMatch[i][0].distance;
    const float dist2 = nnMatch[i][1].distance;

    if (dist1 < MATCH_RATIO_THRESHOLD * dist2) {
        ratioMatched.push_back(first);
    }
}

return ratioMatched;
}
```

The preceding function not only invokes our matcher (for example, a
BFMatcher(NORM_HAMMING)) regularly, it also performs the **ratio test**. This simple test is a
very fundamental concept in many computer vision algorithms that rely on feature
matching (such as SfM, panorama stitching, sparse tracking, and more). Instead of looking
for a single match for a feature from image *A* in image *B*, we look for two matches in image
B and make sure there is *no confusion*. Confusion in matching may arise if two potential
matching-feature descriptors are too similar (in terms of their distance metric) and we
cannot tell which of them is the correct match for the query, so we discard them both to
prevent confusion.

Next, we implement a **reciprocity filter**. This filter only allows feature matches that match
(with a ratio test) in *A* to *B*, as well as *B* to *A*. Essentially, this is making sure there's a one-
to-one match between features in image *A* and those in image *B*: a symmetric match. The
reciprocity filter removes even more ambiguity and contributes to a cleaner, more robust
match:

```
// Match with ratio test filter
vector<DMatch> match = matchWithRatioTest(matcher, descriptors[imgi],
descriptors[imgj]);

// Reciprocity test filter
vector<DMatch> matchRcp = matchWithRatioTest(matcher, descriptors[imgj],
descriptors[imgi]);
vector<DMatch> merged;
for (const DMatch& dmrecip : matchRcp) {
    bool found = false;
    for (const DMatch& dm : match) {
        // Only accept match if 1 matches 2 AND 2 matches 1.
        if (dmrecip.queryIdx == dm.trainIdx and dmrecip.trainIdx ==
```

```
            dm.queryIdx) {
                merged.push_back(dm);
                found = true;
                break;
            }
        }
        if (found) {
            continue;
        }
    }
```

Lastly, we apply the **epipolar constraint**. Every two images that have a valid rigid transformation between them would comply with the epipolar constraint over their feature points, $x_L^T F x_R = 0$, and those who don't pass this test (with sufficient success) are likely not a good match and may contribute to noise. We achieve this by calculating the fundamental matrix with a voting algorithm (RANSAC) and checking for the ratio of inliers to outliers. We apply a threshold to discard matches with a low survival rate with respect to the original match:

```
// Fundamental matrix filter
vector<uint8_t> inliersMask(merged.size());
vector<Point2f> imgiPoints, imgjPoints;
for (const DMatch& m : merged) {
    imgiPoints.push_back(keypoints[imgi][m.queryIdx].pt);
    imgjPoints.push_back(keypoints[imgj][m.trainIdx].pt);
}
findFundamentalMat(imgiPoints, imgjPoints, inliersMask);

vector<DMatch> final;
for (size_t m = 0; m < merged.size(); m++) {
    if (inliersMask[m]) {
        final.push_back(merged[m]);
    }
}

if ((float)final.size() / (float)match.size() < PAIR_MATCH_SURVIVAL_RATE) {
    CV_LOG_INFO(TAG, "Final match '" + imgi + "'->'" + imgj + "' has less
than "+to_string(PAIR_MATCH_SURVIVAL_RATE)+" inliers from orignal. Skip");
    continue;
}
```

We can see the effect of each of the filtering steps, raw match, ratio, reciprocity, and epipolar, in the following figure:

Finding feature tracks

The concept of **feature tracks** was introduced in SfM literature as early as 1992 in Tomasi and Kanade's work (*Shape and Motion from Image Streams*, 1992) and made famous in Snavely and Szeliski's seminal photo tourism work from 2007 for large-scale unconstrained reconstructions. Tracks are simply the 2D positions of a single scene feature, an interesting point, over a number of views. Tracks are important since they maintain consistency across frames than can be composed into a global optimization problem, as Snavely suggested. Tracks are specifically important to us since OpenCV's `sfm` module allows to reconstruct a scene by providing just the 2D tracks across all the views:

Having already found a pair-wise match between all views, we have the required information to find tracks within those matched features. If we follow feature i in the first image to the second image through the match, then from the second image to the third image through their own match, and so on, we would end up with its track. This sort of bookkeeping can easily become too hard to implement in a straightforward fashion with standard data structures. However, it can be simply done if we represent all the matches in a **match graph**. Each node in the graph would be a feature detected in a single image, and edges would be the matches we recovered. From the feature nodes of the first image, we would have many edges to the feature nodes of the second image, third image, fourth image, and so on (for matches not discarded by our filters). Since our matches are reciprocal (symmetric), the graph can be undirected. Moreover, the reciprocity test ensures that for feature i in the first image, there is **only one** matching feature j in the second image, and vice versa: feature j will only match back to feature i.

The following is a visual example of such a match graph. The node colors represent the image from which the feature point (node) has originated. Edges represent a match between image features. We can notice the very strong pattern of a feature matching chain from the first image to the last:

To code the match graph, we can use the **Boost Graph Library** (**BGL**), which has an extensive API for graph processing and algorithms. Constructing the graph is straightforward; we simply augment the nodes with the image ID and feature ID, so later we can trace back the origin:

```cpp
using namespace boost;

struct ImageFeature {
    string image;
    size_t featureID;
};
typedef adjacency_list < listS, vecS, undirectedS, ImageFeature > Graph;
typedef graph_traits < Graph >::vertex_descriptor Vertex;
map<pair<string, int>, Vertex> vertexByImageFeature;

Graph g;

// Add vertices - image features
for (const auto& imgi : keypoints) {
    for (size_t i = 0; i < imgi.second.size(); i++) {
        Vertex v = add_vertex(g);
        g[v].image = imgi.first;
        g[v].featureID = i;
        vertexByImageFeature[make_pair(imgi.first, i)] = v;
    }
}

// Add edges - feature matches
for (const auto& match : matches) {
    for (const DMatch& dm : match.second) {
        Vertex& vI = vertexByImageFeature[make_pair(match.first.first,
dm.queryIdx)];
        Vertex& vJ = vertexByImageFeature[make_pair(match.first.second,
dm.trainIdx)];
        add_edge(vI, vJ, g);
```

```
        }
    }
```

Looking at a visualization of the resulting graph (using `boost::write_graphviz()`), we can see many cases where our matching is erroneous. A bad match chain will involve more than one feature from the same image in the chain. We marked a few such instances in the following figure; notice some chains have two or more nodes with the same color:

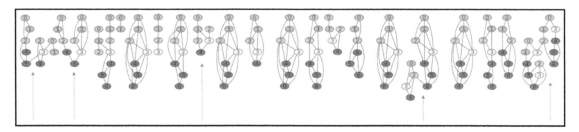

We can notice the chains are essentially connected components in the graph. Extracting the components is simple using `boost::connected_components()`:

```
// Get connected components
std::vector<int> component(num_vertices(gFiltered), -1);
int num = connected_components(gFiltered, &component[0]);
map<int, vector<Vertex> > components;
for (size_t i = 0; i != component.size(); ++i) {
    if (component[i] >= 0) {
        components[component[i]].push_back(i);
    }
}
```

We can filter out the bad components (with more than one feature from any one image) to get a clean match graph.

3D reconstruction and visualization

Having obtained the tracks in principle, we need to align them in a data structure that OpenCV's SfM module expects. Unfortunately, the `sfm` module is not very well documented, so this part we have to figure out on our own from the source code. We will be invoking the following function under the `cv::sfm::` namespace, which can be found in `opencv_contrib/modules/sfm/include/opencv2/sfm/reconstruct.hpp`:

```
void reconstruct(InputArrayOfArrays points2d, OutputArray Ps, OutputArray
points3d, InputOutputArray K, bool is_projective = false);
```

The `opencv_contrib/modules/sfm/src/simple_pipeline.cpp` file has a major hint as to what that function expects as input:

```cpp
static void
parser_2D_tracks( const std::vector<Mat> &points2d, libmv::Tracks &tracks )
{
  const int nframes = static_cast<int>(points2d.size());
  for (int frame = 0; frame < nframes; ++frame) {
    const int ntracks = points2d[frame].cols;
    for (int track = 0; track < ntracks; ++track) {
      const Vec2d track_pt = points2d[frame].col(track);
      if ( track_pt[0] > 0 && track_pt[1] > 0 )
        tracks.Insert(frame, track, track_pt[0], track_pt[1]);
    }
  }
}
```

In general, the `sfm` module uses a reduced version of `libmv` (`https://developer.blender.org/tag/libmv/`), which is a well-established SfM package used for 3D reconstruction for cinema production with the Blender 3D (`https://www.blender.org/`) graphics software.

We can tell the tracks need to be placed in a vector of multiple individual `cv::Mat`, where each contains an aligned list of `cv::Vec2d` as columns, meaning it has two rows of `double`. We can also deduce that missing (unmatched) feature points in a track will have a negative coordinate. The following snippet will extract tracks in the desired data structure from the match graph:

```cpp
vector<Mat> tracks(nViews); // Initialize to number of views

// Each component is a track
const size_t nViews = imagesFilenames.size();
tracks.resize(nViews);
for (int i = 0; i < nViews; i++) {
    tracks[i].create(2, components.size(), CV_64FC1);
    tracks[i].setTo(-1.0); // default is (-1, -1) - no match
}
int i = 0;
for (auto c = components.begin(); c != components.end(); ++c, ++i) {
    for (const int v : c->second) {
        const int imageID = imageIDs[g[v].image];
        const size_t featureID = g[v].featureID;
        const Point2f p = keypoints[g[v].image][featureID].pt;
        tracks[imageID].at<double>(0, i) = p.x;
        tracks[imageID].at<double>(1, i) = p.y;
    }
}
```

We follow up with running the reconstruction function, collecting the sparse 3D point cloud and the color for each 3D point, and afterward, visualize the results (using functions from `cv::viz::`):

```
cv::sfm::reconstruct(tracks, Rs, Ts, K, points3d, true);
```

This will produce a sparse reconstruction with a point cloud and camera positions, visualized in the following image:

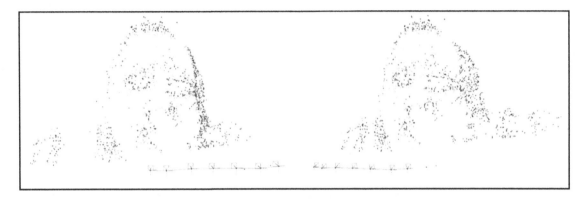

Re-projecting the 3D points back on the 2D images we can validate a correct reconstruction:

See the entire code for reconstruction and visualization in the accompanying source repository.

Notice the reconstruction is very sparse; we only see 3D points where features have matched. This doesn't make for a very appealing effect when getting the geometry of objects in the scene. In many cases, SfM pipelines do not conclude with a sparse reconstruction, which is not useful for many applications, such as 3D scanning. Next, we will see how to get a **dense** reconstruction.

MVS for dense reconstruction

With the sparse 3D point cloud and the positions of the cameras, we can proceed with dense reconstruction using MVS. We already learned the basic concept of MVS in the first section; however, we do not need to implement this from scratch, but rather we can use the **OpenMVS** project. To use OpenMVS for cloud densifying, we must save our project in a specialized format. OpenMVS provides a class for saving and loading .mvs projects, the MVS::Interface class, defined in MVS/Interface.h.

Let's start with the camera:

```
MVS::Interface interface;
MVS::Interface::Platform p;

// Add camera
MVS::Interface::Platform::Camera c;
c.K = Matx33d(K_); // The intrinsic matrix as refined by the bundle
adjustment
c.R = Matx33d::eye(); // Camera doesn't have any inherent rotation
c.C = Point3d(0,0,0); // or translation
c.name = "Camera1";
const Size imgS = images[imagesFilenames[0]].size();
c.width = imgS.width; // Size of the image, to normalize the intrinsics
c.height = imgS.height;
p.cameras.push_back(c);
```

When adding the camera poses (views), we must take care. OpenMVS expects to get the rotation and **center** of the camera, and not the camera pose matrix for point projection $[R|t]$. We therefore must translate the translation vector to represent the center of the camera by applying the inverse rotation $-R^t t$:

```
// Add views
p.poses.resize(Rs.size());
for (size_t i = 0; i < Rs.size(); ++i) {
    Mat t = -Rs[i].t() * Ts[i]; // Camera *center*
    p.poses[i].C.x = t.at<double>(0);
    p.poses[i].C.y = t.at<double>(1);
    p.poses[i].C.z = t.at<double>(2);
    Rs[i].convertTo(p.poses[i].R, CV_64FC1);

    // Add corresponding image (make sure index aligns)
    MVS::Interface::Image image;
    image.cameraID = 0;
    image.poseID = i;
    image.name = imagesFilenames[i];
    image.platformID = 0;
```

```
    interface.images.push_back(image);
}
p.name = "Platform1";
interface.platforms.push_back(p);
```

After adding the point cloud to the `Interface` as well, we can proceed with the cloud densifying in the command line:

```
$ ${openMVS}/build/bin/DensifyPointCloud -i crazyhorse.mvs
18:48:32 [App ] Command line: -i crazyhorse.mvs
18:48:32 [App ] Camera model loaded: platform 0; camera 0; f 0.896x0.896;
poses 7
18:48:32 [App ] Image loaded 0: P1000965.JPG
18:48:32 [App ] Image loaded 1: P1000966.JPG
18:48:32 [App ] Image loaded 2: P1000967.JPG
18:48:32 [App ] Image loaded 3: P1000968.JPG
18:48:32 [App ] Image loaded 4: P1000969.JPG
18:48:32 [App ] Image loaded 5: P1000970.JPG
18:48:32 [App ] Image loaded 6: P1000971.JPG
18:48:32 [App ] Scene loaded from interface format (11ms):
7 images (7 calibrated) with a total of 5.25 MPixels (0.75 MPixels/image)
1557 points, 0 vertices, 0 faces
18:48:32 [App ] Preparing images for dense reconstruction completed: 7
images (125ms)
18:48:32 [App ] Selecting images for dense reconstruction completed: 7
images (5ms)
Estimated depth-maps 7 (100%, 1m44s705ms)
Filtered depth-maps 7 (100%, 1s671ms)
Fused depth-maps 7 (100%, 421ms)
18:50:20 [App ] Depth-maps fused and filtered: 7 depth-maps, 1653963
depths, 263027 points (16%%) (1s684ms)
18:50:20 [App ] Densifying point-cloud completed: 263027 points
(1m48s263ms)
18:50:21 [App ] Scene saved (489ms):
7 images (7 calibrated)
263027 points, 0 vertices, 0 faces
18:50:21 [App ] Point-cloud saved: 263027 points (46ms)
```

This process might take a few minutes to complete. However, once it's done, the results are very impressive. The dense point cloud has a whopping **263,027 3D points**, compared to just 1,557 in the sparse cloud. We can visualize the dense OpenMVS project using the `Viewer` app bundled in OpenMVS:

OpenMVS has several more functions to complete the reconstruction, such as extracting a triangular mesh from the dense point cloud.

Summary

This chapter focused on SfM and its implementation with OpenCV's `sfm` contributed module and OpenMVS. We explored some theoretical concepts in multiple view geometry, and several practical matters: extracting key feature points, matching them, creating and analyzing the match graph, running the reconstruction, and finally performing MVS to densify the sparse 3D point cloud.

In the next chapter, we will see how to use OpenCV's `face contrib` module to detect facial landmarks in photos, as well as detecting the direction a face is pointing with the `solvePnP` function.

Face Landmark and Pose with the Face Module

3

Face landmark detection is the process of finding points of interest in an image of a human face. It recently saw a spur of interest in the computer vision community, as it has many compelling applications; for example, detecting emotion through facial gestures, estimating gaze direction, changing facial appearance (**face swap**), augmenting faces with graphics, and puppeteering of virtual characters. We can see many of these applications in today's smartphones and PC web-camera programs. To achieve these applications, the landmark detector must find dozens of points on the face, such as corners of the mouth, corners of eyes, the silhouette of the jaws, and many more. To that end, many algorithms were developed, and a few were implemented in OpenCV. In this chapter, we will discuss the process of face landmark (also known as **facemark**) detection using the `cv::face` module, which provides an API for inference, as well as training of a facemark detector. We will see how to apply the facemark detector to locating the direction of the face in 3D.

The following topics will be covered in this chapter:

- Introducing face landmark detection history and theory, and an explanation of the algorithms implemented in OpenCV
- Utilizing OpenCV's `face` module for face landmark detection
- Estimating the approximate direction of the face by leveraging 2D–3D information

Technical requirements

The following technologies and installations are required to build the code in this chapter:

- OpenCV v4 (compiled with the `face contrib` module)
- Boost v1.66+

Build instructions for the preceding components listed, as well as the code to implement the concepts presented in this chapter, will be provided in the accompanying code repository.

To run the facemark detector, a pre-trained model is required. Although training the detector model is certainly possible with the APIs provided in OpenCV, some pre-trained models are offered for download. One such model can be obtained from `https://raw.githubusercontent.com/kurnianggoro/GSOC2017/master/data/lbfmodel.yaml`, supplied by the contributor of the algorithm implementation to OpenCV (during the 2017 **Google Summer of Code (GSoC)**).

The facemark detector can work with any image; however, we can use a prescribed dataset of facial photos and videos that are used to benchmark facemark algorithms. Such a dataset is **300-VW**, available through **Intelligent Behaviour Understanding Group (iBUG)**, a computer vision group at Imperial College London: `https://ibug.doc.ic.ac.uk/resources/300-VW/`. It contains hundreds of videos of facial appearances in media, carefully annotated with 68 facial landmark points. This dataset can be used for training the facemark detector, as well as to understand the performance level of the pre-trained model we use. The following is an excerpt from one of the 300-VW videos with ground truth annotation:

Image reproduced under Creative Commons license

The code files for this book can be downloaded from `https://github.com/PacktPublishing/Mastering-OpenCV-4-Third-Edition`.

Theory and context

Facial landmark detection algorithms automatically find the locations of key landmark points on facial images. Those key points are usually prominent points locating a facial component, such as eye corner or mouth corner, to achieve a higher-level understanding of the face shape. To detect a decent range of facial expressions, for example, points around the jawline, mouth, eyes, and eyebrows are needed. Finding facial landmarks proves to be a difficult task for a variety of reasons: great variation between subjects, illumination conditions, and occlusions. To that end, computer vision researchers proposed dozens of landmark detection algorithms over the past three decades.

A recent survey of facial landmark detection (Wu and Ji, 2018) suggests separating landmark detectors into three groups: holistic methods, **constrained local model (CLM)** methods, and regression methods:

- Wu and Ji pose the **holistic methods** as ones that model the complete appearance of the face's pixel intensities
- **CLM methods** examine *local* patches around each landmark in combination with a global model
- **Regression methods** iteratively try to predict landmark locations using a cascade of small updates learned by regressors

Active appearance models and constrained local models

A canonical example of a holistic method is the **active appearance model (AAM)** from the late '90s, usually attributed to the work of T.F. Cootes (1998). In AAM, the goal is to iteratively match a known face rendering (from the training data) to the target input image, which upon convergence gives the shape, and thus, landmarks. The AAM method and its derivatives were extremely popular, and still take up a fair share of attention. However AAM's successor, CLM methods, have shown far better performance under illumination changes and occlusions, and rapidly took the lead. Mostly attributed to the work of Cristinacce and Cootes (2006) and Saragih et al. (2011), CLM methods model the pixel intensity appearance of each landmark locally (patch), as well as incorporating a global shape beforehand to cope with occlusions and false local detections.

CLMs can be generally described as looking to minimize, where p is a facial shape *pose* that can be decomposed to its D landmark $x_d(p)$ points, as follows:

$$\hat{p} = \arg\min_p Q(p) + \sum_{d=1}^{D} \text{Distance}(x_d(p), I)$$

Facial poses are primarily obtained by way of **principal component analysis (PCA)**, and the landmarks are the result of the inverse PCA operation. Using PCA is useful, since most facial shape poses are strongly correlated, and the full landmark position space is highly redundant. A distance function (denoted Distance) is used to determine how close a given landmark model point is to the image observation I. In many cases, the distance function is a patch-to-patch similarity measure (template matching), or usage of edge-based features, such as the **histogram of gradients (HOG)**. The term $Q(p)$ is used for regularization over improbable or extreme face shape poses.

Regression methods

In contrast, *regression methods* employ a more simplistic, but powerful approach. These methods use machine learning, by way of regression, an *update step* to an initial positioning of the landmarks and iterate until the positions converge, where $\hat{S}^{(t)}$ is the shape at time t, and $r_t(I, \hat{S}^{(t)})$ is the result of running the regressor r on the image I and the current shape, demonstrated as follows:

$$\hat{S}^{(t+1)} = \hat{S}^{(t)} + r_t(I, \hat{S}^{(t)})$$

By cascading these update operations, the final landmark positions are obtained.

This approach allows consuming enormous amounts of training data and letting go of the handcrafted models for the local similarity and global constraints that are the center of CLM methods. The prevailing regression method is **gradient boosting trees (GBT)**, which offer very fast inference, simple implementations, and are parallelizable as a forest.

There are yet newer approaches to facial landmark detection, utilizing deep learning. These new methods either directly regress the position of the facial landmarks from the image by employing **convolutional neural networks (CNN)**, or use a hybrid approach of CNNs with a 3D model and cascaded-regression methods.

OpenCV's `face` module (first introduced in OpenCV v3.0) that contains implementations for AAM, Ren et al. (2014) and Kazemi et al. (2014) regression type methods. In this chapter, we will employ Ren et al.'s (2014) method, since it presents the best results given the pre-trained model provided by the contributors. Ren et al.'s method learns the best **local binary features** (LBF), a very short binary code that describes the visual appearance around a point for each landmark, as well as to learn the shape update step by regression.

Facial landmark detection in OpenCV

Landmark detection starts with **face detection**, finding faces in the image and their extents (bounding boxes). Facial detection has long been considered a solved problem, and OpenCV contains one of the first robust face detectors freely available to the public. In fact, OpenCV, in its early days, was majorly known and used for its fast face detection feature, implementing the canonical Viola-Jones boosted cascade classifier algorithm (Viola et al. 2001, 2004), and providing a pre-trained model. While face detection has grown much since those early days, the fastest and easiest method for detecting faces in OpenCV is still to use the bundled cascade classifiers, by means of the `cv::CascadeClassifier` class provided in the `core` module.

We implement a simple helper function to detect faces with the cascade classifier, shown as follows:

```
void faceDetector(const Mat& image,
                  std::vector<Rect> &faces,
                  CascadeClassifier &face_cascade) {
    Mat gray;

    // The cascade classifier works best on grayscale images
    if (image.channels() > 1) {
        cvtColor(image, gray, COLOR_BGR2GRAY);
    } else {
        gray = image.clone();
    }

    // Histogram equalization generally aids in face detection
    equalizeHist(gray, gray);

    faces.clear();

    // Run the cascade classifier
    face_cascade.detectMultiScale(
        gray,
        faces,
```

```
        1.4, // pyramid scale factor
        3,   // lower thershold for neighbors count
        // here we hint the classifier to only look for one face
        CASCADE_SCALE_IMAGE + CASCADE_FIND_BIGGEST_OBJECT);
}
```

We may want to tweak the two parameters that govern the face detection: pyramid scale factor and number of neighbors. The pyramid scale factor is used to create a pyramid of images within which the detector will try to find faces. This is how multi-scale detection is achieved, since the bare detector has a fixed aperture. In each step of the image pyramid, the image is downscaled by this factor, so a small factor (closer to 1.0) will result in many images, longer runtime, but more accurate results. We also have control of the lower threshold for a number of neighbors. This comes into play when the cascade classifier has multiple positive face classifications in close proximity. Here, we instruct the overall classification to only return a face bound if it has at least three neighboring positive face classifications. A lower number (an integer, close to 1) will return more detections, but will also introduce false positives.

We must initialize the cascade classifier from the OpenCV-provided models (XML files of the serialized models are provided in the $OPENCV_ROOT/data/haarcascades directory). We use the standard trained classifier on frontal faces, demonstrated as follows:

```
const string cascade_name =
"$OPENCV_ROOT/data/haarcascades/haarcascade_frontalface_default.xml";

CascadeClassifier face_cascade;
if (not face_cascade.load(cascade_name)) {
    cerr << "Cannot load cascade classifier from file: " << cascade_name <<
endl;
    return -1;
}

// ... obtain an image in img

vector<Rect> faces;
faceDetector(img, faces, face_cascade);

// Check if any faces were detected or not
if (faces.size() == 0) {
    cerr << "Cannot detect any faces in the image." << endl;
    return -1;
}
```

A visualization of the results of the face detector is shown in the following screenshot:

The facemark detector will work around the detected faces, beginning at the bounding boxes. However, first we must initialize the `cv::face::Facemark` object, demonstrated as follows:

```
#include <opencv2/face.hpp>

using namespace cv::face;

// ...

const string facemark_filename = "data/lbfmodel.yaml";
Ptr<Facemark> facemark = createFacemarkLBF();
facemark->loadModel(facemark_filename);
cout << "Loaded facemark LBF model" << endl;
```

The `cv::face::Facemark` abstract API is used for all the landmark detector flavors, and offers base functionality for implementation for inference and training according to the specific algorithm. Once loaded, the `facemark` object can be used with its `fit` function to find the face shape, shown as follows:

```
vector<Rect> faces;
faceDetector(img, faces, face_cascade);

// Check if faces detected or not
if (faces.size() != 0) {
    // We assume a single face so we look at the first only
    cv::rectangle(img, faces[0], Scalar(255, 0, 0), 2);

    vector<vector<Point2f> > shapes;

    if (facemark->fit(img, faces, shapes)) {
        // Draw the detected landmarks
        drawFacemarks(img, shapes[0], cv::Scalar(0, 0, 255));
    }
} else {
    cout << "Faces not detected." << endl;
}
```

A visualization of the results of the landmark detector (using `cv::face::drawFacemarks`) is shown in the following screenshot:

Measuring error

Visually, the results seem very good. However, since we have the ground truth data, we may elect to analytically compare it to the detection and get an error estimate. We can use a standard mean Euclidean distance metric ($\frac{1}{n}\sum_i^n \|X_i - \hat{y}_i\|_{L_2}$) to tell how close each predicted landmark is to the ground truth on average:

```
float MeanEuclideanDistance(const vector<Point2f>& A, const
vector<Point2f>& B) {
    float med = 0.0f;
    for (int i = 0; i < A.size(); ++i) {
        med += cv::norm(A[i] - B[i]);
    }
    return med / (float)A.size();
}
```

A visualization of the results with the prediction (red) and ground truth (green) overlaid, shown in the following screenshot:

We can see the average error over all landmarks is roughly only one pixel for these particular video frames.

Estimating face direction from landmarks

Having obtained the facial landmarks, we can attempt to find the direction of the face. The 2D face landmark points essentially conform to the shape of the head. So, given a 3D model of a generic human head, we can find approximate corresponding 3D points for a number of facial landmarks, as shown in the following photo:

Estimated pose calculation

From these 2D–3D correspondences, we can calculate 3D pose (rotation and translation) of the head, with respect to the camera, by way of the **Point-n-Perspective** (**PnP**) algorithm. The details of the algorithm and object pose detection are beyond the scope of this chapter; however, we can quickly rationalize why just a handful of 2D–3D point correspondences are suffice to achieve this. The camera that took the preceding picture has a **rigid** transformation, meaning it has moved a certain distance from the object, as well as rotated somewhat, with respect to it. In very broad terms, we can then write the relationship between points on the image (near the camera) and the object as follows:

$$\begin{pmatrix} x \\ y \\ 1 \end{pmatrix} = s \begin{pmatrix} f_x & 0 & c_x \\ 0 & f_y & c_y \\ 0 & 0 & 1 \end{pmatrix} \begin{pmatrix} r_1 & r_2 & r_3 & t_1 \\ r_4 & r_5 & r_6 & t_2 \\ r_7 & r_8 & r_9 & t_3 \end{pmatrix} \begin{pmatrix} U \\ V \\ W \\ 1 \end{pmatrix}$$

This is an equation where U, V, W are the object's 3D position, and x, y are points in the image. This equation also includes a projection, governed by the camera intrinsic parameters (focal length f and center point c), that transforms the 3D points to 2D image points, up to scale s. Say we are given the intrinsic parameters by calibrating the camera, or we approximate them, we are left to find 12 coefficients for the rotation and translation. If we had enough 2D and 3D corresponding points, we can write a system of linear equations, where each point can contribute two equations, to solve for all of these coefficients. In fact, it was shown that we don't need six points, since the rotation has less than nine degrees of freedom, we can make do with just four points. OpenCV provides an implementation to find the rotation and translation with its `cv::solvePnP` functions of the `calib3d` module.

We line up the 3D and 2D points and employ `cv::solvePnP`:

```
vector<Point3f> objectPoints {
        {8.27412, 1.33849, 10.63490},      //left eye corner
        {-8.27412, 1.33849, 10.63490},     //right eye corner
        {0, -4.47894, 17.73010},           //nose tip
        {-4.61960, -10.14360, 12.27940},   //right mouth corner
        {4.61960, -10.14360, 12.27940},    //left mouth corner
};
vector<int> landmarksIDsFor3DPoints {45, 36, 30, 48, 54}; // 0-index

// ...
vector<Point2f> points2d;
for (int pId : landmarksIDsFor3DPoints) {
    points2d.push_back(shapes[0][pId] / scaleFactor);
}

solvePnP(objectPoints, points2d, K, Mat(), rvec, tvec, true);
```

The K matrix for the camera intrinsics we estimate from size the preceding image.

Projecting the pose on the image

After obtaining the rotation and translation, we project four points from the object coordinate space to the preceding image: tip of the nose, x axis direction, y axis direction, and z axis direction, and draw the arrows in the preceding image:

```
vector<Point3f> objectPointsForReprojection {
        objectPoints[2],                   // tip of nose
        objectPoints[2] + Point3f(0,0,15), // nose and Z-axis
        objectPoints[2] + Point3f(0,15,0), // nose and Y-axis
        objectPoints[2] + Point3f(15,0,0)  // nose and X-axis
};
```

```
//...

vector<Point2f> projectionOutput(objectPointsForReprojection.size());
projectPoints(objectPointsForReprojection, rvec, tvec, K, Mat(),
projectionOutput);
arrowedLine(out, projectionOutput[0], projectionOutput[1],
Scalar(255,255,0));
arrowedLine(out, projectionOutput[0], projectionOutput[2],
Scalar(0,255,255));
arrowedLine(out, projectionOutput[0], projectionOutput[3],
Scalar(255,0,255));
```

This results in a visualization of the direction the face is pointing, as shown in the following screenshots:

Summary

In this chapter, we learned how to use OpenCV's `face contrib` module and the `cv::Facemark` API to detect facial landmarks in the image, and then use the landmarks with `cv::solvePnP()` to find the approximate direction of the face. The APIs are simple and straightforward, but pack a powerful punch. With knowledge of landmark detection, many exciting applications can be implemented, such as augmented reality, face swap, identification, and puppeteering.

4
Number Plate Recognition with Deep Convolutional Networks

This chapter introduces us to the steps needed to create an application for **Automatic Number Plate Recognition (ANPR)**. There are different approaches and techniques based on different situations; for example, an infrared camera, fixed car position, and light conditions. We can proceed to construct an ANPR application to detect automobile license plates in a photograph taken between two and three meters from a car, in ambiguous light conditions, and with a non-parallel ground with minor perspective distortions in the automobile's plate.

The main purpose of this chapter is to introduce us to image segmentation and feature extraction, pattern recognition basics, and two important pattern recognition algorithms, the **Support Vector Machine (SVM)** and **deep neural network (DNN)**, using **convolutional networks**. In this chapter, we will cover the following topics:

- ANPR
- Plate detection
- Plate recognition

Introduction to ANPR

ANPR, sometimes known by other terms, such as **Automatic License Plate Recognition (ALPR)**, **Automatic Vehicle Identification (AVI)**, or **car plate recognition (CPR)**, is a surveillance method that uses **optical character recognition (OCR)** and other methods such as segmentation and detection to read vehicle registration plates.

The best results in an ANPR system can be obtained with an **infrared** (**IR**) camera, because the segmentation steps for detection and OCR segmentation are easy and clean, and they minimize errors. This is due to the laws of light, the basic one being that the angle of incidence equals **Angle reflection**. We can see this basic reflection when we see a smooth surface, such as a plane mirror. Reflection off rough surfaces such as paper leads to a type of reflection known as s**catter or diffuse reflection**. However, the majority of the country plates have a special characteristic named **Retroreflection**: the surface of the plate is made with a material that is covered with thousands of tiny hemispheres that cause light to be reflected back to the source, as we can see in the following diagram:

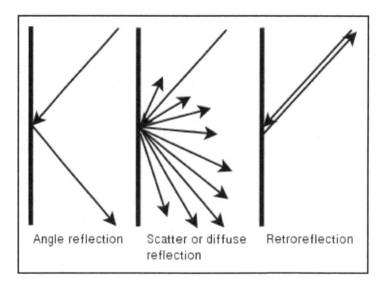

If we use a camera with a filter-coupled, structured infrared light projector, we can retrieve just the infrared light, and then we have a very high-quality image to segment, with which we can subsequently detect and recognize the plate number independent of any lighting environment, as shown in the following image:

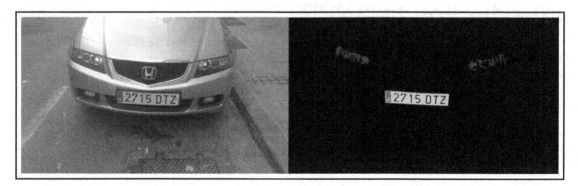

We will not use IR photographs in this chapter; we will use regular photographs so that we do not obtain the best results, and we get a higher level of detection errors and higher false recognition rate than if we used an IR camera. However, the steps for both are the same.

Each country has different license plate sizes and specifications. It is useful to know these specifications in order to get the best results and reduce errors. Algorithms used in this chapter are designed for explaining the basics of ANPR and designed for license plates used in Spain, but we can extend it to any country or specification.

In this chapter, we will work with license plates from Spain. In Spain, there are three different sizes and shapes of license plates, but we will only use the most common (large) license plate, which has a width of 520 mm and a height of 110 mm. Two groups of characters are separated by a 41 mm space, and a 14 mm space separates each individual character. The first group of characters is four numeric digits, and the second group three letters excluding the vowels *A*, *E*, *I*, *O* or *U*, or the letters *N* or *Q*. All characters have dimensions of 45 mm by 77 mm.

This data is important for character segmentation, since we can check both the character and blank spaces to verify that we get a character and no other image segment:

ANPR algorithm

Before explaining the ANPR code, we need to define the main steps and tasks in the ANPR algorithm. ANPR is divided into two main steps, plate detection and plate recognition:

- Plate detection has the purpose of detecting the location of the plate in the whole camera frame.
- When a plate is detected in an image, the plate segment is passed to the second step (plate recognition), which uses an OCR algorithm to determine the alphanumeric characters on the plate.

In the following diagram, we can see the two main algorithm steps, plate detection and plate recognition. After these steps, the program paints in the camera image the plate's characters that have been detected. The algorithms can return bad results, or may not return any result:

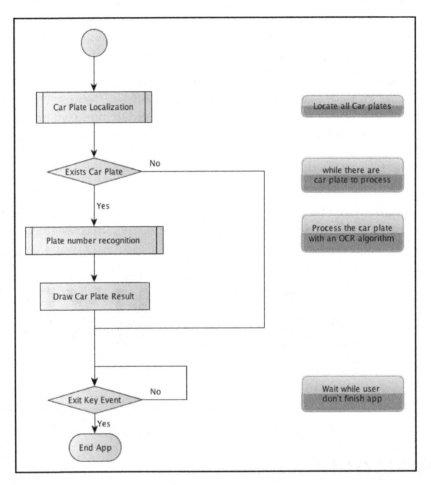

In each step shown in the previous diagram, we will define three additional steps that are commonly used in pattern recognition algorithms. These steps are as follows:

1. **Segmentation**: This step detects and removes each patch/region of interest in the image.
2. **Feature extraction**: This step extracts from each patch a set of characteristics.
3. **Classification**: This step extracts each character from the plate recognition step, or classifies each image patch into a *plate* or *no plate* in the plate detection step.

In the following diagram, we can see these pattern recognition steps in the application as a whole:

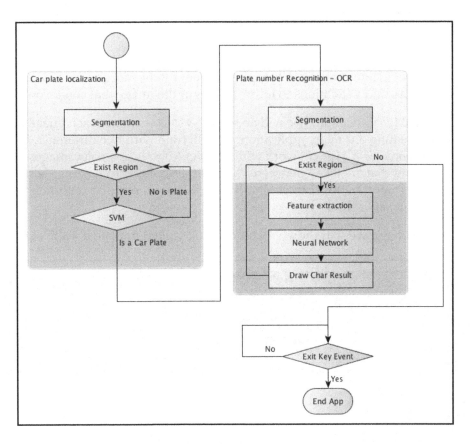

Aside from the main application, whose purpose is to detect and recognize a car plate number, we will briefly explain two more tasks that are usually not explained:

- How to train a pattern recognition system
- How to evaluate it

These tasks, however, can be more important than the main application, because if we do not train the pattern recognition system correctly, our system can fail and not work correctly; different patterns need different training and evaluation processes. We need to evaluate our system with different environments, conditions, and features to get the best results. These two tasks are sometimes done together, since different features can produce different results, which we can see in the evaluation section.

Plate detection

In this step, we have to detect all the plates in a current camera frame. To do this task, we divide it in to two main steps: segmentation and segment classification. The feature step is not explained because we use the image patch as a vector feature.

In the first step (segmentation), we will apply different filters, morphological operations, contour algorithms, and validations to retrieve parts of the image that could contain a plate.

In the second step (classification), we will apply an SVM classifier to each image patch, our feature. Before creating our main application, we will train with two different classes: *plate* and *non-plate*. We will work with parallel frontal view color images with 800 pixels of width and that are taken between two and four meters from a car. These requirements are important for correct segmentation. We can perform detection if we create a multi-scale image algorithm.

In the following image, we will shown each process involved in plate detection:

The processes involved are as follows:

- Sobel filter
- Threshold operation
- Close morphological operation
- Mask of one of filled area
- In red, possible detected plates (feature images)
- Plates detected by SVM classifier

Segmentation

Segmentation is the process of dividing an image into multiple segments. This process is to simplify the image for analysis and make feature extraction easier.

One important feature of plate segmentation is the high number of vertical edges in a license plate, assuming that the image was taken frontally and the plate is not rotated and without perspective distortion. This feature can be exploited during the first segmentation step to eliminate regions that don't have any vertical edges.

Before finding vertical edges, we need to convert the color image to a grayscale image (because color can't help us in this task) and remove possible noise generated from the camera or other ambient noise. We will apply a 5x5 gaussian blur and remove noise. If we don't apply a noise removal method, we can get a lot of vertical edges that produce fail detection:

```
//convert image to gray
Mat img_gray;
cvtColor(input, img_gray, CV_BGR2GRAY);
blur(img_gray, img_gray, Size(5,5));
```

To find the vertical edges, we will use a Sobel filter and find the first horizontal derivate. The derivate is a mathematical function that allows us to find vertical edges on an image. The definition of the Sobel function in OpenCV is as follows:

```
void Sobel(InputArray src, OutputArray dst, int ddepth, int xorder, int
yorder, int ksize=3, double scale=1, double delta=0, int
borderType=BORDER_DEFAULT )
```

Here, ddepth is the destination image depth; xorder is the order of the derivate by *x*; yorder is the order of the derivate by *y*; ksize is the kernel size of one, three, five, or seven; scale is an optional factor for computed derivative values; delta is an optional value added to the result; and borderType is the pixel interpolation method.

Then, for our case, we can use xorder=1, yorder=0, and ksize=3:

```
//Find vertical lines. Car plates have high density of vertical
lines
Mat img_sobel;
Sobel(img_gray, img_sobel, CV_8U, 1, 0, 3, 1, 0);
```

After applying a `Sobel` filter, we will apply a threshold filter to obtain a binary image with a threshold value obtained through Otsu's method. Otsu's algorithm needs an 8-bit input image, and Otsu's method automatically determines the optimal threshold value:

```
//threshold image
Mat img_threshold;
threshold(img_sobel, img_threshold, 0, 255,
CV_THRESH_OTSU+CV_THRESH_BINARY);
```

To define Otsu's method in the threshold function, we will combine the type parameter with the `CV_THRESH_OTSU` value, and the threshold value parameter is ignored.

 When the `CV_THRESH_OTSU` value is defined, the threshold function returns the optimal threshold value obtained by Otsu's algorithm.

By applying a close morphological operation, we can remove blank spaces between each vertical edge line and connect all regions that have a high number of edges. In this step, we have possible regions that can contain plates.

First, we will define our structural element to use in our morphological operation. We will use the `getStructuringElement` function to define a structural rectangular element with a `17` by `3` dimension size in our case; this may be different in other image sizes:

```
Mat element = getStructuringElement(MORPH_RECT, Size(17, 3));
```

Then, we will use this structural element in a close morphological operation using the `morphologyEx` function:

```
morphologyEx(img_threshold, img_threshold, CV_MOP_CLOSE, element);
```

After applying these functions, we have regions in the image that could contain a plate; however, most of the regions do not contain license plates. These regions can be split by means of connected component analysis, or by using the `findContours` function. This last function retrieves the contours of a binary image with different methods and results. We only need to get the external contours with any hierarchical relationship and any polygonal approximation results:

```
//Find contours of possibles plates
 vector< vector< Point>> contours;
 findContours(img_threshold,
     contours, // a vector of contours
     CV_RETR_EXTERNAL, // retrieve the external contours
     CV_CHAIN_APPROX_NONE); // all pixels of each contours
```

For each contour detected, extract the bounding rectangle of minimal area. OpenCV brings up the `minAreaRect` function for this task. This function returns a rotated `RotatedRect` rectangle class. Then, using a vector iterator over each contour, we can get the rotated rectangle and make some preliminary validations before we classify each region:

```
//Start to iterate to each contour founded
 vector<vector<Point>>::iterator itc= contours.begin();
 vector<RotatedRect> rects;

 //Remove patch that has no inside limits of aspect ratio and
 area.
 while (itc!=contours.end()) {
     //Create bounding rect of object
     RotatedRect mr= minAreaRect(Mat(*itc));
     if(!verifySizes(mr)){
         itc= contours.erase(itc);
     }else{
         ++itc;
         rects.push_back(mr);
     }
 }
```

We make basic validations for the regions detected based on their area and aspect ratio. We will consider that a region can be a plate if the aspect ratio is approximately *520/110 = 4.727272* (plate width divided by plate height), with an error margin of 40% and an area based on a minimum of 15 pixels and a maximum of 125 pixels for the height of the plate. These values are calculated depending on the image size and camera position:

```
bool DetectRegions::verifySizes(RotatedRect candidate ){
    float error=0.4;
    //Spain car plate size: 52x11 aspect 4,7272
    const float aspect=4.7272;
    //Set a min and max area. All other patchs are discarded
    int min= 15*aspect*15; // minimum area
    int max= 125*aspect*125; // maximum area
    //Get only patches that match to a respect ratio.
    float rmin= aspect-aspect*error;
    float rmax= aspect+aspect*error;

    int area= candidate.size.height * candidate.size.width;
    float r= (float)candidate.size.width
    /(float)candidate.size.height;
    if(r<1)
        r= 1/r;

    if(( area < min || area > max ) || ( r < rmin || r > rmax )){
```

```
            return false;
        }else{
            return true;
        }
    }
```

We can make even more improvements using the license plate's white background property. All plates have the same background color, and we can use a flood fill algorithm to retrieve the rotated rectangle for precise cropping.

The first step to crop the license plate is to get several seeds near the last rotated rectangle center. Then, we will get the minimum size of the plate between the width and height, and use it to generate random seeds near the patch center.

We want to select the white region, and we need several seeds to touch at least one white pixel. Then, for each seed, we use a `floodFill` function to draw a new mask image to store the new closest cropping region:

```
for(int i=0; i< rects.size(); i++){
 //For better rect cropping for each possible box
 //Make floodFill algorithm because the plate has white background
 //And then we can retrieve more clearly the contour box
 circle(result, rects[i].center, 3, Scalar(0,255,0), -1);
 //get the min size between width and height
 float minSize=(rects[i].size.width < rects[i].size.height)?
 rects[i].size.width:rects[i].size.height;
 minSize=minSize-minSize*0.5;
 //initialize rand and get 5 points around center for floodFill algorithm
 srand ( time(NULL) );
 //Initialize floodFill parameters and variables
 Mat mask;
 mask.create(input.rows + 2, input.cols + 2, CV_8UC1);
 mask= Scalar::all(0);
 int loDiff = 30;
 int upDiff = 30;
 int connectivity = 4;
 int newMaskVal = 255;
 int NumSeeds = 10;
 Rect ccomp;
 int flags = connectivity + (newMaskVal << 8 ) + CV_FLOODFILL_FIXED_RANGE +
CV_FLOODFILL_MASK_ONLY;
 for(int j=0; j<NumSeeds; j++){
     Point seed;
     seed.x=rects[i].center.x+rand()%(int)minSize-(minSize/2);
     seed.y=rects[i].center.y+rand()%(int)minSize-(minSize/2);
     circle(result, seed, 1, Scalar(0,255,255), -1);
     int area = floodFill(input, mask, seed, Scalar(255,0,0), &ccomp,
```

```
Scalar(loDiff, loDiff, loDiff), Scalar(upDiff, upDiff, upDiff), flags);
```

The `floodFill` function fills a connected component with a color into a mask image starting from a point seed, and sets the maximum lower and upper brightness/color difference between the pixel to fill and the pixel's neighbors or pixel seed:

```
int floodFill(InputOutputArray image, InputOutputArray mask, Point seed,
Scalar newVal, Rect* rect=0, Scalar loDiff=Scalar(), Scalar
upDiff=Scalar(), int flags=4 )
```

The `newval` parameter is the new color we want to incorporate into the image when filling. The `loDiff` and `upDiff` parameters are the maximum lower and maximum upper brightness/color difference between the pixel to fill and the pixel neighbors or pixel seed.

The parameter flag is a combination of the following bits:

- **Lower bits**: These bits contain the connectivity values, four (by default) or eight, used within the function. Connectivity determines which neighbors of a pixel are considered.
- **Upper bits**: These can be 0 or a combination of the following values: `CV_FLOODFILL_FIXED_RANGE` and `CV_FLOODFILL_MASK_ONLY`.

`CV_FLOODFILL_FIXED_RANGE` sets the difference between the current pixel and the seed pixel. `CV_FLOODFILL_MASK_ONLY` will only fill the image mask and not change the image itself.

Once we have a crop mask, we will get a minimal area rectangle from the image mask points and check the validity size again. For each mask, a white pixel gets the position and uses the `minAreaRect` function to retrieve the closest crop region:

```
//Check new floodFill mask match for a correct patch.
//Get all points detected for get Minimal rotated Rect
vector<Point> pointsInterest;
Mat_<uchar>::iterator itMask= mask.begin<uchar>();
Mat_<uchar>::iterator end= mask.end<uchar>();
for( ; itMask!=end; ++itMask)
    if(*itMask==255)
        pointsInterest.push_back(itMask.pos());
    RotatedRect minRect = minAreaRect(pointsInterest);
    if(verifySizes(minRect)){
```

The segmentation process is finished, and we have valid regions. Now, we can crop each detected region, remove possible rotation, crop the image region, resize the image, and equalize the light of the cropped image regions.

First, we need to generate the transform matrix with `getRotationMatrix2D` to remove possible rotations in the detected region. We need to pay attention to height, because `RotatedRect` can be returned and rotated at 90 degrees. So, we have to check the rectangle aspect and, if it is less than 1, we need to rotate it by 90 degrees:

```
//Get rotation matrix
float r= (float)minRect.size.width / (float)minRect.size.height;
float angle=minRect.angle;
if(r<1)
    angle=90+angle;
Mat rotmat= getRotationMatrix2D(minRect.center, angle,1);
```

With the transform matrix, we now can rotate the input image by an affine transformation (an affine transformation preserves parallel lines) with the `warpAffine` function, where we set the input and destination images, the transform matrix, the output size (same as the input in our case), and the interpolation method to use. We can define the border method and border value if required:

```
//Create and rotate image
Mat img_rotated;
warpAffine(input, img_rotated, rotmat, input.size(),
CV_INTER_CUBIC);
```

After we rotate the image, we will crop the image with `getRectSubPix`, which crops and copies an image portion of width and height centered on a point. If the image is rotated, we need to change the width and height sizes with the C++ `swap` function:

```
//Crop image
Size rect_size=minRect.size;
if(r < 1)
    swap(rect_size.width, rect_size.height);
Mat img_crop;
getRectSubPix(img_rotated, rect_size, minRect.center, img_crop);
```

Cropped images are not good for use in training and classification since they do not have the same size. Also, each image contains different light conditions, accentuating the differences between them. To resolve this, we resize all the images to the same width and height, and apply a light histogram equalization:

```
Mat resultResized;
resultResized.create(33,144, CV_8UC3);
resize(img_crop, resultResized, resultResized.size(), 0, 0, INTER_CUBIC);
//Equalize croped image
Mat grayResult;
cvtColor(resultResized, grayResult, CV_BGR2GRAY);
blur(grayResult, grayResult, Size(3,3));
```

```
equalizeHist(grayResult, grayResult);
```

For each detected region, we store the cropped image and its position in a vector:

```
output.push_back(Plate(grayResult,minRect.boundingRect()));
```

Now that we have possible detected regions, we have to classify whether each possible region is a plate or not. In the next section, we are going to learn how to create a classification based on SVM.

Classification

After we preprocess and segment all possible parts of an image, we now need to decide whether each segment is (or is not) a license plate. To do this, we will use an SVM algorithm.

An SVM is a pattern recognition algorithm included in a family of supervised learning algorithms that was originally created for binary classification. Supervised learning is the machine learning algorithm technique that is trained with labeled data. We need to train the algorithm with an amount of data that is labeled; each dataset needs to have a class.

The SVM creates one or more hyperplanes, which are used to discriminate each class of data.

A classic example is a 2D point set that defines two classes; the SVM searches the optimal line that differentiates each class:

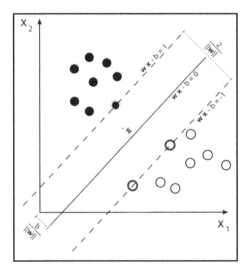

The first task before any classification is to train our classifier; this is a job to be undertaken prior to the main application and is referred to as "offline training." This is not an easy job because it requires a sufficient amount of data to train the system, but a bigger dataset does not always imply the best results. In our case, we do not have enough data due to the fact that there are no public license plate databases. Because of this, we need to take hundreds of car photos, and then preprocess and segment all of them.

We trained our system with 75 license plate images and 35 images without license plates, containing a 144 x 33 pixel resolution. We can see a sample of this data in the following image. This is not a large dataset, but sufficient to obtain decent results for our chapter. In a real application, we would need to train with more data:

To easily understand how machine learning works, we will proceed to use the image pixel features of the classifier algorithm (keep in mind that there are better methods and features to train an SVM, such as **principal components analysis (PCA)**, Fourier transform, and texture analysis).

We need to create the images to train our system using the DetectRegions class and set the savingRegions variable to true in order to save the images. We can use the segmentAllFiles.sh bash script to repeat the process on all image files in a folder. This can be taken from the source code of the book.

To make this easier, we will store all image training data that is processed and prepared into an XML file for use directly with the SVM function. The trainSVM.cpp application creates this file using the folders and number of image files.

Training data for a machine learning OpenCV algorithm is stored in an *NxM* matrix, with *N* samples and *M* features. Each dataset is saved as a row in the training matrix.

The classes are stored in another matrix with nx1 size, where each class is identified by a float number.

OpenCV has an easy way to manage a data file in the XML or YAML formats with the FileStorage class. This class lets us store and read OpenCV variables and structures, or our custom variables. With this function, we can read the training data matrix and training classes and save them in SVM_TrainingData and SVM_Classes:

```
FileStorage fs;
fs.open("SVM.xml", FileStorage::READ);
Mat SVM_TrainingData;
Mat SVM_Classes;
fs["TrainingData"] >>SVM_TrainingData;
fs["classes"] >>SVM_Classes;
```

Now, we have the training data in the SVM_TrainingData variable and labels in SVM_Classes. Then, we only have to create the training data object that connects data and labels to be used in our machine learning algorithm. To do this, we will use the TrainData class as an OpenCV pointer Ptr class as follows:

```
Ptr<TrainData> trainData = TrainData::create(SVM_TrainingData, ROW_SAMPLE,
SVM_Classes);
```

We will create the classifier object using the SVM class using the Ptr or with OpenCV 4 using the std::shared_ptr OpenCV class:

```
Ptr<SVM> svmClassifier = SVM::create()
```

Now, we need to set the SVM parameters, which define the basic parameters to use in an SVM algorithm. To do this, we only have to change some object variables. After different experiments, we will choose the next parameter's setup:

```
svmClassifier->setTermCriteria(TermCriteria(TermCriteria::MAX_ITER, 1000,
0.01));
svmClassifier->setC(0.1);
svmClassifier->setKernel(SVM::LINEAR);
```

We chose `1000` iterations for training, a `C` param variable optimization of `0.1`, and finally a kernel function.

We only need to train our classifier with the `train` function and the training data:

```
svmClassifier->train(trainData);
```

Our classifier is ready to predict a possible cropped image using the predict function of our SVM class; this function returns the class identifier `i`. In our case, we will label the *plate* class with one and the *no plate* class with zero. Then, for each detected region that can be a plate, we will use SVM to classify it as *plate* or *no plate*, and save only the correct responses. The following code is a part of a main application called online processing:

```
vector<Plate> plates;
for(int i=0; i< posible_regions.size(); i++)
{
    Mat img=posible_regions[i].plateImg;
    Mat p= img.reshape(1, 1);//convert img to 1 row m features
    p.convertTo(p, CV_32FC1);
    int response = (int)svmClassifier.predict( p );
    if(response==1)
        plates.push_back(posible_regions[i]);
}
```

Plate recognition

The second step in license plate recognition aims to retrieve the characters of the license plate with OCR. For each detected plate, we proceed to segment the plate for each character and use an **artificial neural network** machine learning algorithm to recognize the character. Also, in this section, you will learn how to evaluate a classification algorithm.

OCR segmentation

First, we will obtain a plate image patch as an input to the OCR segmentation function with an equalized histogram. We then need to apply only a threshold filter and use this threshold image as the input of a **Find contours** algorithm. We can observe this process in the following image:

This segmentation process is coded as follows:

```
Mat img_threshold;
threshold(input, img_threshold, 60, 255, CV_THRESH_BINARY_INV);
if(DEBUG)
    imshow("Threshold plate", img_threshold);
    Mat img_contours;
    img_threshold.copyTo(img_contours);
    //Find contours of possibles characters
    vector< vector< Point>> contours;
    findContours(img_contours, contours, // a vector of contours
        CV_RETR_EXTERNAL, // retrieve the external contours
        CV_CHAIN_APPROX_NONE); // all pixels of each contours
```

We used the CV_THRESH_BINARY_INV parameter to invert the threshold output by turning the white input values black and the black input values white. This is needed to get the contours of each character, because the contours algorithm searches for white pixels.

For each detected contour, we can make a size verification and remove all regions where the size is smaller or the aspect is not correct. In our case, the characters have a 45/77 aspect, and we can accept a 35% error of aspect for rotated or distorted characters. If an area is higher than 80%, we will consider that region to be a black block and not a character. For counting the area, we can use the countNonZero function, which counts the number of pixels with a value higher than zero:

```
bool OCR::verifySizes(Mat r){
    //Char sizes 45x77
    float aspect=45.0f/77.0f;
    float charAspect= (float)r.cols/(float)r.rows;
    float error=0.35;
    float minHeight=15;
    float maxHeight=28;
```

```
    //We have a different aspect ratio for number 1, and it can be ~0.2
    float minAspect=0.2;
    float maxAspect=aspect+aspect*error;
    //area of pixels
    float area=countNonZero(r);
    //bb area
    float bbArea=r.cols*r.rows;
    //% of pixel in area
    float percPixels=area/bbArea;
    if(percPixels < 0.8 && charAspect > minAspect && charAspect <
    maxAspect && r.rows >= minHeight && r.rows < maxHeight)
        return true;
    else
        return false;
}
```

If a segmented character is verified, we have to preprocess it to set the same size and position for all characters, and save it in a vector with the auxiliary `CharSegment` class. This class saves the segmented character image and the position that we need to order the characters, because the find contour algorithm does not return the contours in the correct order required.

Character classification using a convolutional neural network

Before we start to work with a convolutional neural network and deep learning, we are going to introduce these topics and the tools to create our DNN.

Deep learning is part of the machine learning family and can be supervised, semi-supervised, or unsupervised. DNNs are not a new concept in the scientific community. The term was introduced into the machine learning community in 1986 by Rina Dechter, and into artificial neural networks by Igor Aizenberg in the year 2000. But research in this area was started in the early 1980, where studies such as neocognitron were the inspiration for convolutional neural networks.

But it wasn't before 2009 that deep learning started its revolution. In 2009, as well as new research algorithms, advances in hardware renewed interest in deep learning using NVidia GPUs to speed up training algorithms that previously could take days or months, and are now 100x faster.

A convolutional neural network, ConvNet, or CNN, is a class of Deep Learning algorithm based on a feed-forward network and applied mainly to computer vision. CNNs use a variation of the multilayer perceptron, allowing us to extract shift invariant features automatically. CNNs use relatively little preprocessing compared to a hand classical machine learning engineered. Feature extraction is a major advantage over other machine learning algorithms.

Convolutional neural networks consist of an input and output layer with multiple hidden layers, like a classical artificial neural network, with the difference that the input normally is the raw pixels of the image and the hidden layers consist of convolutional layers and pooling layers, fully connected or normalized.

Now, we are going to briefly explain the most frequently used layers in a convolutional neural network:

- **Convolutional:** This layer applies a convolution operation filter to the input, passing the result to the next layers. This layer works like a typical computer vision filter (sobel, canny, and so on), but the kernel filters are learned in the training phase. The main benefit of using this layer is to reduce the common fully connected feedforward neural networks, for example, a 100 x 100 image has 10,000 weights, but, using CNN, the problem is reduced to the kernel size; for example, applying a kernel of 5 x 5 and 32 different filters, there are only *5*5*32=800*. At the same time, the filters explode all the possibilities of feature extraction.

- **Pooling:** This layer combines the outputs of a group of neurons into a single one. The most common is max pooling, which returns the maximum value of the group of input neurons. Another frequently used approach in deep learning is average pooling. This layer brings to the CNN the possibility of extracting higher-level features in layers following.

- **Flatten:** Flatten is not a DNN layer, but is a common operation to convert a matrix to a simple vector; this step is required to apply other layers and, finally, get the classification.

- **Fully connected:** This is the same as the traditional multi-layer perceptron, where every neuron in the previous layer is connected to the next layer with an activation function.

- **Dropout:** This layer is a regularization for reducing overfitting; it's a frequently used layer for performing accuracy on the model.

- **Loss layer:** This is normally the last layer in a DNN, and specifies how to train and calculate errors to perform the predictions. A very common loss layer is Softmax for classification.

OpenCV deep learning is not designed to train deep learning models, and it's not supported because there are very stable and powerful open source projects focused only on deep learning, such as TensorFlow, Caffe, and Torch. Then, OpenCV has an interface to import and read the most important models.

Then, we are going to develop our CNN for OCR classification in TensorFlow, which is one of the most frequently used and popular software libraries for deep learning, originally developed by Google researchers and engineers.

Creating and training a convolutional neural network with TensorFlow

This section will explore how to train a new TensorFlow model, but before we start to create our model, we have to check our image dataset and generate the resources that we need to train our models.

Preparing the data

We have 30 characters and numbers, distributed along 702 images in our dataset with the following distribution. We can check that there are more than 30 images for numbers, but some letters such as **K**, **M**, and **P**, have fewer images samples:

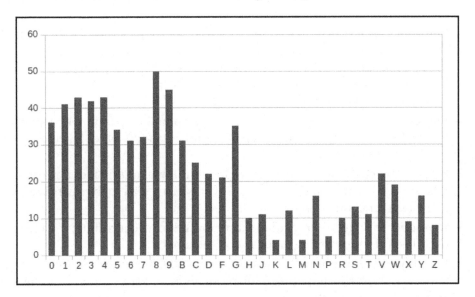

In the following image, we can see a small sample of images from our dataset:

This dataset is very small for deep learning. Deep learning requires a huge amount of samples and is a common technique. In some cases, use a dataset augmentation over the original dataset. Dataset augmentation is a way of creating new samples by applying different transformations, such as rotations, flipping the image, perspective distortions, and adding noise.

There are multiple ways to augment a dataset: we can create our own script or use open source libraries for this task. We are going to use Augmentor (https://github.com/mdbloice/Augmentor). Augmentor is a Python library that allows us to create the number of samples we require by applying the transformations we think are more convenient for our problem.

To install Augmentor through `pip`, we have to execute the following command:

```
pip install Augmentor
```

After installing the library, we create a small Python script to generate and increase the number of samples changing variable `number_samples` and apply the following: random distortion; a shear; and skew and rotation distortion, as we can see in the next Python script:

```
import Augmentor
number_samples = 20000
p = Augmentor.Pipeline("./chars_seg/chars/")
p.random_distortion(probability=0.4, grid_width=4, grid_height=4,
magnitude=1)
p.shear(probability=0.5, max_shear_left=5, max_shear_right=5)
p.skew_tilt(probability=0.8, magnitude=0.1)
p.rotate(probability=0.7, max_left_rotation=5, max_right_rotation=5)
p.sample(number_samples)
```

This script will generate an output folder where all the images will be stored, maintaining the same paths as the original path. We need to generate two datasets, one for training, and another to test our algorithm. Then, we are going to generate one of 20,000 images for training and 2,000 for test by changing the `number_samples`.

Now that we have sufficient images, we have to feed them into the TensorFlow algorithm. TensorFlow allows multiple input data formats, such as a CSV file with images and labels, Numpy data files, and the recommended TFRecordDataset.

 Visit `http://blog.damiles.com/2018/06/18/tensorflow-tfrecodataset.html` for more info about why it is better to use TFRecordDataset instead of CSV files with image references.

Before generating TFRecordDataset, we need to have installed the TensorFlow software. We can install it using `pip` with the following command for the CPU:

```
pip install tensorflow
```

Or, if you have an NVIDIA card with Cuda support, you can use the GPU distribution:

```
pip install tensorflow-gpu
```

Now, we can create the dataset file to train our model using the script provided, `create_tfrecords_from_dir.py`, passing two parameters, the input folder where the images are located, and the output file. We have to call this script twice, once for training and another for testing, to generate both files separately. We can see an example of the call in the next snippet:

```
python ./create_tfrecords_from_dir.py -i ../data/chars_seg/DNN_data/test -o
../data/chars_seg/DNN_data/test.tfrecords
python ./create_tfrecords_from_dir.py -i ../data/chars_seg/DNN_data/train -
o ../data/chars_seg/DNN_data/train.tfrecords
```

The script generates `test.tfrecords` and `train.tfrecords` files, where the labels are numbers assigned automatically and ordered by folder name. The `train` folder must have the following structure:

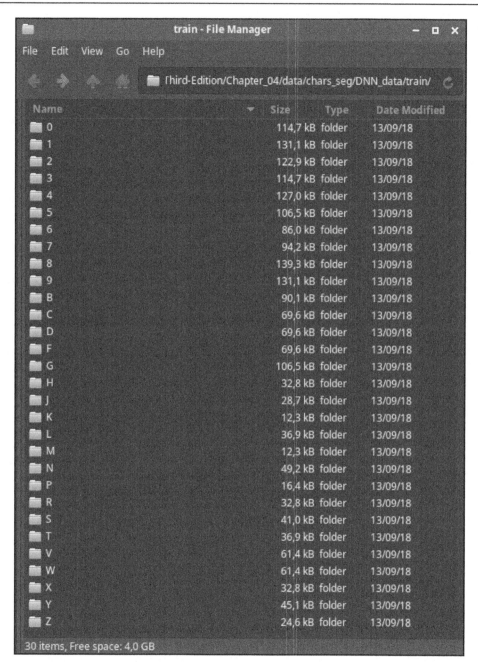

Now, we have the datasets and we are ready to create our model and start to train and evaluate.

Creating a TensorFlow model

TensorFlow is an open source software library that focuses on high-performance numerical computation and deep learning with access and support to CPUs, GPUs, and TPUs (Tensor Process Units, new Google hardware specialized for deep learning purposes). This library is not an easy library and has a high learning curve, but the introduction of Keras (a library on top of TensorFlow) as a part of TensorFlow makes the learning curve easier, but still requires a huge learning curve itself.

In this chapter, we cannot explain how to use TensorFlow because we will require a separate book for this topic alone, but we are going to explain the structure of the CNN we are going to use. We will show how to use an online visual tool called TensorEditor to generate, in a few minutes, TensorFlow code that we can download and train locally on our computer, or use the same online tool to train our model if we don't have enough computer processing power. If you want to read about and learn TensorFlow, we suggest you read any of the relevant Packt Publishing books or the TensorFlow tutorials.

The CNN layer structure that we are going to create is a simple convolutional network:

- **Convolutional Layer 1:** 32 filters of 5 x 5 with ReLU activation function
- **Pooling Layer 2:** Max pooling with 2 x 2 filters and a stride of 2
- **Convolutional Layer 3:** 64 filters of 5 x 5 with ReLU activation function
- **Pooling Layer 4:** Max pooling with 2 x 2 filter and a stride of 2
- **Dense Layer 5:** 1,024 neurons
- **Dropout Layer 6:** Dropout regularization with a rate of 0.4
- **Dense Layer 7:** 30 neurons, one for each number and character
- **SoftMax Layer 8:** Softmax layer loss function with gradient descent optimizer with a learning rate of 0.001 and 20,000 training steps.

We can see a basic graph of the model we have to generate in the following diagram:

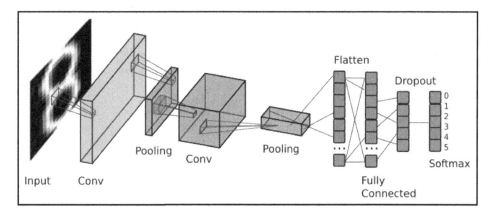

TensorEditor is an online tool that allows us to create models for TensorFlow and train on the cloud, or download the Python 2.7 code and execute it locally. After registering for the online free tool, we can generate the model, as shown in the following diagram:

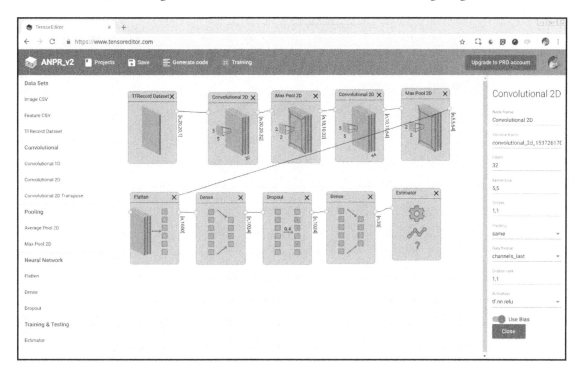

To add a layer, we choose it by clicking on the left-hand menu and it will appear on the editor. We can drag and drop to change its position and double-click to change its parameters. Clicking on the small dots of each node, allows us to link each node/layer. This editor shows us the parameters we choose visually and the output size of each layer; we can see in the following image that the convolutional layer has a kernel of 5 x 5 x 32 and an output of **n x 20 x 20 x 32**; the n variable means that we can compute one or multiple images at the same time for each training epoch:

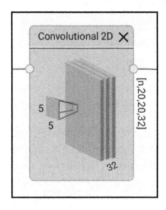

After creating the CNN layer structure in TensorEditor, we can now download the TensorFlow code by clicking on **Generate code** and downloading the Python code, as shown in the following screenshot:

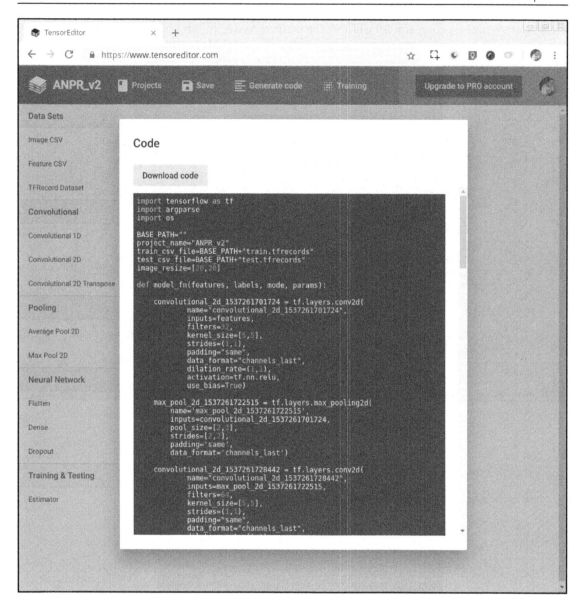

Now, we can start training our algorithm using TensorFlow with the following command:

```
python code.py --job-dir=./model_output
```

Here, the `--job-dir` parameter defines the output folder in which we store the output model trained. In the terminal, we can see the output of each iteration, together with the loss result and accuracy. We can see an example in the following screenshot:

Output of the algorithm training command

We can use TensorBoard, a TensorFlow tool, which gives us information about the training and graphs. To activate TensorBoard, we have to use this command:

```
tensorboard --logdir ./model_output
```

Here, the `--logdir` parameter, where we save our model and checkpoints, must be identified. After launching TensorBoard, we can access it with this URL: `http://localhost:6006`. This awesome tool shows us the graph generated by TensorFlow, where we can explore every operation and variable, clicking on each node, as we can see in the next screenshot:

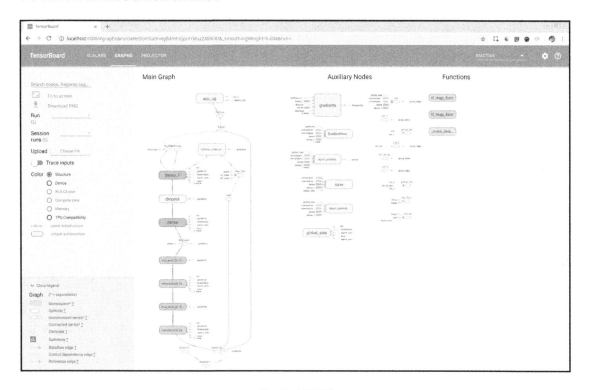

TensorBoard GRAPHS

Or, we can explore the results obtained, such as for loss values in each epoch step or accuracy metrics. The results obtained with the training model per epoch are shown in the following screenshot:

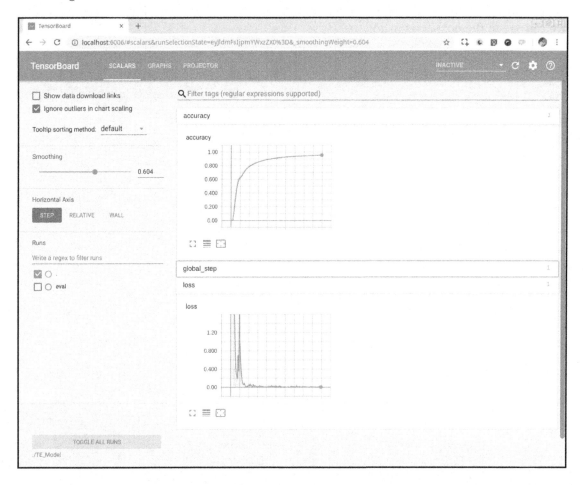

Training on an i7 6700HQ CPU with 8 GB RAM takes a long time, around 50 hours; a bit more than two days of training. If you use a basic NVIDIA GPU, this task can be reduced to around 2-3 hours.

If you want to train in TensorEditor, it can take 10-15 minutes and will download the model after training the models, with the possibility of downloading the full output model or a frozen and optimized model. The concept of freezing will be described in the following section, *Preparing a model for OpenCV*. We can see the result of training in TensorEditor in the next screenshot:

Training in TensorEditor

Analyzing the results obtained, we attain an accuracy level of around 96%, much better than the old algorithm explained in the second edition of this book, where we attained an accuracy level of only 92% using feature extraction and a simple artificial neural network.

After we finish training, all models and variables are stored in the job folder defined when we launched the TensorFlow script. Now, we have to prepare the finished result to integrate and import it into OpenCV.

Preparing a model for OpenCV

TensorFlow generates multiple files when we train a new model, generating files for events that store accuracy and loss, and other metrics obtained in each step; also, some files will store the variable results obtained for each step or checkpoint. These variables are the weights that networks learn in training. But it's not convenient to share all these files in production, as OpenCV would not be able to manage them. At the same time, there are nodes that are used only for training and not for inference. We have to remove these nodes from the model, nodes such as dropouts layers or training input iterators.

To put our model into production, we need to do the following:

- Freeze our graph
- Remove nodes/layers that are not required
- Optimize for inference

Freezing takes the graph definition and a set of checkpoints and merges them together into a single file, converting the variables into constants. To freeze our model, we have to move into the saved model folder and execute the following script provided by TensorFlow:

```
freeze_graph --input_graph=graph.pbtxt --input_checkpoint=model.ckpt-20000
--output_graph frozen_graph.pb --output_node_names=softmax_tensor
```

Now, we generate a new file called *frozen_graph.pb*, which is the merged and frozen graph. Then, we have to remove the input layers used for training purposes. If we review the graph using TensorBoard, we can see that our input to the first convolutional neural network is the `IteratorGetNext` node, which we have to cut and set as a single layer input of a 20 x 20 pixel image of one channel. Then, we can use the TensorFlow *transform_graph* application, which allows us to change the graph, cutting or modifying the TensorFlow model graph. To remove the layer connected to the ConvNet, we execute the following code:

```
transform_graph --in_graph="frozen_graph.pb" --
out_graph="frozen_cut_graph.pb" --inputs="IteratorGetNext" --
outputs="softmax_tensor" --transforms='strip_unused_nodes(type=half,
shape="1,20,20,1") fold_constants(ignore_errors=true) fold_batch_norms
fold_old_batch_norms sort_by_execution_order'
```

It's very important to add the `sort_by_execution_order` parameter to ensure that the layers are stored in order in the model graph, to allow OpenCV to correctly import the model. OpenCV sequentially imports the layers from the graph model, checking that all previous layers, operations, or variables are imported; if not, we will receive an import error. TensorEditor doesn't take care of the execution order in the graph to construct and execute it.

After executing `transform_graph`, we have a new model saved as `frozen_cut_graph.pb`. The final step requires us to optimize the graph, removing all training operations and layers such as dropout. We are going to use the following command to optimize our model for production/inference; this application is provided by TensorFlow:

```
optimize_for_inference.py --input frozen_cut_graph.pb --output
frozen_cut_graph_opt.pb --frozen_graph True --input_names IteratorGetNext -
-output_names softmax_tensor
```

The output of this is a file called `frozen_cut_graph_opt.pb`. This file is our final model, which we can import and use in our OpenCV code.

Import and use model in OpenCV C++ code

Importing a deep learning model into OpenCV is very easy; we can import models from TensorFlow, Caffe, Torch, and Darknet. All imports are very similar, but, in this chapter, we are going to learn how to import a TensorFlow model.

To import a TensorFlow model, we can use the `readNetFromTensorflow` method, which accepts two parameters: the first parameter is the model in protobuf format, and the second is the text graph definition in protobuf format, too. The second parameter is not required, but in our case, we have to prepare our model for inference, and we have to optimize it to import to OpenCV too. Then, we can import the model with the following code:

```
dnn::Net dnn_net= readNetFromTensorflow("frozen_cut_graph_opt.pb");
```

To classify each detected segment of our plate, we have to put each image segment into our `dnn_net` and obtain the probabilities. This is the full code to classify each segment:

```
for(auto& segment : segments){
    //Preprocess each char for all images have same sizes
    Mat ch=preprocessChar(segment.img);
    // DNN classify
    Mat inputBlob;
    blobFromImage(ch, inputBlob, 1.0f, Size(20, 20), Scalar(), true,
false);
    dnn_net.setInput(inputBlob);

    Mat outs;
    dnn_net.forward(outs);
    cout << outs << endl;
    double max;
    Point pos;
    minMaxLoc( outs, NULL, &max, NULL, &pos);
    cout << "---->" << pos << " prob: " << max << " " <<
strCharacters[pos.x] << endl;
    input->chars.push_back(strCharacters[pos.x]);
    input->charsPos.push_back(segment.pos);
}
```

We are going to explain this code a bit more. First, we have to preprocess each segment to get the same-sized image with 20 x 20 pixels. This preprocessed image must be converted as a blob saved in a `Mat` structure. To convert it to a blob, we are going to use the `blobFromImage` function, which creates four-dimensional data with optional resize, scale, crop, or swap channel blue and red. The function has the following parameters:

```
void cv::dnn::blobFromImage (
```

```
        InputArray image,
        OutputArray blob,
        double scalefactor = 1.0,
        const Size & size = Size(),
        const Scalar & mean = Scalar(),
        bool swapRB = false,
        bool crop = false,
        int ddepth = CV_32F
    )
```

The definitions of each one are as follows:

- `image`: Input image (with one, three, or four channels).
- `blob`: Output blob mat.
- `size`: Spatial size for the output image.
- `mean`: Scalar with mean values, which are subtracted from channels. Values are intended to be in (mean-R, mean-G, mean-B) order if the image has BGR ordering and `swapRB` is `true`.
- `scalefactor`: Multiplier for image values.
- `swapRB`: A flag that indicates the need to swap the first and last channels in a three-channel image.
- `crop`: A flag that indicates whether the image will be cropped after resizing
- `ddepth`: Depth of output `blob`. Choose `CV_32F` or `CV_8U`.

This generated blob can be added as an input to our DNN using `dnn_net.setInput(inputBlob)`.

Once the input blob is set up for our network, we only need to pass the input forward to obtain our results. This is the purpose of the `dnn_net.forward(outs)` function, which returns a `Mat` with the softmax prediction results. The result obtained is a row of `Mat` where each column is the label; then, to get the label with the highest probability, we only need to get the max position of this `Mat`. We can use the `minMaxLoc` function to retrieve the label value, and if we so desire, the probability value too.

Finally, to close the ANPR application, we only have to save, in the input plate data, the new segment position and the label obtained.

If we execute the application, we will obtain a result like this:

Summary

In this chapter, you learned how an Automatic Number Plate Recognition program works and its two important steps: plate localization and plate recognition.

In the first step, you learned how to segment an image by looking for patches where we may have a plate, and using simple heuristics and the SVM algorithm to make a binary classification for patches with *plates* and *no plates*.

In the second step, you learned how to segment using the find contours algorithm, create a deep learning model with TensorFlow, and train and import it into OpenCV. You also learned how to increase the number of samples in your dataset using augmentation techniques.

In the next chapter, you will learn how to create a face recognition application using eigenfaces and deep learning.

5
Face Detection and Recognition with the DNN Module

In this chapter, we are going to learn the main techniques of face detection and recognition. Face detection is the process whereby faces are located in a whole image. In this chapter, we are going to cover different techniques to detect faces in images, from classic algorithms using cascade classifiers with Haar features to newer techniques using deep learning. Face recognition is the process of identifying a person that appears in an image. We are going to cover the following topics in this chapter:

- Face detection with different methods
- Face preprocessing
- Training a machine learning algorithm from collected faces
- Face recognition
- Finishing touches

Introduction to face detection and face recognition

Face recognition is the process of putting a label to a known face. Just like humans learn to recognize their family, friends, and celebrities just by seeing their face, there are many techniques for recognize a face in computer vision.

These generally involve four main steps, defined as follows:

1. **Face detection**: This is the process of locating a face region in an image (the large rectangle near the center of the following screenshot). This step does not care who the person is, just that it is a human face.
2. **Face preprocessing**: This is the process of adjusting the face image to look clearer and similar to other faces (a small grayscale face in the top center of the following screenshot).
3. **Collecting and learning faces**: This is a process of saving many preprocessed faces (for each person that should be recognized), and then learning how to recognize them.
4. **Face recognition**: This is the process that checks which of the collected people are most similar to the face in the camera (a small rectangle in the top right of the following screenshot).

Note that the phrase **face recognition** is often used by the general public to refer to finding the positions of faces (that is, face detection, as described in *step 1*), but this book will use the formal definition of face recognition referring to *step 4*, and face detection referring to *Step 1*.

The following screenshot shows the final `WebcamFaceRec` project, including a small rectangle at the top-right corner highlighting the recognized person. Also, notice the confidence bar that is next to the preprocessed face (a small face at the top center of the rectangle marking the face), which in this case shows roughly 70 percent confidence that it has recognized the correct person:

Current face detection techniques are quite reliable in real-world conditions, whereas current face recognition techniques are much less reliable when used in real-world conditions. For example, it is easy to find research papers showing face recognition accuracy rates above 95 percent, but when testing those same algorithms yourself, you may often find that accuracy is lower than 50 percent. This comes from the fact that current face recognition techniques are very sensitive to exact conditions in images, such as the type of lighting, direction of lighting and shadows, exact orientation of the face, expression of the face, and the current mood of the person. If they are all kept constant when training (collecting images), as well as when testing (from the camera image), then face recognition should work well, but if the person was standing to the left-hand side of the lights in a room when training, and then stood to the right-hand side while testing with the camera, it may give quite bad results. So, the dataset used for training is very important.

Face preprocessing aims to reduce these problems by making sure the face always appears to have similar brightness and contrast, and perhaps making sure the features of the face will always be in the same position (such as aligning the eyes and/or nose to certain positions). A good face preprocessing stage will help improve the reliability of the whole face recognition system, so this chapter will place some emphasis on face preprocessing methods.

Despite the big claims about using face recognition for security in the media, it is unlikely that the current face recognition methods alone are reliable enough for any true security system. However, they can be used for purposes that don't need high reliability, such as playing personalized music for different people entering a room, or a robot that says your name when it sees you. There are also various practical extensions to face recognition, such as gender recognition, age recognition, and emotion recognition.

Face detection

Until the year 2000, there were many different techniques used for finding faces, but all of them were either very slow, very unreliable, or both. A major change came in 2001 when Viola and Jones invented the Haar-based cascade classifier for object detection, and in 2002 when it was improved by Lienhart and Maydt. The result is an object detector that is both fast (it can detect faces in real time on a typical desktop with a VGA webcam) and reliable (it detects approximately 95 percent of frontal faces correctly). This object detector revolutionized the field of face recognition (as well as that of robotics and computer vision in general), as it finally allowed real-time face detection and face recognition, especially as Lienhart himself wrote the object detector that comes free with OpenCV! It works not only for frontal faces but also side-view faces (referred to as profile faces), eyes, mouths, noses, company logos, and many other objects.

This object detector was extended in OpenCV v2.0 to also use LBP features for detection based on the work done by Ahonen, Hadid, and Pietikäinen in 2006, as LBP-based detectors are potentially several times faster than Haar-based detectors, and don't have the licensing issues that many Haar detectors have.

OpenCV has implemented deep learning from v3.4 and it's more stable in v4.0. In this chapter, we will show how to use **Single Shot Multibox Detector (SSD)** algorithm for face detection.

The basic idea of the Haar-based face detector is that if you look at most frontal faces, the region with the eyes should be darker than the forehead and cheeks, the region with the mouth should be darker than the cheeks, and so on. It typically performs about 20 stages of comparisons like this to decide whether it is a face or not, but it must do this at each possible position in the image, and for each possible size of the face, so in fact, it often does thousands of checks per image. The basic idea of the LBP-based face detector is similar to the Haar-based one, but it uses histograms of pixel intensity comparisons, such as edges, corners, and flat regions.

Rather than have a person decide which comparisons would best define a face, both Haar and LBP-based face detectors can be automatically trained to find faces from a large set of images, with the information stored as XML files to be used later. These cascade classifier detectors are typically trained using at least 1,000 unique face images and 10,000 non-face images (for example, photos of trees, cars, and text), and the training process can take a long time even on a multi-core desktop (typically a few hours for LBP, but one week for Haar!). Luckily, OpenCV comes with some pretrained Haar and LBP detectors for you to use! In fact, you can detect frontal faces, profile (side-view) faces, eyes, or noses just by loading different cascade classifier XML files into the object detector and choosing between the Haar and LBP detector, based on which XML file you choose.

Implementing face detection using OpenCV cascade classifiers

As mentioned previously, OpenCV v2.4 comes with various pretrained XML detectors that you can use for different purposes. The following table lists some of the most popular XML files:

Type of cascade classifier	XML filename
Face detector (default)	`haarcascade_frontalface_default.xml`
Face detector (fast Haar)	`haarcascade_frontalface_alt2.xml`
Face detector (fast LBP)	`lbpcascade_frontalface.xml`

Profile (side-looking) face detector	haarcascade_profileface.xml
Eye detector (separate for left and right)	haarcascade_lefteye_2splits.xml
Mouth detector	haarcascade_mcs_mouth.xml
Nose detector	haarcascade_mcs_nose.xml
Whole person detector	haarcascade_fullbody.xml

Haar-based detectors are stored in the `data/haarcascades` folder and LBP-based detectors are stored in the `datal/bpcascades` folder of the OpenCV root folder, such as `C:\\opencv\\data\\lbpcascades`.

For our face recognition project, we want to detect frontal faces, so let's use the LBP face detector because it is the fastest and doesn't have patent licensing issues. Note that the pretrained LBP face detector that comes with OpenCV v2.x is not tuned as well as the pretrained Haar face detectors, so if you want more reliable face detection then you may want to train your own LBP face detector or use a Haar face detector.

Loading a Haar or LBP detector for object or face detection

To perform object or face detection, first you must load the pretrained XML file using OpenCV's `CascadeClassifier` class as follows:

```
CascadeClassifier faceDetector;
faceDetector.load(faceCascadeFilename);
```

This can load Haar or LBP detectors just by giving a different filename. A very common mistake when using this is to provide the wrong folder or filename, but depending on your build environment, the `load()` method will either return `false` or generate a C++ exception (and exit your program with an assert error). So it is best to surround the `load()` method with a `try... catch` block, and display an error message to the user if something went wrong. Many beginners skip checking for errors, but it is crucial to show a help message to the user when something did not load correctly; otherwise, you may spend a very long time debugging other parts of your code before eventually realizing something did not load. A simple error message can be displayed as follows:

```
CascadeClassifier faceDetector;
try {
  faceDetector.load(faceCascadeFilename);
} catch (cv::Exception e) {}
if ( faceDetector.empty() ) {
  cerr << "ERROR: Couldn't load Face Detector (";
  cerr << faceCascadeFilename << ")!" << endl;
  exit(1);
}
```

Accessing the webcam

To grab frames from a computer's webcam, or even from a video file, you can simply call the `VideoCapture::open()` function with the camera number or video filename, then grab the frames using the C++ stream operator, as mentioned in the, *Accessing the webcam* section in `Chapter 1`, *Cartoonifier and Skin Changer for Raspberry Pi*.

Detecting an object using the Haar or LBP classifier

Now that we have loaded the classifier (just once during initialization), we can use it to detect faces in each new camera frame. But first, we should do some initial processing of the camera image just for face detection by performing the following steps:

1. **Grayscale color conversion**: Face detection only works on grayscale images. So we should convert the color camera frame to grayscale.

2. **Shrinking the camera image**: The speed of face detection depends on the size of the input image (it is very slow for large images but fast for small images), and yet detection is still fairly reliable, even at low resolutions. So we should shrink the camera image to a more reasonable size (or use a large value for `minFeatureSize` in the detector, as explained in the following sections).

3. **Histogram equalization**: Face detection is not as reliable in low light conditions. So we should perform histogram equalization to improve the contrast and brightness.

Grayscale color conversion

We can easily convert an RGB color image to grayscale using the `cvtColor()` function. But we should only do this if we know we have a color image (that is, it is not a grayscale camera), and we must specify the format of our input image (usually three-channel BGR on desktop or four-channel BGRA on mobile). So, we should allow three different input color formats, as shown in the following code:

```
Mat gray;
if (img.channels() == 3) {
  cvtColor(img, gray, COLOR_BGR2GRAY);
}
else if (img.channels() == 4) {
  cvtColor(img, gray, COLOR_BGRA2GRAY);
}
else {
  // Access the grayscale input image directly.
  gray = img;
}
```

Shrinking the camera image

We can use the `resize()` function to shrink an image to a certain size or scale factor. Face detection usually works quite well for any image whose size is greater than 240 x 240 pixels (unless you need to detect faces that are far away from the camera), because it will look for any faces larger than the `minFeatureSize` (typically 20 x 20 pixels). So let's shrink the camera image to be 320 pixels wide; it doesn't matter if the input is a VGA webcam or a five megapixel HD camera. It is also important to remember and enlarge the detection results, because if you detect faces in a shrunken image, then the results will also be shrunken. Note that instead of shrinking the input image, you could use a large value for the `minFeatureSize` variable in the detector instead. We must also ensure the image does not become fatter or thinner. For example, a widescreen 800 x 400 image when shrunk to 300 x 200 would make a person look thin. So, we must keep the aspect ratio (the ratio of width to height) of the output the same as the input. Let's calculate how much to shrink the image width by, then apply the same scale factor to the height as well, as follows:

```
const int DETECTION_WIDTH = 320;
// Possibly shrink the image, to run much faster.
Mat smallImg;
float scale = img.cols / (float) DETECTION_WIDTH;
if (img.cols > DETECTION_WIDTH) {
  // Shrink the image while keeping the same aspect ratio.
  int scaledHeight = cvRound(img.rows / scale);
  resize(img, smallImg, Size(DETECTION_WIDTH, scaledHeight));
}
else {
  // Access the input directly since it is already small.
  smallImg = img;
}
```

Histogram equalization

We can easily perform histogram equalization to improve the contrast and brightness of an image, using the `equalizeHist()` function. Sometimes this will make the image look strange, but in general it should improve the brightness and contrast, and help face detection. The `equalizeHist()` function is used as follows:

```
// Standardize the brightness & contrast, such as
// to improve dark images.
Mat equalizedImg;
equalizeHist(inputImg, equalizedImg);
```

Detecting the face

Now that we have converted the image to grayscale, shrunk the image, and equalized the histogram, we are ready to detect the faces using the `CascadeClassifier::detectMultiScale()` function! There are many parameters, listed as follows, that we pass to this function:

- `minFeatureSize`: This parameter determines the minimum face size that we care about, typically 20 x 20 or 30 x 30 pixels, but this depends on your use case and image size. If you are performing face detection on a webcam or smartphone where the face will always be very close to the camera, you could enlarge this to 80 x 80 to have much faster detection, or if you want to detect far away faces, such as on a beach with friends, then leave this as 20 x 20.
- `searchScaleFactor`: This parameter determines how many different sizes of faces to look for; typically it would be `1.1` for good detection, or `1.2` for faster detection, which does not find the face as often.
- `minNeighbors`: This parameter determines how sure the detector should be that it has detected a face; its typically a value of `3`, but you can set it higher if you want more reliable faces, even if many faces are not detected.
- `flags`: This parameter allows you to specify whether to look for all faces (default), or only look for the largest face (`CASCADE_FIND_BIGGEST_OBJECT`). If you only look for the largest face, it should run faster. There are several other parameters you can add to make the detection about 1% or 2% faster, such as `CASCADE_DO_ROUGH_SEARCH` or `CASCADE_SCALE_IMAGE`.

The output of the `detectMultiScale()` function will be a `std::vector` of the `cv::Rect` type object. For example, if it detects two faces, then it will store an array of two rectangles in the output. The `detectMultiScale()` function is used as follows:

```
int flags = CASCADE_SCALE_IMAGE; // Search for many faces.
Size minFeatureSize(20, 20);      // Smallest face size.
float searchScaleFactor = 1.1f;   // How many sizes to search.
int minNeighbors = 4;             // Reliability vs many faces.

// Detect objects in the small grayscale image.
std::vector<Rect> faces;
faceDetector.detectMultiScale(img, faces, searchScaleFactor,
            minNeighbors, flags, minFeatureSize);
```

We can see whether any faces were detected by looking at the number of elements stored in our vector of rectangles, that is, by using the `objects.size()` function.

As mentioned earlier, if we gave a shrunken image to the face detector, the results will also be shrunken, so we need to enlarge them if we want to see the face regions for the original image. We also need to make sure faces on the border of the image stay completely within the image, as OpenCV will now raise an exception if this happens, as shown by the following code:

```
// Enlarge the results if the image was temporarily shrunk.
if (img.cols > scaledWidth) {
  for (auto& object:objects ) {
    object.x = cvRound(object.x * scale);
    object.y = cvRound(object.y * scale);
    object.width = cvRound(object.width * scale);
    object.height = cvRound(object.height * scale);
  }
}
// If the object is on a border, keep it in the image.
for (auto& object:objects) {
  if (object.x < 0)
    object.x = 0;
  if (object.y < 0)
    object.y = 0;
  if (object.x + object.width > img.cols)
    object.x = img.cols - object.width;
  if (object.y + object.height > img.rows)
    object.y = img.rows - object.height;
}
```

Note that the preceding code will look for all faces in the image, but if you only care about one face, then you could change the `flags` variable as follows:

```
int flags = CASCADE_FIND_BIGGEST_OBJECT |
            CASCADE_DO_ROUGH_SEARCH;
```

The `WebcamFaceRec` project includes a wrapper around OpenCV's Haar or LBP detector, to make it easier to find a face or eye within an image, for example:

```
Rect faceRect;    // Stores the result of the detection, or -1.
int scaledWidth = 320;     // Shrink the image before detection.
detectLargestObject(cameraImg, faceDetector, faceRect, scaledWidth);
if (faceRect.width > 0)
cout << "We detected a face!" << endl;
```

Now that we have a face rectangle, we can use it in many ways, such as to extract or crop the face from the original image. The following code allows us to access the face:

```
// Access just the face within the camera image.
Mat faceImg = cameraImg(faceRect);
```

The following photo shows the typical rectangular region given by the face detector:

Implementing face detection using the OpenCV deep learning module

From OpenCV 3.4, the deep learning module was available as a contrib source (https://github.com/opencv/opencv_contrib), but from version 4.0, deep learning is part of OpenCV core. This means that OpenCV deep learning is stable and in good maintenance.

We can use a pretrained Caffe model based on the SSD deep learning algorithm for faces. This algorithm allows us to detect multiple objects in an image in a single deep learning network, returning a class and bounding box per object detected.

To load the pretrained Caffe, model we need to load two files:

- Proto file or configuration model; in our case, the file is saved in data/deploy.prototxt
- Binary trained model, which has the weights of each variable; in our case, the file is saved in data/res10_300x300_ssd_iter_140000_fp16.caffemodel

The following code allows us to load the model into OpenCV:

```
dnn::Net net = readNetFromCaffe("data/deploy.prototxt",
"data/res10_300x300_ssd_iter_14000_fp16.caffemodel");
```

After loading the deep learning network, per each frame that we capture with the webcam, we have to convert as a blob image that deep learning network can understand. We have to use the `blobFromImage` function as follows:

```
Mat inputBlob = blobFromImage(frame, 1.0, Size(300, 300), meanVal, false,
false);
```

Where the first parameter is the input image, the second is a scaled factor for each pixel value, the third is the output spatial size, the fourth is a `Scalar` value to be subtracted from each channel, the fifth is a flag to swap the *B* and *R* channels, and the last parameter, and if we set the last parameter to true, it crops the image after resized.

Now, we have prepared the input image for the deep neural network; to set it to the net, we have to call the following function:

```
net.setInput(inputBlob);
```

Finally, we can call to network to predict as follows:

```
Mat detection = net.forward();
```

Face preprocessing

As mentioned earlier, face recognition is extremely vulnerable to changes in lighting conditions, face orientation, face expression, and so on, so it is very important to reduce these differences as much as possible. Otherwise, the face recognition algorithm will often think there is more similarity between the faces of two different people in the same conditions, than between two images of the same person.

The easiest form of face preprocessing is just to apply histogram equalization using the `equalizeHist()` function, like we just did for face detection. This may be sufficient for some projects where the lighting and positional conditions won't change by much. But for reliability in real-world conditions, we need many sophisticated techniques, including facial feature detection (for example, detecting eyes, nose, mouth, and eyebrows). For simplicity, this chapter will just use eye detection and ignore other facial features such as the mouth and nose, which are less useful.

The following photo shows an enlarged view of a typical preprocessed face, using the techniques that will be covered in this section:

Eye detection

Eye detection can be very useful for face preprocessing, because for frontal faces, you can always assume a person's eyes should be horizontal and on opposite sides of the face, and should have a fairly standard position and size within a face, despite changes in facial expressions, lighting conditions, camera properties, distance to camera, and so on.

It is also useful to discard false positives, when the face detector says it has detected a face and it is actually something else. It is rare that the face detector and two eye detectors will all be fooled at the same time, so if you only process images with a detected face and two detected eyes, then it will not have many false positives (but will also give fewer faces for processing, as the eye detector will not work as often as the face detector).

Some of the pretrained eye detectors that come with OpenCV v2.4 can detect an eye whether it is open or closed, whereas some of them can only detect open eyes.

Eye detectors that detect open or closed eyes are as follows:

- `haarcascade_mcs_lefteye.xml` (and `haarcascade_mcs_righteye.xml`)
- `haarcascade_lefteye_2splits.xml` (and `haarcascade_righteye_2split s.xml`)

Eye detectors that detect open eyes only are as follows:

- `haarcascade_eye.xml`
- `haarcascade_eye_tree_eyeglasses.xml`

As the open or closed eye detectors specify which eye they are trained on, you need to use a different detector for the left and the right eye, whereas the detectors for just open eyes can use the same detector for left or right eyes.

The `haarcascade_eye_tree_eyeglasses.xml` detector can detect the eyes if the person is wearing glasses, but is not reliable if they don't wear glasses.

If the XML filename says *left eye*, it means the actual left eye of the person, so in the camera image it would normally appear on the right-hand side of the face, not on the left-hand side!

The list of four eye detectors mentioned is ranked in approximate order from most reliable to least reliable, so if you know you don't need to find people with glasses, then the first detector is probably the best choice.

Eye search regions

For eye detection, it is important to crop the input image to just show the approximate eye region, just like doing face detection and then cropping to just a small rectangle where the left eye should be (if you are using the left eye detector), and the same for the right rectangle for the right eye detector.

If you just do eye detection on a whole face or whole photo, then it will be much slower and less reliable. Different eye detectors are better suited to different regions of the face; for example, the `haarcascade_eye.xml` detector works best if it only searches in a very tight region around the actual eye, whereas the `haarcascade_mcs_lefteye.xml` and `haarcascade_lefteye_2splits.xml` detect work best when there is a large region around the eye.

The following table lists some good search regions of the face for different eye detectors (when using the LBP face detector), using relative coordinates within the detected face rectangle (`EYE_SX` is the eye search *x* position, `EYE_SY` is the eye search *y* position, `EYE_SW` is the eye search width, and `EYE_SH` is the eye search height):

Cascade classifier	EYE_SX	EYE_SY	EYE_SW	EYE_SH
haarcascade_eye.xml	0.16	0.26	0.30	0.28
haarcascade_mcs_lefteye.xml	0.10	0.19	0.40	0.36
haarcascade_lefteye_2splits.xml	0.12	0.17	0.37	0.36

Here is the source code to extract the left eye and right eye regions from a detected face:

```
int leftX = cvRound(face.cols * EYE_SX);
int topY = cvRound(face.rows * EYE_SY);
int widthX = cvRound(face.cols * EYE_SW);
int heightY = cvRound(face.rows * EYE_SH);
int rightX = cvRound(face.cols * (1.0-EYE_SX-EYE_SW));

Mat topLeftOfFace = faceImg(Rect(leftX, topY, widthX, heightY));
Mat topRightOfFace = faceImg(Rect(rightX, topY, widthX, heightY));
```

The following photo shows the ideal search regions for the different eye detectors, where the `haarcascade_eye.xml` and `haarcascade_eye_tree_eyeglasses.xml` files are best with the small search region, and the `haarcascade_mcs_*eye.xml` and `haarcascade_*eye_2splits.xml` files are best with larger search regions. Note that the detected face rectangle is also shown, to give an idea of how large the eye search regions are compared to the detected face rectangle:

The approximate detection properties of the different eye detectors while using the eye search regions are given in the following table:

Cascade classifier	Reliability*	Speed**	Eyes found	Glasses
haarcascade_mcs_lefteye.xml	80%	18 msec	Open or closed	no
haarcascade_lefteye_2splits.xml	60%	7 msec	Open or closed	no
haarcascade_eye.xml	40%	5 msec	Open only	no
haarcascade_eye_tree_eyeglasses.xml	15%	10 msec	Open only	yes

Reliability values show how often both eyes will be detected after LBP frontal face detection, when no eyeglasses are worn and both eyes are open. If the eyes are closed, then the reliability may drop, and if eyeglasses are worn, then both reliability and speed will drop.

Speed values are in milliseconds for images scaled to the size of 320 x 240 pixels on an Intel Core i7 2.2 GHz (averaged across 1,000 photos). Speed is typically much faster when eyes are found than when eyes are not found, as it must scan the entire image, but `haarcascade_mcs_lefteye.xml` is still much slower than the other eye detectors.

For example, if you shrink a photo to 320 x 240 pixels, perform a histogram equalization on it, use the LBP frontal face detector to get a face, then extract the *left eye region* and *right eye region* from the face using the `haarcascade_mcs_lefteye.xml` values, then perform a histogram equalization on each eye region. Then, if you use the `haarcascade_mcs_lefteye.xml` detector on the left eye (which is actually in the top-right of your image) and use the `haarcascade_mcs_righteye.xml` detector on the right eye (the top-left part of your image), each eye detector should work in roughly 90 percent of photos with LBP-detected frontal faces. So if you want both eyes detected, then it should work in roughly 80 percent of photos with LBP-detected frontal faces.

Note that while it is recommended to shrink the camera image before detecting faces, you should detect eyes at the full camera resolution, because eyes will obviously be much smaller than faces, so you need as much resolution as you can get.

Based on the table, it seems that when choosing an eye detector to use, you should decide whether you want to detect closed eyes or only open eyes. And remember that you can even use one eye detector, and if it does not detect an eye, then you can try with another one.

For many tasks, it is useful to detect eyes whether they are open or closed, so if speed is not crucial, it is best to search with the `mcs_*eye` detector first, and if it fails, then search with the `eye_2splits` detector.

But for face recognition, a person will appear quite different if their eyes are closed, so it is best to search with the plain `haarcascade_eye` detector first, and if it fails, then search with the `haarcascade_eye_tree_eyeglasses` detector.

We can use the same `detectLargestObject()` function we used for face detection to search for eyes, but instead of asking to shrink the images before eye detection, we specify the full eye region width to get better eye detection. It is easy to search for the left eye using one detector, and if it fails, then try another detector (the same for the right eye). The eye detection is done as follows:

```
CascadeClassifier eyeDetector1("haarcascade_eye.xml");
CascadeClassifier eyeDetector2("haarcascade_eye_tree_eyeglasses.xml");
...
Rect leftEyeRect;     // Stores the detected eye.
// Search the left region using the 1st eye detector.
detectLargestObject(topLeftOfFace, eyeDetector1, leftEyeRect,
topLeftOfFace.cols);
// If it failed, search the left region using the 2nd eye
// detector.
if (leftEyeRect.width <= 0)
  detectLargestObject(topLeftOfFace, eyeDetector2,
           leftEyeRect, topLeftOfFace.cols);
// Get the left eye center if one of the eye detectors worked.
Point leftEye = Point(-1,-1);
if (leftEyeRect.width <= 0) {
  leftEye.x = leftEyeRect.x + leftEyeRect.width/2 + leftX;
  leftEye.y = leftEyeRect.y + leftEyeRect.height/2 + topY;
}

// Do the same for the right eye
...

// Check if both eyes were detected.
if (leftEye.x >= 0 && rightEye.x >= 0) {
  ...
}
```

With the face and both eyes detected, we'll perform face preprocessing by combining the following steps:

1. **Geometrical transformation and cropping**: This process includes scaling, rotating, and translating the images so that the eyes are aligned, followed by the removal of the forehead, chin, ears, and background from the face image.
2. **Separate histogram equalization for left and right sides**: This process standardizes the brightness and contrast on both the left- and right-hand sides of the face independently.
3. **Smoothing**: This process reduces the image noise using a bilateral filter.
4. **Elliptical mask**: The elliptical mask removes some remaining hair and background from the face image.

The following photos shows the face preprocessing *Step 1* to *Step 4* applied to a detected face. Notice how the final photo has good brightness and contrast on both sides of the face, whereas the original does not:

Geometrical transformation

It is important that the faces are all aligned together, otherwise the face recognition algorithm might be comparing part of a nose with part of an eye, and so on. The output of the face detection we've just seen will give aligned faces to some extent, but it is not very accurate (that is, the face rectangle will not always be starting from the same point on the forehead).

To have better alignment, we will use eye detection to align the face, so the positions of the two detected eyes line up perfectly in the desired positions. We will do the geometrical transformation using the `warpAffine()` function, which is a single operation that will do the following four things:

- Rotate the face so that the two eyes are horizontal
- Scale the face so that the distance between the two eyes is always the same
- Translate the face so that the eyes are always centered horizontally, and at the desired height
- Crop the outer parts of the face, since we want to crop away the image background, hair, forehead, ears, and chin

Affine warping takes an affine matrix that transforms the two detected eye locations into the two desired eye locations, and then crops to a desired size and position. To generate this affine matrix, we will get the center between the eyes, calculate the angle at which the two detected eyes appear, and look at their distance apart, as follows:

```
// Get the center between the 2 eyes.
Point2f eyesCenter;
eyesCenter.x = (leftEye.x + rightEye.x) * 0.5f;
eyesCenter.y = (leftEye.y + rightEye.y) * 0.5f;
```

```
// Get the angle between the 2 eyes.
double dy = (rightEye.y - leftEye.y);
double dx = (rightEye.x - leftEye.x);
double len = sqrt(dx*dx + dy*dy);

// Convert Radians to Degrees.
double angle = atan2(dy, dx) * 180.0/CV_PI;

// Hand measurements shown that the left eye center should
// ideally be roughly at (0.16, 0.14) of a scaled face image.
const double DESIRED_LEFT_EYE_X = 0.16;
const double DESIRED_RIGHT_EYE_X = (1.0f - 0.16);

// Get the amount we need to scale the image to be the desired
// fixed size we want.
const int DESIRED_FACE_WIDTH = 70;
const int DESIRED_FACE_HEIGHT = 70;
double desiredLen = (DESIRED_RIGHT_EYE_X - 0.16);
double scale = desiredLen * DESIRED_FACE_WIDTH / len;
```

Now, we can transform the face (rotate, scale, and translate) to get the two detected eyes to be in the desired eye positions in an ideal face, as follows:

```
// Get the transformation matrix for the desired angle & size.
Mat rot_mat = getRotationMatrix2D(eyesCenter, angle, scale);
// Shift the center of the eyes to be the desired center.
double ex = DESIRED_FACE_WIDTH * 0.5f - eyesCenter.x;
double ey = DESIRED_FACE_HEIGHT * DESIRED_LEFT_EYE_Y -
  eyesCenter.y;
rot_mat.at<double>(0, 2) += ex;
rot_mat.at<double>(1, 2) += ey;
// Transform the face image to the desired angle & size &
// position! Also clear the transformed image background to a
// default grey.
Mat warped = Mat(DESIRED_FACE_HEIGHT, DESIRED_FACE_WIDTH,
  CV_8U, Scalar(128));
warpAffine(gray, warped, rot_mat, warped.size());
```

Separate histogram equalization for left and right sides

In real-world conditions, it is common to have strong lighting on one half of the face and weak lighting on the other. This has an enormous effect on the face recognition algorithm, as the left- and right-hand sides of the same face will seem like very different people. So, we will perform histogram equalization separately on the left and right halves of the face, to have a standardized brightness and contrast on each side of the face.

If we simply applied histogram equalization on the left half and then again on the right half, we would see a very distinct edge in the middle because the average brightness is likely to be different on the left and the right side. So to remove this edge, we will apply the two histogram equalizations gradually from the left or right-hand side toward the center, and mix it with a whole face histogram equalization.

Then, the far left-hand side will use the left histogram equalization, the far right-hand side will use the right histogram equalization, and the center will use a smooth mix of the left and right values and the whole face equalized value.

The following screenshot shows how the left-equalized, whole-equalized, and right-equalized images are blended together:

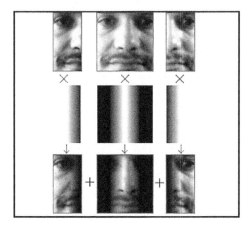

To perform this, we need copies of the whole face equalized, as well as the left half equalized and the right half equalized, which is done as follows:

```
int w = faceImg.cols;
int h = faceImg.rows;
Mat wholeFace;
equalizeHist(faceImg, wholeFace);
int midX = w/2;
Mat leftSide = faceImg(Rect(0,0, midX,h));
Mat rightSide = faceImg(Rect(midX,0, w-midX,h));
equalizeHist(leftSide, leftSide);
equalizeHist(rightSide, rightSide);
```

Now, we combine the three images together. As the images are small, we can easily access the pixels directly using the `image.at<uchar>(y,x)` function, even if it is slow; so let's merge the three images by directly accessing pixels in the three input images and output images, as follows:

```
for (int y=0; y<h; y++) {
    for (int x=0; x<w; x++) {
        int v;
        if (x < w/4) {
            // Left 25%: just use the left face.
            v = leftSide.at<uchar>(y,x);
        }
        else if (x < w*2/4) {
            // Mid-left 25%: blend the left face & whole face.
            int lv = leftSide.at<uchar>(y,x);
            int wv = wholeFace.at<uchar>(y,x);
            // Blend more of the whole face as it moves
            // further right along the face.
            float f = (x - w*1/4) / (float)(w/4);
            v = cvRound((1.0f - f) * lv + (f) * wv);
        }
        else if (x < w*3/4) {
            // Mid-right 25%: blend right face & whole face.
            int rv = rightSide.at<uchar>(y,x-midX);
            int wv = wholeFace.at<uchar>(y,x);
            // Blend more of the right-side face as it moves
            // further right along the face.
            float f = (x - w*2/4) / (float)(w/4);
            v = cvRound((1.0f - f) * wv + (f) * rv);
        }
        else {
            // Right 25%: just use the right face.
            v = rightSide.at<uchar>(y,x-midX);
        }
        faceImg.at<uchar>(y,x) = v;
    } // end x loop
} //end y loop
```

This separated histogram equalization should significantly help reduce the effect of different lighting on the left- and right-hand sides of the face, but we must understand that it won't completely remove the effect of one-sided lighting, since the face is a complex 3D shape with many shadows.

Smoothing

To reduce the effect of pixel noise, we will use a bilateral filter on the face, as a bilateral filter is very good at smoothing most of an image while keeping edges sharp. Histogram equalization can significantly increase the pixel noise, so we will make the filter strength 20.0 to cover heavy pixel noise, and use a neighborhood of just two pixels as we want to heavily smooth the tiny pixel noise, but not the large image regions, as follows:

```
Mat filtered = Mat(warped.size(), CV_8U);
bilateralFilter(warped, filtered, 0, 20.0, 2.0);
```

Elliptical mask

Although we have already removed most of the image background, forehead, and hair when we did the geometrical transformation, we can apply an elliptical mask to remove some of the corner regions, such as the neck, which might be in shadow from the face, particularly if the face is not looking perfectly straight toward the camera. To create the mask, we will draw a black-filled ellipse onto a white image. One ellipse to perform this has a horizontal radius of 0.5 (that is, it covers the face width perfectly), a vertical radius of 0.8 (as faces are usually taller than they are wide), and centered at the coordinates 0.5, 0.4, as shown in the following screenshot, where the elliptical mask has removed some unwanted corners from the face:

We can apply the mask when calling the `cv::setTo()` function, which would normally set a whole image to a certain pixel value, but as we will give a mask image, it will only set some parts to the given pixel value. We will fill the image in with gray so that it should have less contrast to the rest of the face, as follows:

```
// Draw a black-filled ellipse in the middle of the image.
// First we initialize the mask image to white (255).
Mat mask = Mat(warped.size(), CV_8UC1, Scalar(255));
double dw = DESIRED_FACE_WIDTH;
double dh = DESIRED_FACE_HEIGHT;
Point faceCenter = Point( cvRound(dw * 0.5),
  cvRound(dh * 0.4) );
Size size = Size( cvRound(dw * 0.5), cvRound(dh * 0.8) );
```

```
ellipse(mask, faceCenter, size, 0, 0, 360, Scalar(0),
    CV_FILLED);

// Apply the elliptical mask on the face, to remove corners.
// Sets corners to gray, without touching the inner face.
filtered.setTo(Scalar(128), mask);
```

The following enlarged screenshot shows a sample result from all the face preprocessing stages. Notice it is much more consistent for face recognition at different brightness, face rotations, angles from camera, backgrounds, positions of lights, and so on. This preprocessed face will be used as input to the face recognition stages, both when collecting faces for training and when trying to recognize input faces:

Collecting faces and learning from them

Collecting faces can be just as simple as putting each newly preprocessed face into an array of preprocessed faces from the camera, as well as putting a label into an array (to specify which person the face was taken from). For example, you could use 10 preprocessed faces of the first person and 10 preprocessed faces of a second person, so the input to the face recognition algorithm will be an array of 20 preprocessed faces, and an array of 20 integers (where the first 10 numbers are 0 and the next 10 numbers are 1).

The face recognition algorithm will then learn how to distinguish between the faces of the different people. This is referred to as the training phase, and the collected faces are referred to as the training set. After the face recognition algorithm has finished training, you can then save the generated knowledge to a file or memory and later use it to recognize which person is seen in front of the camera. This is referred to as the testing phase. If you used it directly from a camera input, then the preprocessed face would be referred to as the test image, and if you tested with many images (such as from a folder of image files), it would be referred to as the testing set.

It is important that you provide a good training set that covers the types of variations you expect to occur in your testing set. For example, if you will only test with faces that are looking perfectly straight ahead (such as ID photos), then you only need to provide training images with faces that are looking perfectly straight ahead. But if the person might be looking to the left, or up, then you should make sure the training set also includes faces of that person doing this, otherwise the face recognition algorithm will have trouble recognizing them, as their face will appear quite different. This also applies to other factors, such as facial expression (for example, if the person is always smiling in the training set, but not smiling in the testing set) or lighting direction (for example, a strong light is to the left-hand side in the training set but to the right-hand side in the testing set), then the face recognition algorithm will have difficulty recognizing them. The face preprocessing steps that we just saw will help reduce these issues, but it certainly won't remove these factors, particularly the direction that the face is looking, as it has a large effect on the position of all elements in the face.

One way to obtain a good training set that will cover many different real-world conditions is for each person to rotate their head from looking left, to up, to right, to down, then looking directly straight. Then, the person tilts their head sideways and then up and down, while also changing their facial expression, such as alternating between smiling, looking angry, and having a neutral face. If each person follows a routine such as this while collecting faces, then there is a much better chance of recognizing everyone in real-world conditions.

For even better results, it should be performed again with one or two more locations or directions, such as by turning the camera around 180 degrees, walking in the opposite direction, and then repeating the whole routine, so that the training set would include many different lighting conditions.

So, in general, having 100 training faces for each person is likely to give better results than having just 10 training faces for each person, but if all 100 faces look almost identical, then it will still perform badly, because it is more important that the training set has enough variety to cover the testing set, rather than to just have a large number of faces. So, to make sure the faces in the training set are not all too similar, we should add a noticeable delay between each collected face. For example, if the camera is running at 30 frames per second, then it might collect 100 faces in just several seconds when the person has not had time to move around, so it is better to collect just one face per second while the person moves their face around. Another simple method to improve the variation in the training set is to only collect a face if it is noticeably different from the previously collected face.

Collecting preprocessed faces for training

To make sure there is at least a one-second gap between collecting new faces, we need to measure how much time has passed. This is done as follows:

```
// Check how long since the previous face was added.
double current_time = (double)getTickCount();
double timeDiff_seconds = (current_time -
  old_time) / getTickFrequency();
```

To compare the similarity of two images, pixel by pixel, you can find the relative L2 error, which just involves subtracting one image from the other, summing the squared value of it, and then getting the square root of it. So if the person had not moved at all, subtracting the current face from the previous face should give a very low number at each pixel, but if they had just moved slightly in any direction, subtracting the pixels would give a large number and so the L2 error will be high. As the result is summed over all pixels, the value will depend on the image resolution. So to get the mean error, we should divide this value by the total number of pixels in the image. Let's put this in a handy function, getSimilarity(), as follows:

```
double getSimilarity(const Mat A, const Mat B) {
  // Calculate the L2 relative error between the 2 images.
  double errorL2 = norm(A, B, CV_L2);
  // Scale the value since L2 is summed across all pixels.
  double similarity = errorL2 / (double)(A.rows * A.cols);
  return similarity;
}

...

// Check if this face looks different from the previous face.
double imageDiff = MAX_DBL;
if (old_prepreprocessedFaceprepreprocessedFace.data) {
  imageDiff = getSimilarity(preprocessedFace,
    old_prepreprocessedFace);
}
```

This similarity will often be less than 0.2 if the image did not move much, and higher than 0.4 if the image did move, so let's use 0.3 as our threshold for collecting a new face.

There are many tricks we can perform to obtain more training data, such as using mirrored faces, adding random noise, shifting the face by a few pixels, scaling the face by a percentage, or rotating the face by a few degrees (even though we specifically tried to remove these effects when preprocessing the face!). Let's add mirrored faces to the training set, so that we have both a larger training set and a reduction in the problems of asymmetrical faces, or if a user is always oriented slightly to the left or right during training but not testing. This is done as follows:

```
// Only process the face if it's noticeably different from the
// previous frame and there has been a noticeable time gap.
if ((imageDiff > 0.3) && (timeDiff_seconds > 1.0)) {
  // Also add the mirror image to the training set.
  Mat mirroredFace;
  flip(preprocessedFace, mirroredFace, 1);

  // Add the face & mirrored face to the detected face lists.
  preprocessedFaces.push_back(preprocessedFace);
  preprocessedFaces.push_back(mirroredFace);
  faceLabels.push_back(m_selectedPerson);
  faceLabels.push_back(m_selectedPerson);

  // Keep a copy of the processed face,
  // to compare on next iteration.
  old_prepreprocessedFace = preprocessedFace;
  old_time = current_time;
}
```

This will collect the `std::vector` arrays, `preprocessedFaces`, and `faceLabels` for a preprocessed face, as well as the label or ID number of that person (assuming it is in the integer `m_selectedPerson` variable).

To make it more obvious to the user that we have added their current face to the collection, you could provide a visual notification by either displaying a large white rectangle over the whole image, or just displaying their face for just a fraction of a second so they realize a photo was taken. With OpenCV's C++ interface, you can use the + overloaded `cv::Mat` operator to add a value to every pixel in the image and have it clipped to 255 (using `saturate_cast`, so it doesn't overflow from white back to black!). Assuming `displayedFrame` will be a copy of the color camera frame that should be shown, insert this after the preceding code for face collection:

```
// Get access to the face region-of-interest.
Mat displayedFaceRegion = displayedFrame(faceRect);
// Add some brightness to each pixel of the face region.
displayedFaceRegion += CV_RGB(90,90,90);
```

Training the face recognition system from collected faces

After you have collected enough faces for each person to recognize, you must train the system to learn the data using a machine learning algorithm suited for face recognition. There are many different face recognition algorithms in the literature, the simplest of which are Eigenfaces and artificial neural networks. Eigenfaces tends to work better than ANNs, and despite its simplicity, it tends to work almost as well as many more complex face recognition algorithms, so it has become very popular as the basic face recognition algorithm for beginners, as well as for new algorithms to be compared to.

Any reader who wishes to work further on face recognition is recommended to read the theory behind the following:

- Eigenfaces (also referred to as **principal component analysis (PCA)**)
- Fisherfaces (also referred to as **linear discriminant analysis (LDA)**)
- Other classic face recognition algorithms (many are available at http://www. facerec.org/algorithms/)
- Newer face recognition algorithms in recent computer vision research papers (such as CVPR and ICCV at http://www.cvpapers.com/), as there are hundreds of face recognition papers published each year

However, you don't need to understand the theory of these algorithms in order to use them as shown in this book. Thanks to the OpenCV team and Philipp Wagner's libfacerec contribution, OpenCV v2.4.1 provided cv::Algorithm as a simple and generic method to perform face recognition using one of several different algorithms (even selectable at runtime) without necessarily understanding how they are implemented. You can find the available algorithms in your version of OpenCV by using the Algorithm::getList() function, such as with the following code:

```
vector<string> algorithms;
Algorithm::getList(algorithms);
cout << "Algorithms: " << algorithms.size() << endl;
for (auto& algorithm:algorithms) {
  cout << algorithm << endl;
}
```

Here are the three face recognition algorithms available in OpenCV v2.4.1:

- `FaceRecognizer.Eigenfaces`: Eigenfaces, also referred to as PCA, first used by Turk and Pentland in 1991
- `FaceRecognizer.Fisherfaces`: Fisherfaces, also referred to as LDA, invented by Belhumeur, Hespanha, and Kriegman in 1997
- `FaceRecognizer.LBPH`: Local Binary Pattern Histograms, invented by Ahonen, Hadid, and Pietikäinen in 2004

 More information on these face recognition algorithm implementations can be found with documentation, samples, and Python equivalents for each of them on Philipp Wagner's websites (`http://bytefish.de/blog` and `http://bytefish.de/dev/libfacerec/`).

These face recognition-algorithms are available through the `FaceRecognizer` class in OpenCV's `contrib` module. Due to dynamic linking, it is possible that your program is linked to the `contrib` module, but it is not actually loaded at runtime (if it was deemed as not required). So it is recommended to call the `cv::initModule_contrib()` function before trying to access the `FaceRecognizer` algorithms. This function is only available from OpenCV v2.4.1, so it also ensures that the face recognition algorithms are at least available to you at compile time:

```
// Load the "contrib" module is dynamically at runtime.
bool haveContribModule = initModule_contrib();
if (!haveContribModule) {
  cerr << "ERROR: The 'contrib' module is needed for ";
  cerr << "FaceRecognizer but hasn't been loaded to OpenCV!";
  cerr << endl;
  exit(1);
}
```

To use one of the face recognition algorithms, we must create a `FaceRecognizer` object using the `cv::Algorithm::create<FaceRecognizer>()` function. We pass the name of the face recognition algorithm we want to use as a string to this `create` function. This will give us access to that algorithm, if it is available in the OpenCV version. So, it may be used as a runtime error check to ensure the user has OpenCV v2.4.1 or newer. An example of this is shown as follows:

```
string facerecAlgorithm = "FaceRecognizer.Fisherfaces";
Ptr<FaceRecognizer> model;
// Use OpenCV's new FaceRecognizer in the "contrib" module:
model = Algorithm::create<FaceRecognizer>(facerecAlgorithm);
if (model.empty()) {
  cerr << "ERROR: The FaceRecognizer [" << facerecAlgorithm;
```

```
    cerr << "] is not available in your version of OpenCV. ";
    cerr << "Please update to OpenCV v2.4.1 or newer." << endl;
    exit(1);
}
```

Once we have loaded the `FaceRecognizer` algorithm, we simply call the `FaceRecognizer::train()` function with our collected face data, as follows:

```
// Do the actual training from the collected faces.
model->train(preprocessedFaces, faceLabels);
```

This one line of code will run the whole face recognition training algorithm that you selected (for example, Eigenfaces, Fisherfaces, or potentially other algorithms). If you have just a few people with less than 20 faces, then this training should return very quickly, but if you have many people with many faces, it is possible that the `train()` function will take several seconds, or even minutes, to process all the data.

Viewing the learned knowledge

While it is not necessary, it is quite useful to view the internal data structures that the face recognition algorithm generated when learning your training data, particularly if you understand the theory behind the algorithm you selected and want to verify it worked, or find out why it is not working as you hoped. The internal data structures can be different for different algorithms, but luckily they are the same for Eigenfaces and Fisherfaces, so let's just look at those two. They are both based on 1D eigenvector matrices that appear somewhat like faces when viewed as 2D images; therefore, it is common to refer to eigenvectors as Eigenfaces when using the **Eigenface** algorithm or as Fisherfaces when using the **Fisherface** algorithm.

In simple terms, the basic principle of Eigenfaces is that it will calculate a set of special images (Eigenfaces), and blending ratios (Eigenvalues), which when combined in different ways, can generate each of the images in the training set, but can also be used to differentiate the many face images in the training set from each other. For example, if some of the faces in the training set had a moustache and some did not, then there would be at least one eigenface that shows a moustache, and so the training faces with a moustache would have a high blending ratio for that eigenface to show that they contained a moustache, and the faces without a moustache would have a low blending ratio for that eigenvector.

If the training set has five people with twenty faces for each person, then there would be 100 Eigenfaces and Eigenvalues to differentiate the 100 total faces in the training set, and in fact these would be sorted, so the first few Eigenfaces and Eigenvalues would be the most critical differentiators, and the last few Eigenfaces and Eigenvalues would just be random pixel noises that don't actually help to differentiate the data. So it is common practice to discard some of the last Eigenfaces, and just keep the first 50 or so Eigenfaces.

In comparison, the basic principle of Fisherfaces is that instead of calculating a special eigenvector and eigenvalue for each image in the training set, it only calculates one special eigenvector and eigenvalue for each person. So, in the preceding example that has five people with twenty faces for each person, the Eigenfaces algorithm would use 100 Eigenfaces and Eigenvalues, whereas the Fisherfaces algorithm would use just five Fisherfaces and Eigenvalues.

To access the internal data structures of the Eigenfaces and Fisherfaces algorithms, we must use the `cv::Algorithm::get()` function to obtain them at runtime, as there is no access to them at compile time. The data structures are used internally as part of mathematical calculations, rather than for image processing, so they are usually stored as floating-point numbers typically ranging between 0.0 and 1.0, rather than 8-bit `uchar` pixels ranging from 0 to 255, similar to pixels in regular images. Also, they are often either a 1D row or column matrix, or they make up one of the many 1D rows or columns of a larger matrix. So, before you can display many of these internal data structures, you must reshape them to be the correct rectangular shape, and convert them to 8-bit `uchar` pixels between 0 and 255. As the matrix data might range from 0.0 to 1.0, or -1.0 to 1.0, or anything else, you can use the `cv::normalize()` function with the `cv::NORM_MINMAX` option to make sure it outputs data ranging between 0 and 255, no matter what the input range may be. Let's create a function to perform this reshaping to a rectangle and conversion to 8-bit pixels for us, as follows:

```
// Convert the matrix row or column (float matrix) to a
// rectangular 8-bit image that can be displayed or saved.
// Scales the values to be between 0 to 255.
Mat getImageFrom1DFloatMat(const Mat matrixRow, int height)
{
  // Make a rectangular shaped image instead of a single row.
  Mat rectangularMat = matrixRow.reshape(1, height);
  // Scale the values to be between 0 to 255 and store them
  // as a regular 8-bit uchar image.
  Mat dst;
  normalize(rectangularMat, dst, 0, 255, NORM_MINMAX,
    CV_8UC1);
  return dst;
}
```

To make it easier to debug OpenCV code and even more so, when internally debugging the `cv::Algorithm` data structure, we can use the `ImageUtils.cpp` and `ImageUtils.h` files to display information about a `cv::Mat` structure easily, as follows:

```
Mat img = ...;
printMatInfo(img, "My Image");
```

You will see something similar to the following printed on your console:

My Image: 640w480h 3ch 8bpp, range[79,253][20,58][18,87]

This tells you that it is 640 elements wide and 480 high (that is, a 640 x 480 image or a 480 x 640 matrix, depending on how you view it), with three channels per pixel that are 8-bits each (that is, a regular BGR image), and it shows the minimum and maximum values in the image for each of the color channels.

 It is also possible to print the actual contents of an image or matrix by using the `printMat()` function instead of the `printMatInfo()` function. This is quite handy for viewing matrices and multichannel-float matrices, as these can be quite tricky to view for beginners.
The `ImageUtils` code is mostly for OpenCV's C interface, but is gradually including more of the C++ interface over time. The most recent version can be found at http://shervinemami.info/openCV.html.

Average face

Both the Eigenfaces and Fisherfaces algorithms first calculate the average face that is the mathematical average of all the training images, so they can subtract the average image from each facial image to have better face recognition results. So, let's view the average face from our training set. The average face is named mean in the Eigenfaces and Fisherfaces implementations, shown as follows:

```
Mat averageFace = model->get<Mat>("mean");
printMatInfo(averageFace, "averageFace (row)");
// Convert a 1D float row matrix to a regular 8-bit image.
averageFace = getImageFrom1DFloatMat(averageFace, faceHeight);
printMatInfo(averageFace, "averageFace");
imshow("averageFace", averageFace);
```

You should now see an average face image on your screen similar to the following (enlarged) photo, which is a combination of a man, a woman, and a baby. You should also see similar text to this shown on your console:

```
averageFace (row): 4900w1h 1ch 64bpp, range[5.21,251.47]
averageFace: 70w70h 1ch 8bpp, range[0,255]
```

The image will appear as shown in the following screenshot:

Notice that `averageFace (row)` was a single-row matrix of 64-bit floats, whereas `averageFace` is a rectangular image with 8-bit pixels, covering the full range from 0 to 255.

Eigenvalues, Eigenfaces, and Fisherfaces

Let's view the actual component values in the Eigenvalues (as text), shown as follows:

```
Mat eigenvalues = model->get<Mat>("eigenvalues");
printMat(eigenvalues, "eigenvalues");
```

For Eigenfaces, there is one Eigenvalue for each face, so if we have three people with four faces each, we get a column vector with 12 Eigenvalues sorted from best to worst as follows:

```
eigenvalues: 1w18h 1ch 64bpp, range[4.52e+04,2.02836e+06]
2.03e+06
1.09e+06
5.23e+05
4.04e+05
2.66e+05
2.31e+05
1.85e+05
1.23e+05
9.18e+04
7.61e+04
6.91e+04
4.52e+04
```

For Fisherfaces, there is just one eigenvalue for each extra person, so if there are three people with four faces each, we just get a row vector with two Eigenvalues as follows:

```
eigenvalues: 2w1h 1ch 64bpp, range[152.4,316.6]
317, 152
```

To view the eigenvectors (as Eigenface or Fisherface images), we must extract them as columns from the big eigenvector matrix. As data in OpenCV and C/C++ is normally stored in matrices using row-major order, it means that to extract a column, we should use the `Mat::clone()` function to ensure the data will be continuous, otherwise we can't reshape the data into a rectangle. Once we have a continuous column, `Mat`, we can display the eigenvectors using the `getImageFrom1DFloatMat()` function just like we did for the average face:

```
// Get the eigenvectors
Mat eigenvectors = model->get<Mat>("eigenvectors");
printMatInfo(eigenvectors, "eigenvectors");

// Show the best 20 Eigenfaces
for (int i = 0; i < min(20, eigenvectors.cols); i++) {
  // Create a continuous column vector from eigenvector #i.
  Mat eigenvector = eigenvectors.col(i).clone();

  Mat eigenface = getImageFrom1DFloatMat(eigenvector,
    faceHeight);
  imshow(format("Eigenface%d", i), eigenface);
}
```

The following screenshot displays eigenvectors as images. You can see that for three people with four faces, there are 12 Eigenfaces (left-hand side of the screenshot), or two Fisherfaces (right-hand side of the screenshot):

Notice that both Eigenfaces and Fisherfaces seem to have a resemblance to some facial features, but they don't really look like faces. This is simply because the average face was subtracted from them, so they just show the differences for each Eigenface from the average face. The numbering shows which Eigenface it is, because they are always ordered from the most significant Eigenface to the least significant Eigenface, and if you have 50 or more Eigenfaces, then the later Eigenfaces will often just show random image noise and therefore should be discarded.

Face recognition

Now that we have trained the Eigenfaces or Fisherfaces machine learning algorithm with our set of training images and face labels, we are finally ready to figure out who a person is, just from a facial image! This last step is referred to as face recognition or face identification.

Face identification – recognizing people from their faces

Thanks to OpenCV's `FaceRecognizer` class, we can identify the person in a photo simply by calling the `FaceRecognizer::predict()` function on a facial image as follows:

```
int identity = model->predict(preprocessedFace);
```

This `identity` value will be the label number that we originally used when collecting faces for training, for example, zero for the first person, one for the second person, and so on.

The problem with this identification is that it will always predict one of the given people, even if the input photo is of an unknown person, or of a car. It would still tell you which person is the most likely person in that photo, so it can be difficult to trust the result! The solution is to obtain a confidence metric so we can judge how reliable the result is, and if it seems that the confidence is too low, then we assume it is an unknown person.

Face verification—validating that it is the claimed person

To confirm whether the result of the prediction is reliable or it should be taken as an unknown person, we perform **face verification** (also referred to as **face authentication**) to obtain a confidence metric showing whether the single face image is similar to the claimed person (as opposed to face identification, which we just performed, comparing the single face image with many people).

OpenCV's `FaceRecognizer` class can return a confidence metric when you call the `predict()` function, but unfortunately the confidence metric is simply based on the distance in eigen-subspace, so it is not very reliable. The method we will use is to reconstruct the facial image using the *eigenvectors* and Eigenvalues, and compare this reconstructed image with the input image. If the person had many of their faces included in the training set, then the reconstruction should work quite well from the learned eigenvectors and Eigenvalues, but if the person did not have any faces in the training set (or did not have any that have similar lighting and facial expressions to the test image), then the reconstructed face will look very different from the input face, signaling that it is probably an unknown face.

Remember we said earlier that the Eigenfaces and Fisherfaces algorithms are based on the notion that an image can be roughly represented as a set of eigenvectors (special face images) and Eigenvalues (blending ratios). So if we combine all the eigenvectors with the Eigenvalues from one of the faces in the training set, then we should obtain a fairly close replica of that original training image. The same applies with other images that are similar to the training set; if we combine the trained eigenvectors with the Eigenvalues from a similar test image, we should be able to reconstruct an image that is somewhat a replica of the test image.

Once again, OpenCV's `FaceRecognizer` class makes it quite easy to generate a reconstructed face from any input image, by using the `subspaceProject()` function to project onto the eigenspace and the `subspaceReconstruct()` function to go back from the eigenspace to the image space. The trick is that we need to convert it from a floating-point row matrix to a rectangular 8-bit image (like we did when displaying the average face and Eigenfaces), but we don't want to normalize the data, as it is already in the ideal scale to compare with the original image. If we normalized the data, it would have a different brightness and contrast from the input image, and it would become difficult to compare the image similarity just by using the L2 relative error. This is done as follows:

```
// Get some required data from the FaceRecognizer model.
Mat eigenvectors = model->get<Mat>("eigenvectors");
Mat averageFaceRow = model->get<Mat>("mean");
```

```
// Project the input image onto the eigenspace.
Mat projection = subspaceProject(eigenvectors, averageFaceRow,
    preprocessedFace.reshape(1,1));

// Generate the reconstructed face back from the eigenspace.
Mat reconstructionRow = subspaceReconstruct(eigenvectors,
    averageFaceRow, projection);

// Make it a rectangular shaped image instead of a single row.
Mat reconstructionMat = reconstructionRow.reshape(1,
    faceHeight);

// Convert the floating-point pixels to regular 8-bit uchar.
Mat reconstructedFace = Mat(reconstructionMat.size(), CV_8U);
reconstructionMat.convertTo(reconstructedFace, CV_8U, 1, 0);
```

The following screenshot shows two typical reconstructed faces. The face on the left-hand side was reconstructed well because it was from a known person, whereas the face on the right-hand side was reconstructed badly because it was from an unknown person, or a known person but with unknown lighting conditions/facial expression/face direction:

We can now calculate how similar this reconstructed face is to the input face by using the getSimilarity() function we created previously for comparing two images, where a value less than 0.3 implies that the two images are very similar. For Eigenfaces, there is one eigenvector for each face, so reconstruction tends to work well, and therefore we can typically use a threshold of 0.5, but Fisherfaces has just one eigenvector for each person, so reconstruction will not work as well, and therefore it needs a higher threshold, say 0.7. This is done as follows:

```
similarity = getSimilarity(preprocessedFace, reconstructedFace);
if (similarity > UNKNOWN_PERSON_THRESHOLD) {
    identity = -1;    // Unknown person.
}
```

Now, you can just print the identity to the console, or use it wherever your imagination takes you! Remember that this face recognition method and this face verification method are only reliable in the conditions that you train them for. So to obtain good recognition accuracy, you will need to ensure that the training set of each person covers the full range of lighting conditions, facial expressions, and angles that you expect to test with. The face preprocessing stage helped reduce some differences with lighting conditions and in-plane rotation (if the person tilts their head toward their left or right shoulder), but for other differences, such as out-of-plane rotation (if the person turns their head toward the left-hand side or right-hand side), it will only work if it is covered well in your training set.

Finishing touches—saving and loading files

You could potentially add a command-line-based method that processes input files and saves them to disk, or even perform face detection, face preprocessing, and/or face recognition as a web service. For these types of projects, it is quite easy to add the desired functionality by using the `save` and `load` functions of the `FaceRecognizer` class. You may also want to save the trained data, and then load it on program startup.

Saving the trained model to an XML or YML file is very easy, and is shown as follows:

```
model->save("trainedModel.yml");
```

You may also want to save the array of preprocessed faces and labels, if you want to add more data to the training set later.

For example, here is some sample code for loading the trained model from a file. Note that you must specify the face recognition algorithm (for example, `FaceRecognizer.Eigenfaces` or `FaceRecognizer.Fisherfaces`) that was originally used to create the trained model:

```
string facerecAlgorithm = "FaceRecognizer.Fisherfaces";
model = Algorithm::create<FaceRecognizer>(facerecAlgorithm);
Mat labels;
try {
  model->load("trainedModel.yml");
  labels = model->get<Mat>("labels");
} catch (cv::Exception &e) {}
if (labels.rows <= 0) {
  cerr << "ERROR: Couldn't load trained data from "
          "[trainedModel.yml]!" << endl;
  exit(1);
}
```

Finishing touches—making a nice and interactive GUI

While the code given so far in this chapter is sufficient for a whole face recognition system, there still needs to be a way to put the data into the system and a way to use it. Many face recognition systems for research will choose the ideal input to be text files, listing where the static image files are stored on the computer, as well as other important data, such as the true name or identity of the person, and perhaps true pixel coordinates of regions of the face (such as the ground truth of where the face and eye centers actually are). This would either be collected manually or by another face recognition system.

The ideal output would then be a text file comparing the recognition results with the ground truth, so that statistics may be obtained for comparing the face recognition system with other face recognition systems.

However, as the face recognition system in this chapter is designed for learning as well as practical fun purposes, rather than competing with the latest research methods, it is useful to have an easy-to-use GUI that allows face collection, training, and testing interactively from the webcam in real time. So this section will show you an interactive GUI that provides these features. The reader is expected to either use the GUI that comes with this book, or modify it for their own purposes, or ignore this GUI and design their own to perform the face recognition techniques discussed so far.

As we need the GUI to perform multiple tasks, let's create a set of modes or states that the GUI will have, with buttons or mouse clicks for the user to change modes:

- **Startup**: This state loads and initializes the data and webcam.
- **Detection**: This state detects faces and shows them with preprocessing, until the user clicks on the **Add Person** button.
- **Collection**: This state collects faces for the current person, until the user clicks anywhere in the window. This also shows the most recent face of each person. The user clicks either one of the existing people or the **Add Person** button to collect faces for different people.
- **Training**: In this state, the system is trained with the help of all the collected faces of all the collected people.
- **Recognition**: This consists of highlighting the recognized person and showing a confidence meter. The user clicks either one of the people or the **Add Person** button to return to mode 2 (*Collection*).

To quit, the user can hit the *Esc* key in the window at any time. Let's also add a **Delete All** mode that restarts a new face recognition system, and a **Debug** button that toggles the display of extra debug information. We can create an enumerated `mode` variable to show the current mode.

Drawing the GUI elements

To display the current mode on the screen, let's create a function to draw text easily. OpenCV comes with a `cv::putText()` function with several fonts and anti-aliasing, but it can be tricky to place the text in the location that you want. Luckily, there is also a `cv::getTextSize()` function to calculate the bounding box around the text, so we can create a wrapper function to make it easier to place text.

We want to be able to place text along any edge of the window, make sure it is completely visible, and also to allow placing multiple lines or words of text next to each other without overwriting. So here is a wrapper function to allow you to specify either left-justified or right-justified, as well as to specify top-justified or bottom-justified, and return the bounding box so we can easily draw multiple lines of text on any corner or edge of the window:

```
// Draw text into an image. Defaults to top-left-justified
// text, so give negative x coords for right-justified text,
// and/or negative y coords for bottom-justified text.
// Returns the bounding rect around the drawn text.
Rect drawString(Mat img, string text, Point coord, Scalar
  color, float fontScale = 0.6f, int thickness = 1,
  int fontFace = FONT_HERSHEY_COMPLEX);
```

Now to display the current mode on the GUI, as the background of the window will be the camera feed, it is quite possible that if we simply draw text over the camera feed, it might be the same color as the camera background! So, let's just draw a black shadow of text that is just one pixel apart from the foreground text we want to draw. Let's also draw a line of helpful text below it, so the user knows the steps to follow. Here is an example of how to draw some text using the `drawString()` function:

```
string msg = "Click [Add Person] when ready to collect faces.";
// Draw it as black shadow & again as white text.
float txtSize = 0.4;
int BORDER = 10;
drawString (displayedFrame, msg, Point(BORDER, -BORDER-2),
  CV_RGB(0,0,0), txtSize);
Rect rcHelp = drawString(displayedFrame, msg, Point(BORDER+1,
  -BORDER-1), CV_RGB(255,255,255), txtSize);
```

The following partial screenshot shows the mode and information at the bottom of the GUI window, overlaid on top of the camera image:

We mentioned that we want a few GUI buttons, so let's create a function to draw a GUI button easily, as follows:

```cpp
// Draw a GUI button into the image, using drawString().
// Can give a minWidth to have several buttons of same width.
// Returns the bounding rect around the drawn button.
Rect drawButton(Mat img, string text, Point coord,
  int minWidth = 0)
{
  const int B = 10;
  Point textCoord = Point(coord.x + B, coord.y + B);
  // Get the bounding box around the text.
  Rect rcText = drawString(img, text, textCoord,
    CV_RGB(0,0,0));
  // Draw a filled rectangle around the text.
  Rect rcButton = Rect(rcText.x - B, rcText.y - B,
    rcText.width + 2*B, rcText.height + 2*B);
  // Set a minimum button width.
  if (rcButton.width < minWidth)
    rcButton.width = minWidth;
  // Make a semi-transparent white rectangle.
  Mat matButton = img(rcButton);
  matButton += CV_RGB(90, 90, 90);
  // Draw a non-transparent white border.
  rectangle(img, rcButton, CV_RGB(200,200,200), 1, LINE_AA);

  // Draw the actual text that will be displayed.
  drawString(img, text, textCoord, CV_RGB(10,55,20));

  return rcButton;
}
```

Now, we create several clickable GUI buttons using the `drawButton()` function, which will always be shown at the top-left of the GUI, as shown in the following partial screenshot:

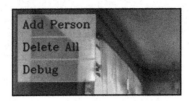

As we mentioned, the GUI program has some modes that it switches between (as a finite state machine), beginning with the Startup mode. We will store the current mode as the `m_mode` variable.

Startup mode

In the Startup mode, we just need to load the XML detector files to detect the face and eyes and initialize the webcam, which we've already covered. Let's also create a main GUI window with a mouse callback function that OpenCV will call whenever the user moves or clicks their mouse in our window. It may also be desirable to set the camera resolution to something reasonable; for example, 640 x 480, if the camera supports it. This is done as follows:

```
// Create a GUI window for display on the screen.
namedWindow(windowName);

// Call "onMouse()" when the user clicks in the window.
setMouseCallback(windowName, onMouse, 0);

// Set the camera resolution. Only works for some systems.
videoCapture.set(CAP_PROP_FRAME_WIDTH, 640);
videoCapture.set(CAP_PROP_FRAME_HEIGHT, 480);

// We're already initialized, so let's start in Detection mode.
m_mode = MODE_DETECTION;
```

Detection mode

In the Detection mode, we want to continuously detect faces and eyes, draw rectangles or circles around them to show the detection result, and show the current preprocessed face. In fact, we will want these to be displayed no matter which mode we are in. The only thing special about the Detection mode is that it will change to the next mode (*Collection*) when the user clicks the **Add Person** button.

If you remember from the detection step, in this chapter, the output of our detection stage will be as follows:

- `Mat preprocessedFace`: The preprocessed face (if face and eyes were detected)
- `Rect faceRect`: The detected face region coordinates
- `Point leftEye, rightEye`: The detected left and right eye center coordinates

So, we should check whether a preprocessed face was returned, and draw a rectangle and circles around the face and eyes if they were detected, as follows:

```
bool gotFaceAndEyes = false;
if (preprocessedFace.data)
  gotFaceAndEyes = true;

if (faceRect.width > 0) {
  // Draw an anti-aliased rectangle around the detected face.
  rectangle(displayedFrame, faceRect, CV_RGB(255, 255, 0), 2,
    CV_AA);

  // Draw light-blue anti-aliased circles for the 2 eyes.
  Scalar eyeColor = CV_RGB(0,255,255);
  if (leftEye.x >= 0) {   // Check if the eye was detected
    circle(displayedFrame, Point(faceRect.x + leftEye.x,
      faceRect.y + leftEye.y), 6, eyeColor, 1, LINE_AA);
  }
  if (rightEye.x >= 0) {   // Check if the eye was detected
    circle(displayedFrame, Point(faceRect.x + rightEye.x,
      faceRect.y + rightEye.y), 6, eyeColor, 1, LINE_AA);
  }
}
```

We will overlay the current preprocessed face at the top center of the window as follows:

```
int cx = (displayedFrame.cols - faceWidth) / 2;
if (preprocessedFace.data) {
  // Get a BGR version of the face, since the output is BGR.
  Mat srcBGR = Mat(preprocessedFace.size(), CV_8UC3);
  cvtColor(preprocessedFace, srcBGR, COLOR_GRAY2BGR);

  // Get the destination ROI.
  Rect dstRC = Rect(cx, BORDER, faceWidth, faceHeight);
  Mat dstROI = displayedFrame(dstRC);

  // Copy the pixels from src to dst.
  srcBGR.copyTo(dstROI);
}
```

```
// Draw an anti-aliased border around the face.
rectangle(displayedFrame, Rect(cx-1, BORDER-1, faceWidth+2,
    faceHeight+2), CV_RGB(200,200,200), 1, LINE_AA);
```

The following screenshot shows the displayed GUI when in the Detection mode. The preprocessed face is shown at the top center, and the detected face and eyes are marked:

Collection mode

We enter the Collection mode when the user clicks on the **Add Person** button to signal that they want to begin collecting faces for a new person. As mentioned previously, we have limited the face collection to one face per second, and then only if it has changed noticeably from the previously collected face. And remember, we decided to collect not only the preprocessed face, but also the mirror image of the preprocessed face.

In the Collection mode, we want to show the most recent face of each known person and let the user click on one of those people to add more faces to them, or click the **Add Person** button to add a new person to the collection. The user must click somewhere in the middle of the window to continue to the next mode (*Training mode*).

So, first we need to keep a reference to the latest face that was collected for each person. We'll do this by updating the m_latestFaces array of integers, which just stores the array index of each person from the big preprocessedFaces array (that is, the collection of all faces of the all the people). As we also store the mirrored face in that array, we want to reference the second-last face, not the last face. This code should be appended to the code that adds a new face (and mirrored face) to the preprocessedFaces array:

```
// Keep a reference to the latest face of each person.
m_latestFaces[m_selectedPerson] = preprocessedFaces.size() - 2;
```

We just have to remember to always grow or shrink the m_latestFaces array whenever a new person is added or deleted (for example, due to the user clicking on the **Add Person** button). Now, let's display the most recent face for each of the collected people on the right-hand side of the window (both in the Collection mode and Recognition mode later) as follows:

```
m_gui_faces_left = displayedFrame.cols - BORDER - faceWidth;
m_gui_faces_top = BORDER;
for (int i=0; i<m_numPersons; i++) {
  int index = m_latestFaces[i];
  if (index >= 0 && index < (int)preprocessedFaces.size()) {
    Mat srcGray = preprocessedFaces[index];
    if (srcGray.data) {
      // Get a BGR face, since the output is BGR.
      Mat srcBGR = Mat(srcGray.size(), CV_8UC3);
      cvtColor(srcGray, srcBGR, COLOR_GRAY2BGR);

      // Get the destination ROI
      int y = min(m_gui_faces_top + i * faceHeight,
      displayedFrame.rows - faceHeight);
      Rect dstRC = Rect(m_gui_faces_left, y, faceWidth,
      faceHeight);
      Mat dstROI = displayedFrame(dstRC);

      // Copy the pixels from src to dst.
      srcBGR.copyTo(dstROI);
    }
  }
}
```

We also want to highlight the current person being collected, using a thick red border around their face. This is done as follows:

```
if (m_mode == MODE_COLLECT_FACES) {
   if (m_selectedPerson >= 0 &&
      m_selectedPerson < m_numPersons) {
      int y = min(m_gui_faces_top + m_selectedPerson *
      faceHeight, displayedFrame.rows - faceHeight);
      Rect rc = Rect(m_gui_faces_left, y, faceWidth, faceHeight);
      rectangle(displayedFrame, rc, CV_RGB(255,0,0), 3, LINE_AA);
   }
}
```

The following partial screenshot shows the typical display when faces for several people have been collected. The user can click on any of the people at the top right to collect more faces for that person:

Training mode

When the user finally clicks in the middle of the window, the face recognition algorithm will begin training on all the collected faces. But it is important to make sure there have been enough faces or people collected, otherwise the program may crash. In general, this just requires making sure there is at least one face in the training set (which implies there is at least one person). But the Fisherfaces algorithm looks for comparisons between people, so if there are less than two people in the training set, it will also crash. So, we must check whether the selected face recognition algorithm is Fisherfaces. If it is, then we require at least two people with faces, otherwise we require at least one person with a face. If there isn't enough data, then the program goes back to the Collection mode so the user can add more faces before training.

To check there are at least two people with collected faces, we can make sure that when a user clicks on the **Add Person** button, a new person is only added if there isn't any empty person (that is, a person that was added but does not have any collected faces yet). If there are just two people, and we are using the Fisherfaces algorithm, then we must make sure an m_latestFaces reference was set for the last person during the Collection mode. Then, m_latestFaces[i] is initialized to −1 when there still haven't been any faces added to that person, and it becomes 0 or higher once faces for that person have been added. This is done as follows:

```
// Check if there is enough data to train from.
bool haveEnoughData = true;
if (!strcmp(facerecAlgorithm, "FaceRecognizer.Fisherfaces")) {
  if ((m_numPersons < 2) ||
  (m_numPersons == 2 && m_latestFaces[1] < 0) ) {
    cout << "Fisherfaces needs >= 2 people!" << endl;
    haveEnoughData = false;
  }
}
if (m_numPersons < 1 || preprocessedFaces.size() <= 0 ||
  preprocessedFaces.size() != faceLabels.size()) {
  cout << "Need data before it can be learnt!" << endl;
  haveEnoughData = false;
}

if (haveEnoughData) {
  // Train collected faces using Eigenfaces or Fisherfaces.
  model = learnCollectedFaces(preprocessedFaces, faceLabels,
          facerecAlgorithm);

  // Now that training is over, we can start recognizing!
  m_mode = MODE_RECOGNITION;
}
else {
  // Not enough training data, go back to Collection mode!
  m_mode = MODE_COLLECT_FACES;
}
```

The training may take a fraction of a second, or it may take several seconds or even minutes, depending on how much data is collected. Once the training of collected faces is complete, the face recognition system will automatically enter the *Recognition mode.*

Recognition mode

In the Recognition mode, a confidence meter is shown next to the preprocessed face, so the user knows how reliable the recognition is. If the confidence level is higher than the unknown threshold, it will draw a green rectangle around the recognized person to show the result easily. The user can add more faces for further training if they click on the **Add Person** button or one of the existing people, which causes the program to return to the Collection mode.

Now, we have obtained the recognized identity and the similarity with the reconstructed face, as mentioned earlier. To display the confidence meter, we know that the L2 similarity value is generally between 0 and 0.5 for high confidence, and between 0.5 and 1.0 for low confidence, so we can just subtract it from 1.0 to get the confidence level between 0.0 to 1.0.

Then, we just draw a filled rectangle using the confidence level as the ratio, shown as follows:

```
int cx = (displayedFrame.cols - faceWidth) / 2;
Point ptBottomRight = Point(cx - 5, BORDER + faceHeight);
Point ptTopLeft = Point(cx - 15, BORDER);

// Draw a gray line showing the threshold for "unknown" people.
Point ptThreshold = Point(ptTopLeft.x, ptBottomRight.y -
  (1.0 - UNKNOWN_PERSON_THRESHOLD) * faceHeight);
rectangle(displayedFrame, ptThreshold, Point(ptBottomRight.x,
ptThreshold.y), CV_RGB(200,200,200), 1, CV_AA);

// Crop the confidence rating between 0 to 1 to fit in the bar.
double confidenceRatio = 1.0 - min(max(similarity, 0.0), 1.0);
Point ptConfidence = Point(ptTopLeft.x, ptBottomRight.y -
  confidenceRatio * faceHeight);

// Show the light-blue confidence bar.
rectangle(displayedFrame, ptConfidence, ptBottomRight,
  CV_RGB(0,255,255), CV_FILLED, CV_AA);

// Show the gray border of the bar.
rectangle(displayedFrame, ptTopLeft, ptBottomRight,
  CV_RGB(200,200,200), 1, CV_AA);
```

To highlight the recognized person, we draw a green rectangle around their face as follows:

```
if (identity >= 0 && identity < 1000) {
  int y = min(m_gui_faces_top + identity * faceHeight,
    displayedFrame.rows - faceHeight);
  Rect rc = Rect(m_gui_faces_left, y, faceWidth, faceHeight);
  rectangle(displayedFrame, rc, CV_RGB(0,255,0), 3, CV_AA);
}
```

The following partial screenshot shows a typical display when running in Recognition mode, showing the confidence meter next to the preprocessed face at the top center, and highlighting the recognized person in the top right corner:

Checking and handling mouse clicks

Now that we have all our GUI elements drawn, we need to process mouse events. When we initialized the display window, we told OpenCV that we want a mouse event callback to our onMouse function.

We don't care about mouse movement, only the mouse clicks, so first we skip the mouse events that aren't for the left mouse button click as follows:

```
void onMouse(int event, int x, int y, int, void*)
{
  if (event != CV_EVENT_LBUTTONDOWN)
    return;

  Point pt = Point(x,y);

  ... (handle mouse clicks)
  ...
}
```

As we obtained the drawn rectangle bounds of the buttons when drawing them, we just check whether the mouse click location is in any of our button regions by calling OpenCV's `inside()` function. Now, we can check for each button we have created.

When the user clicks on the **Add Person** button, we add one to the `m_numPersons` variable, allocate more space in the `m_latestFaces` variable, select the new person for the collection, and begin the Collection mode (no matter which mode we were previously in).

But there is one complication: to ensure that we have at least one face for each person when training, we will only allocate space for a new person if there isn't already a person with zero faces. This will ensure that we can always check the value of `m_latestFaces[m_numPersons-1]` to see if a face has been collected for every person. This is done as follows:

```
if (pt.inside(m_btnAddPerson)) {
  // Ensure there isn't a person without collected faces.
  if ((m_numPersons==0) ||
     (m_latestFaces[m_numPersons-1] >= 0)) {
     // Add a new person.
     m_numPersons++;
     m_latestFaces.push_back(-1);
  }
  m_selectedPerson = m_numPersons - 1;
  m_mode = MODE_COLLECT_FACES;
}
```

This method can be used to test for other button clicks, such as toggling the debug flag as follows:

```
else if (pt.inside(m_btnDebug)) {
  m_debug = !m_debug;
}
```

To handle the **Delete All** button, we need to empty various data structures that are local to our main loop (that is, not accessible from the mouse event callback function), so we change to the **Delete All** mode and then we can delete everything from inside the main loop. We must also deal with the user clicking the main window (that is, not a button). If they clicked on one of the people on the right-hand side, then we want to select that person and change to the Collection mode. Or, if they clicked in the main window while in the Collection mode, then we want to change to the Training mode. This is done as follows:

```
else {
  // Check if the user clicked on a face from the list.
  int clickedPerson = -1;
  for (int i=0; i<m_numPersons; i++) {
    if (m_gui_faces_top >= 0) {
      Rect rcFace = Rect(m_gui_faces_left,
      m_gui_faces_top + i * faceHeight, faceWidth, faceHeight);
      if (pt.inside(rcFace)) {
        clickedPerson = i;
        break;
      }
    }
  }
  // Change the selected person, if the user clicked a face.
  if (clickedPerson >= 0) {
    // Change the current person & collect more photos.
    m_selectedPerson = clickedPerson;
    m_mode = MODE_COLLECT_FACES;
  }
  // Otherwise they clicked in the center.
  else {
    // Change to training mode if it was collecting faces.
    if (m_mode == MODE_COLLECT_FACES) {
        m_mode = MODE_TRAINING;
    }
  }
}
```

Summary

This chapter has shown you all the steps required to create a real-time face recognition application, with enough preprocessing to allow some differences between the training set conditions and the testing set conditions, just using basic algorithms. We used face detection to find the location of a face within the camera image, followed by several forms of face preprocessing to reduce the effects of different lighting conditions, camera and face orientations, and facial expressions.

We then trained an Eigenfaces or Fisherfaces machine learning system with the preprocessed faces we collected, and finally we performed face recognition to see who the person is with face verification, providing a confidence metric in case it is an unknown person.

Rather than providing a command-line tool that processes image files in an offline manner, we combined all the preceding steps into a self-contained real-time GUI program to allow immediate use of the face recognition system. You should be able to modify the behavior of the system for your own purposes, such as to allow automatic login on your computer, or if you are interested in improving recognition reliability, then you can read conference papers about recent advances in face recognition to potentially improve each step of the program until it is reliable enough for your specific needs. For example, you could improve the face preprocessing stages, or use a more advanced machine learning algorithm, or an even better face verification algorithm, based on methods at `http://www.facerec.org/algorithms/` and `http://www.cvpapers.com`.

References

- *Rapid Object Detection Using a Boosted Cascade of Simple Features, P. Viola and M.J. Jones, Proceedings of the IEEE Transactions on CVPR 2001, Vol. 1, pp. 511-518*
- *An Extended Set of Haar-like Features for Rapid Object Detection, R. Lienhart and J. Maydt, Proceedings of the IEEE Transactions on ICIP 2002, Vol. 1, pp. 900-903*
- *Face Description with Local Binary Patterns: Application to Face Recognition, T. Ahonen, A. Hadid and M. Pietikäinen, Proceedings of the IEEE Transactions on PAMI 2006, Vol. 28, Issue 12, pp. 2037-2041*
- *Learning OpenCV: Computer Vision with the OpenCV Library, G. Bradski and A. Kaehler, pp. 186-190, O'Reilly Media.*
- *Eigenfaces for recognition, M. Turk and A. Pentland, Journal of Cognitive Neuroscience 3, pp. 71-86*
- *Eigenfaces vs. Fisherfaces: Recognition using class specific linear projection, P.N. Belhumeur, J. Hespanha and D. Kriegman, Proceedings of the IEEE Transactions on PAMI 1997, Vol. 19, Issue 7, pp. 711-720*
- *Face Recognition with Local Binary Patterns, T. Ahonen, A. Hadid and M. Pietikäinen, Computer Vision - ECCV 2004, pp. 469-48*

Introduction to Web Computer Vision with OpenCV.js

6

This chapter introduces you to a new way to develop computer vision algorithms for the web. When a computer vision algorithm has to be written for the World Wide Web, normally it is a C++ program on the server that is executed when a client calls it via a web server, but with OpenCV.js, this way to develop computer vision algorithms is extended not only on the server but also extended to the browser client. The algorithms can be executed in the client browser, allowing developers to have more flexibility and use the benefits of running code in the clients' browsers.

In this chapter, we are going to learn the following:

- What OpenCV.js is and the benefits of client browser code
- Develop basic algorithms for image manipulation
- Work with video or webcam in the browser
- Manipulate frames with OpenCV.js
- Face detection in a web browser using OpenCV.js

What is OpenCV.js?

OpenCV.js is a port of some OpenCV functions using new technology that compiles C++ code into JavaScript. OpenCV uses Emscripten to compile C++ functions into Asm.js or WebAssembly targets. Emscripten is an LLVM-to-JavaScript compiler that compiles from **low-level virtual machine (LLVM)** bitcode to Asm.js or WebAssembly JavaScript, which can be executed in any new web browser. **Emscripten** works as follows:

The increase in web applications, and the news on web HTML5 standards such as WebGL or WebRTC that allow developers access to webcams, create emerging possibilities for new applications. OpenCV brings to web developers more powerful increase on the browser to develop new algorithms with OpenCV.js, allowing the use of computer vision algorithms and giving possibilities of new applications such as: web virtual reality, web augmented reality, face detection and recognition, image manipulation and so much more.

Asm.js is highly optimized and it is designed to be near-native code, achieving speeds 2x (depends on browser and computer) slower than the same native executable application.

Asm.js is a subset of JavaScript that takes a C++ function like this:

```
int f(int i) {
    return i + 1;
}
```

And converts it into JavaScript code like this:

```
function f(i) {
  i = i|0;
  return (i + 1)|0;
}
```

WebAssembly is a new technology and web standard that defines a binary format for executing code in web pages. It is developed to complement JavaScript to speed up applications that must run like native code. This technology is the best choice to increase the performance for computer vision and port OpenCV to JavaScript. For example, see the following C code:

```
int factorial(int n) {
  if (n == 0)
    return 1;
  else
    return n * factorial(n-1);
}
```

This is transformed into a binary encoding like this:

```
20 00
50
04 7E
42 01
05
20 00
20 00
42 01
7D
```

```
10 00
7E
0B
```

This binary encoding that generates WebAssembly allows the size minimization of large files like OpenCV.js for example. That is compiled with WebAssembly and is highly optimized for speed achieving near-native code that is just 1.5x slower.

But, what are the benefits of using OpenCV.js in a client browser instead of a C++ program on the server? One benefit is the ease of porting an application to any operating system without compiling it on each OS. Another very interesting benefit is optimizing computing time and cost; for example, imagine that you create a web application that has to detect and recognize people in front of a webcam, this algorithm takes 100 ms to compute, and it is used by 1,000 users per second, then we require 100 seconds to compute the 1,000 users' queries. If we only put 10 processes in parallel to reply in 100 ms, we need 10 servers to get a fast reply. To save money, we can leave the computer vision on the client browsers using OpenCV.js, and send to the server only the results of the computer vision operation.

Compile OpenCV.js

To compile OpenCV.js, we need to install Emscripten. Emscripten requires the following:

- Python 2.7
- Node.js
- cmake
- Java runtime

We can install these dependencies following the next instructions:

```
# Install Python
sudo apt-get install python2.7

# Install node.js
sudo apt-get install nodejs

# Install CMake (optional, only needed for tests and building Binaryen)
sudo apt-get install cmake

# Install Java (optional, only needed for Closure Compiler minification)
sudo apt-get install default-jre
```

Now, we have to download Emscripten from the GitHub repository:

```
# Get the emsdk repo
git clone https://github.com/juj/emsdk.git

# Enter that directory
cd emsdk
```

Now, we only have to update and install the environment variables required by Emscripten and we can do that following the next steps in the command line:

```
# Download and install the latest SDK tools.
./emsdk install latest

# Make the "latest" SDK "active" for the current user. (writes
~/.emscripten file)
./emsdk activate latest

# Activate PATH and other environment variables in the current terminal
source ./emsdk_env.sh
```

Now, we are ready to compile OpenCV into JavaScript. After downloading OpenCV from GitHub and accessing the OpenCV folder, we have to create a build folder with a name like build_js and execute the next command line to compile OpenCV into Asm.js:

```
python ./platforms/js/build_js.py build_js
```

Or with the --build_wasm parameter to compile for WebAssembly:

```
python ./platforms/js/build_js.py build_js --build_wasm
```

If we require more debug information and exception catching, we can enable it using the --enable_exception parameter.

The binary results are generated in the build_js/bin folder, where you can locate the opencv.js and opencv.wasm files that you can use in your web pages.

Basic introduction to OpenCV.js development

Before starting to develop with OpenCV.js, we require a basic HTML structure with the required HTML elements to work with. In our examples, we are going to use Bootstrap, which is a toolkit to build responsive web applications with multiple predesigned web components and utilities, using HTML, CSS, and JavaScript. We are going to use JQuery library to work easily with HTML elements, events, and callbacks. We can develop the same samples of this chapter without Bootstrap and JQuery, or use other frameworks or libraries like AngularJS, VUE, and so on, but the simplicity of Bootstrap and JQuery will help us understand and write our web page code.

We are going to use the same HTML structure template for all our samples, which consists of a header, a left menu where we put links to each example code, and the main content where we are going to write the example code. The HTML structure looks like this:

```html
<!doctype html>
<html lang="en">
  <head>
    <!-- Required meta tags -->
    <meta charset="utf-8">
    <meta name="viewport" content="width=device-width, initial-scale=1,
shrink-to-fit=no">

    <!-- Bootstrap CSS -->
    <link rel="stylesheet" href="css/bootstrap.min.css">
    <link rel="stylesheet" href="css/custom.css">
    <title>OpenCV Computer vision on Web. Packt Publishing.</title>
  </head>
  <body>
    <nav class="navbar navbar-dark fixed-top flex-md-nowrap p-0 shadow">
        <a class="navbar-brand col-sm-3 col-md-2 mr-0"
href="#">OpenCV.js</a>
        <h1 class="col-md-10">TITLE</h1>
    </nav>
    <div class="container-fluid">
        <div class="row">
            <nav class="col-md-2 d-none d-md-block bg-light sidebar">
                <div class="sidebar-sticky">
                    <ul id="menu" class="nav flex-column">
                        MENU ITEMS LOAD WITH JavaScript
                    </ul>
                </div>
            </nav>
            <main role="main" class="col-md-10 ml-sm-auto col-lg-10 px-4">
```

```
                    EXAMPLE CONTENT
                </main>
            </div>
        </div>

        <!-- Optional JavaScript -->
        <!-- jQuery first, then Popper.js, then Bootstrap JS -->
        <script src="js/jquery-3.3.1.min.js"></script>
        <script src="js/popper.min.js"></script>
        <script src="js/bootstrap.min.js"></script>
        <script src="js/common.js"></script>
        <!-- OPENCV -->
        <script async="" src="js/opencv.js" type="text/JavaScript"
    onload="onOpenCvReady();" onerror="onOpenCvError();"></script>

        <script type="text/JavaScript">
            // OUR EXAMPLE SCRIPT
            function onOpenCvReady() {
                // OPENCV.JS IS LOADED AND READY TO START TO WORK
            }
            function onOpenCvError() {
                // CALLBACK IF ERROR LOADING OPENCV.JS
            }
        </script>
    </body>
</html>
```

If we take a look at this code, the most important parts will be in the EXAMPLE CONTENT part, where we are going to write the HTML elements that will interact with OpenCV.js in the following snippet:

```
<!-- OPENCV -->
    <script async="" src="js/opencv.js" type="text/JavaScript"
onload="onOpenCvReady();" onerror="onOpenCvError();"></script>

    <script type="text/JavaScript">
        // OUR EXAMPLE SCRIPT
        function onOpenCvReady() {
            // OPENCV.JS IS LOADED AND READY TO START TO WORK
        }
        function onOpenCvError() {
            // CALLBACK IF ERROR LOADING OPENCV.JS
        }
    </script>
```

The onOpenCvReady and onOpenCvError callback functions will be called when OpenCV.js is loaded and ready to use or if we have an error loading it, respectively.

Now that we have the main HTML structure created, we are going to start with the first example. In this example, we are going to create the following:

- An **alert box** to show when OpenCV.js is loaded, because OpenCV.js is heavy and will take a few seconds to load on the client browser. So, we are going to load it asynchronously and when it's loaded, we will start to load the other required code and user interfaces.
- An **image** element to load the client image.
- A **canvas** element, which shows the result of our algorithm.
- A **button** to load the file image.

Then, we are going to create the required HTML elements. To create the **alert box**, we are going to use our bootstrap `alert` class, using a `div` HTML element wrapped in a single column of a row. The code to do this is given here:

```
...
<div class="row">
    <div class="col">
        <div id="status" class="alert alert-primary" role="alert">
            <img src="img/ajax-loader.gif" /> Loading OpenCV...</div>
    </div>
</div>
...
```

Now, we are going to create a row block that contains the following elements: **input image** using the `img` element, and **canvas output** result using the `canvas` element.

```
...
<div class="row">
    <div class="col">
        <img id="imageSrc" alt="No Image" class="small"
src="img/white.png">
    </div>
    <div class="col">
        <canvas id="canvasOutput" class="small" height="300px"></canvas>
    </div>
</div>
...
```

To finish, we need to add the file button using the `input` HTML element of type file, as shown in this code:

```
<input type="file" id="fileInput" name="file" accept="image/*">
```

The preceding HTML code looks like this screenshot:

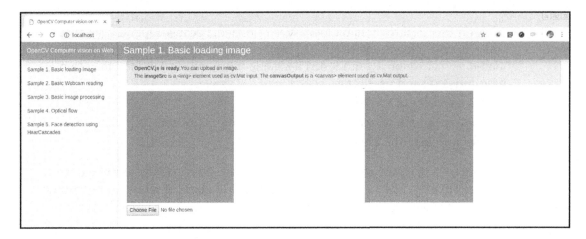

Preview of the image input and canvas output section

We are now ready to start working with OpenCV.js. Now we are going to explain how to load an image, convert it to grayscale, and show it on the browser via the `canvas` element. The first thing we are going to do is to alert the user that OpenCV.js is loaded and we can then start to select an image. We are going to use the `onOpenCvReady` callback function to change the alert box content with the following code:

```
function onOpenCvReady() {
    document.getElementById('status').innerHTML = '<b>OpenCV.js is
ready</b>.' +
        'You can upload an image.<br>' +
        'The <b>imageSrc</b> is a <img> element used as cv.Mat input. ' +
        'The <b>canvasOutput</b> is a <canvas> element used as cv.Mat
output.';
}
```

And if there are any issues loading OpenCV.js, we can use the `onOpenCvError` callback function to show an error in the alert box:

```
function onOpenCvError() {
    let element = document.getElementById('status');
    element.setAttribute('class', 'err');
    element.innerHTML = 'Failed to load opencv.js';
}
```

Now, we can check when the user clicks the file input button to load an image into the `img` HTML element. To create a callback for a file input, we first save the input file button into a variable:

```
let inputElement = document.getElementById('fileInput');
```

And, we create an event when the user clicks and changes the input file value using `addEventListener`, with the first parameter as *change*:

```
inputElement.addEventListener('change', (e) => {
    imgElement.src = URL.createObjectURL(e.target.files[0]);
}, false);
```

When the user clicks on the button, we have to set up the source of our image element using the `src` attribute that we previously saved into the `imgElement` variable:

```
let imgElement = document.getElementById('imageSrc');
```

The finishing step is to process the image loaded in the `img` element (the `imgElement` variable) to convert it into grayscale and show it in the `canvas` output. Then, we create a new event listener for `imgElement`, assigning a function to the `onload` attribute:

```
imgElement.onload = function() {
...
};
```

This function will be called when the image element is loaded. In this function, we will read the image in this element, like OpenCV does, while reading the file using the `imread` function:

```
let mat = cv.imread(imgElement);
```

And later, we convert the `mat` variable image using the `cvtColor` function. As we can see, the functions are very similar to the C++ interfaces:

```
cv.cvtColor(mat, mat, cv.COLOR_BGR2GRAY);
```

Finally, we show the image on the canvas using the `imshow` function, as a C++ interface, but in this case, instead of putting the name of the window we want to show the image in, we put the ID of the canvas we want to show the image on:

```
cv.imshow('canvasOutput', mat);
```

It is a good practice to release all the memory that we do not require, rather than releasing the `mat` variable using the `delete` function:

```
mat.delete();
```

The complete code of the `onload` function looks like this:

```
imgElement.onload = function() {
    let mat = cv.imread(imgElement);
    cv.cvtColor(mat, mat, cv.COLOR_BGR2GRAY);
    cv.imshow('canvasOutput', mat);
    mat.delete();
};
```

And this is the final result in the web page after loading an image:

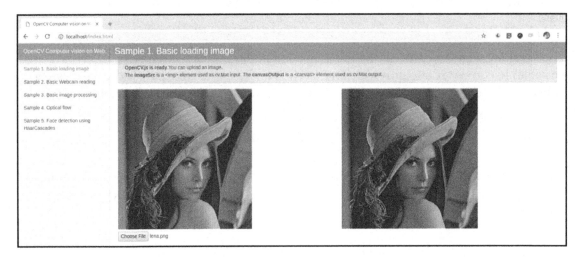

Final output after using the image input and canvas output element

Now, we are ready to continue exploring OpenCV.js, and before working a bit more on processing images or frames, we are going to learn how to read a video streaming from a webcam.

Accessing webcam streams

In the previous section, we learned how to read an image; now, we are going to learn how to read framed images from a webcam stream. To do this, we need the following HTML elements:

- An **alert box** to show when OpenCV.js is loaded; because OpenCV.js is heavy and will take a few seconds to load on the client browser, then we are going to load it asynchronously and when it's loaded, we will start to load the other required code and user interfaces.
- A `video` element to load the client video stream with the ID `videoInput`.
- A `Canvas` element which shows the result of our algorithm.
- A `button` to start processing video frames with the ID `cv_start`, which is initially hidden.

We are going to maintain the same alert box and canvas elements used in the previous sample and add two new elements, a button using the link and a video HTML element, as we can see in the next code snippet:

```html
<div class="row">
    <div class="col">
        <div id="status" class="alert alert-primary" role="alert"><img
src="img/ajax-loader.gif" /> Loading OpenCV...</div>
    </div>
</div>
<a href="#" class="btn btn-primary" style="display: none;"
id="cv_start">Start</a>
<div class="row">
    <div class="col">
        <video id="videoInput" width="320" height="240"></video>
    </div>
    <div class="col">
        <canvas id="canvasOutput" class="small" height="300px"></canvas>
    </div>
</div>
```

Now, the web page looks like this:

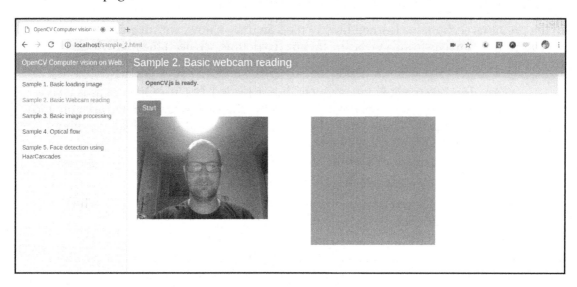

And we only have to develop the interactivity and computer vision processing. First, we have to get a webcam stream to show as a video element. To do this, we need to call the browser we require to access the media devices, in this case, only video stream with the following code:

```
navigator.mediaDevices.getUserMedia({ video: true, audio: false })
```

This code prompt to the user access to webcam media devices, when the users allow the use of the webcam we can get the stream using the promise function `then` or catch any error with `catch` function. In the `then` function we get the stream of a webcam and then we can set the stream into the video source to start the video playing. We can see this in the next code:

```
navigator.mediaDevices.getUserMedia({ video: true, audio: false })
.then(function(stream) {
    video.srcObject = stream;
    video.play();
})
.catch(function(err) {
    console.log("An error occurred! " + err);
});
```

When OpenCV.js is loaded, we are going to show the start button and attach it to the click event:

```
$("#cv_start").show();
$("#cv_start").click(start_cv);
```

The start_cv function initializes the required computer vision variables and starts to process function. We need to initialize the input *mat* and the output *mat* as a matrix with same width and height of video input, to know the width and height of the video input we are going to use the video HTML properties. As we want to process the frames to convert as a gray image the output dst mat will be only 1 channel cv.CV_8UC1 and we need to initialize the video capture as we do in C++ using cv.VideoCapture function, passing as parameter the HTML video element we set before and we want to use as capturing element. We can see this explanation in the next few lines of code:

```
let video = document.getElementById("videoInput"); // video is the ID of
video tag
let src;
let dst;
let cap;

function start_cv(){
    // Init required variables
    src = new cv.Mat(video.height, video.width, cv.CV_8UC4);
    dst = new cv.Mat(video.height, video.width, cv.CV_8UC1);
    cap = new cv.VideoCapture(video);
    // start to process
    processVideo();
}
```

Take care, as the video HTML input has four channels, RGBA, which is different from a C++ video capture from a webcam, which only has three channels.

Next, we are going to grab each frame from the video capture, convert it to a grayscale image, and show it to the user using a canvas element. To read a frame from the video stream, we only need to call the read function and put the mat as the parameter where we want to save the image, like with a C++ interface, as we can see in the next code:

```
cap.read(src);
```

Now we are going to convert the `src` mat to gray and show it in the canvas output, as we did in the previous section:

```
cv.cvtColor(src, dst, cv.COLOR_RGBA2GRAY);
cv.imshow('canvasOutput', dst);
```

In C++, we will use a loop to read the next frame, but if we do this in JavaScript, we will block the rest of the JavaScript code. The best way to grab the next fame to process is to call the processing function again after waiting for a few milliseconds using the `setTimeout` JavaScript function that call a function after the delay is defined as the second parameter. As we wish to have a 30 FPS output, we have to calculate the delay we have to wait before call processing function again is the 1000 milliseconds divided by 30 frames per second we require minus the time spent in our processing function. We can do this calculation using dates, as we can see in the next snippet:

```
let begin = Date.now();
...
// Our processing tasks
...
// calculate the delay.
let delay = 1000/FPS - (Date.now() - begin);
setTimeout(processVideo, delay);
```

We can see a full process function in this piece of code:

```
const FPS = 30;
function processVideo() {
    try {
        let begin = Date.now();
        // start processing.
        cap.read(src);
        cv.cvtColor(src, dst, cv.COLOR_RGBA2GRAY);
        cv.imshow('canvasOutput', dst);
        // schedule the next one.
        let delay = 1000/FPS - (Date.now() - begin);
        setTimeout(processVideo, delay);
    } catch (err) {
        console.log(err);
    }
};
```

And the final result looks like this:

Now, we are going to learn in a bit more depth about some image processing algorithms in OpenCV.js in the following section.

Image processing and basic user interface

Now that we know how to read images and webcam streams, we are going to explain some more basic image processing functions and how to create basic controls to change their parameters. In this section, we are going to create a web page that allows users to choose a filter to apply to a loaded image. The filters that we are going to apply are threshold, Gaussian blur, canny, and histogram equalization. Each filter or algorithm takes different input parameters, which we are going to add to user interfaces to control each one.

First, we are going to generate the required elements to create our application. As the user has the ability to choose the algorithm/filter to apply, we are going to add a `select` HTML element with the possible options to choose from:

```
<select class="form-control" id="filter">
    <option value="0">Choose a filter</option>
    <option value="1">Threshold</option>
    <option value="2">Gaussian Blur</option>
    <option value="3">Canny</option>
    <option value="4">Equalize Histogram</option>
</select>
```

For each option, we are going to show different blocks with elements.

Threshold filter

For threshold, we are going to show an `input` range element, with a default value of 100 and a range between 0 and 200. When we modify this range value, the attached span element will show the value selected. The final code snippet for the threshold HTML template looks like this:

```
<div id="step3_o1" class="step_blocks hide">
    <span class="step">3</span>
    Threshold: <span id="value_sel">100</span>
    <input type="range" class="custom-range" min="0" max="255" value="100"
id="value">
</div>
```

Gaussian filter

For Gaussian, we need a range to select the Gaussian blur kernel; we will use another input range but we have to limit it to only selecting odd values. To do this, we set up the default value as 3 and a step of 2, with a range between 1 and 55:

```
<div id="step3_o2" class="step_blocks hide">
    <span class="step">3</span>
    Kernel Filter size: <span id="value_o2_sel">3x3</span>
    <input type="range" class="custom-range" min="1" max="55" value="3"
step="2" id="value_o2">
 </div>
```

Canny filter

For a canny filter, we need a few more parameters to configure. In a canny filter, we need to define two thresholds and the aperture size. To manage both of them, we are going to create input range elements for each one:

```
<div id="step3_o3" class="step_blocks hide">
    <span class="step">3</span>
    Threshold 1: <span id="value_o3_1_sel">100</span>
    <input type="range" class="custom-range" min="0" max="255" value="100"
id="value_o3_1">
    Threshold 2: <span id="value_o3_2_sel">150</span>
    <input type="range" class="custom-range" min="0" max="255" value="150"
id="value_o3_2">
    Aperture size: <span id="value_o3_sel">3</span>
    <input type="range" class="custom-range" min="3" max="7" value="3"
```

```
step="2" id="value_o3">
</div>
```

Finally, to finish the HTML code, we will add the input image and result in `canvas`, as before:

```
<div class="col">
    Input image<br>
    <img id="imageSrc" class="small" alt="no image">
</div>
<div class="col">
    Result image<br>
    <canvas id="canvasOutput" class="small" height="300px"></canvas>
</div>
```

The HTML result of this code looks like this:

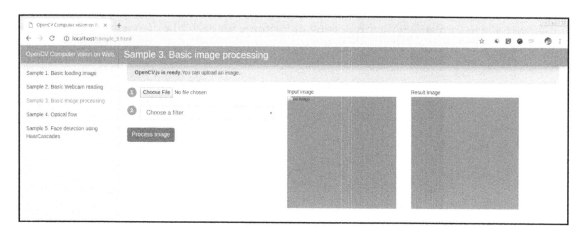

Preview of the canny filter options

Let's go to create the user interaction and image processing function with OpenCV.js.

First, we have to add the same interactivity as the first sample to load the image into the `img` element:

```
let inputElement = document.getElementById('fileInput');
    inputElement.addEventListener('change', (e) => {
    imgElement.src = URL.createObjectURL(e.target.files[0]);
}, false);
```

The most important thing is showing the desired block of filter parameters that user must interact with. If we check the HTML code we wrote for each element block a `hide` class to not show these elements to the user. Then, we have to show the filter parameters when the user chooses the filter with the selected input element. We can use the `onChange` callback event to do this. First, we have to hide all blocks that can be shown using the CSS `".step_blocks"` selector and the JQuery `hide` function. To get the selected option, we only need to get access to the `val` function, and we can benefit from the fact that we named each block with the same ID ending with the corresponding number block and use the `show` JQuery function to draw it. The complete code snippet looks like this:

```
$("#filter").change(function(){
    let filter= parseInt($("#filter").val());
    $(".step_blocks").hide();
    $("#step3_o"+filter).show();
});
```

Now, we have to implement the processing algorithms for each filter we want to apply. The full processing JavaScript code looks like this:

```
function process() {
    let mat = cv.imread(imgElement);
    let mat_result= new cv.Mat();
    let filter= parseInt($("#filter").val());

    switch(filter) {
        case 1:{
            let value= parseInt($("#value").val());
            cv.threshold(mat, mat_result, value, 255, cv.THRESH_BINARY);
            break;}
        case 2:{
            let value= parseInt($("#value_o2").val());
            let ksize = new cv.Size(value, value);
            // You can try more different parameters
            cv.GaussianBlur(mat, mat_result, ksize, 0, 0,
cv.BORDER_DEFAULT);
            break;}
        case 3:{
            let value_t1= parseInt($("#value_o3_1").val());
            let value_t2= parseInt($("#value_o3_2").val());
            let value_kernel= parseInt($("#value_o3").val());
            cv.Canny(mat, mat_result, value_t1,value_t2, value_kernel);
            break;}
        case 4:{
            cv.cvtColor(mat, mat, cv.COLOR_BGR2GRAY);
            cv.equalizeHist(mat, mat_result);
            break;
```

```
            }
        }
        cv.imshow('canvasOutput', mat_result);
        mat.delete();
        mat_result.delete();
    };
```

OK, let's understand the code. First, we read the image from the `img` element using `cv.imread`, and create the mat to store the output result. To find out which filter is selected, we use the ID of the select element to access its value, using `$("#filter").val()` and saving it as a variable named `filter`.

Using a switch statement, we are going to apply different algorithms or filters. We use the following filters, which have the same interfaces as C++, and which we have seen in previous chapters:

- `cv.threshold`
- `cv.GaussianBlur`
- `cv.Canny`
- `cv.equalizeHist`

To access each user interface value, we use JQuery selectors; for example, to access the threshold value input range, we use `$("#value").val()` and parse it to Int. We do the same with the other parameters and functions.

We can see the final result for each filter in the next screenshot:

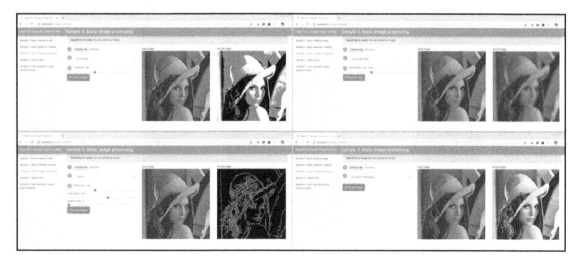

Final output for each filter that we have used

In this section, we learned how to create basic interfaces and apply different image processing algorithms. In the next section, we are going to learn how to create a video tracking using optical flow algorithm.

Optical flow in your browser

In this section, we are going to develop an optical flow over a set of points. To choose the best points to track, we are going to use an OpenCV function to choose them.

In previous chapters, we were going to construct the HTML code that we needed to grab the frames and show the result. Then we require the video element and a canvas to show the processed result, and a start button to process input frames. The HTML code looks like this:

```
<div class="row">
    <div class="col">
    <div id="status" class="alert alert-primary" role="alert"><img
src="img/ajax-loader.gif" /> Loading OpenCV...</div>
</div>
</div>
<a href="#" class="btn btn-primary" style="display: none;"
id="cv_start">Start</a>
<div class="row">
    <div class="col">
        <video id="videoInput" width="320" height="240"></video>
    </div>
    <div class="col">
        <canvas id="canvasOutput" class="small" height="300px"></canvas>
    </div>
</div>
</div>
```

An optical flow algorithm looks for the pattern of motion between two consecutive images caused by the movement of objects or the camera. Optical flow has two main assumptions: the pixel intensities are equal for the same object point, and the neighbor pixels have the same motion. Thanks to these assumptions, the algorithms look for frame *t+dt* the same intensity pattern than frame *t* with a *dx* and *dy*. The main function of this method looks like this:

$$I(x, y, t) = I(x + dx, y + dy, t + dt)$$

Where *I* is the intensity pixel on frame *t* that is calculated from the previous frame.

To optimize the calculations, we can choose the pixels we want to use to calculate the optical flow. We can choose these points manually or use an OpenCV method to choose the bests points. This function is called `goodFeaturesToTrack`.

The first step we have to do is initialize the required variables and choose the best points to track. As we did in the previous sections, we are going to implement all the initializations in the `init_cv` function.

First, we initialize the input and output variables and the video capture using the video element:

```
src = new cv.Mat(video.height, video.width, cv.CV_8UC4);
dst = new cv.Mat(video.height, video.width, cv.CV_8UC1);
cap = new cv.VideoCapture(video);
```

After initializing the required input and output variables we are going to initialize the required variables for an optical flow that are the windows size for look for displacement, the number of pyramid levels and the termination criteria.

```
// Init the required variables for optical flow
winSize = new cv.Size(15, 15);
maxLevel = 2;
criteria = new cv.TermCriteria(cv.TERM_CRITERIA_EPS |
cv.TERM_CRITERIA_COUNT, 10, 0.03);
```

We are going to generate random colors for each point we want to track, to assign each a different color and make them easier to visualize:

```
for (let i = 0; i < maxCorners; i++) {
    color.push(new cv.Scalar(parseInt(Math.random()*255),
parseInt(Math.random()*255),
    parseInt(Math.random()*255), 255));
}
```

Now, we are going to capture the first frame, look for the best points to track, and save it in the mat `p0` as follows:

```
// take first frame and find corners in it
let oldFrame = new cv.Mat(video.height, video.width, cv.CV_8UC4);
cap.read(oldFrame);
oldGray = new cv.Mat();
cv.cvtColor(oldFrame, oldGray, cv.COLOR_RGB2GRAY);
p0 = new cv.Mat();
let none = new cv.Mat();
cv.goodFeaturesToTrack(oldGray, p0, maxCorners, qualityLevel, minDistance,
none, blockSize);
```

We are going to create an image with alpha to draw over the tracking paths:

```
// Create a mask image for drawing purposes
let zeroEle = new cv.Scalar(0, 0, 0, 255);
mask = new cv.Mat(oldFrame.rows, oldFrame.cols, oldFrame.type(), zeroEle);
```

Now, we are ready to start processing every frame and track. We are going to use the `processVideo` function as in the previous section.

First, we have to take a new frame and then calculate the optical flow using the Lukas Kanade algorithm (a widely used differential method for optical flow estimation) with the `calcOpticalFlowPyrLK` function, passing the old frame and new frame in grayscale, and old points and a new mat to save the new points' positions:

```
// start processing.
cap.read(frame);
cv.cvtColor(frame, frameGray, cv.COLOR_RGBA2GRAY);
// calculate optical flow
cv.calcOpticalFlowPyrLK(oldGray, frameGray, p0, p1, st, err, winSize,
maxLevel, criteria);
```

Now, we have in the st variable the state of each point. If we have a state of 0, it means that this point couldn't be processed and must be discarded; if it has a state of 1, we start to track this point and draw, then we are going to loop over st variable and peek and draw only this points:

```
// select good points
let goodNew = [];
let goodOld = [];
for (let i = 0; i < st.rows; i++) {
    if (st.data[i] === 1) {
        goodNew.push(new cv.Point(p1.data32F[i*2], p1.data32F[i*2+1]));
        goodOld.push(new cv.Point(p0.data32F[i*2], p0.data32F[i*2+1]));
    }
}
// draw the tracks
for (let i = 0; i < goodNew.length; i++) {
    cv.line(mask, goodNew[i], goodOld[i], color[i], 2);
    cv.circle(frame, goodNew[i], 5, color[i], -1);
}
cv.add(frame, mask, frame);
cv.imshow('canvasOutput', frame);
```

To finish, the tracking has to update the old frame and old points with the actual state, because some points could not be tracked anymore. The following code shows how to update the old variables:

```
// now update the previous frame and previous points
frameGray.copyTo(oldGray);
p0.delete(); p0 = null;
p0 = new cv.Mat(goodNew.length, 1, cv.CV_32FC2);
for (let i = 0; i < goodNew.length; i++) {
    p0.data32F[i*2] = goodNew[i].x;
    p0.data32F[i*2+1] = goodNew[i].y;
}
```

This is what our code looks like on the web page:

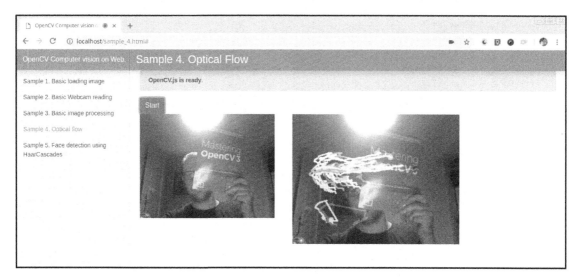

In this section, we learned how to implement a basic optical flow using OpenCV.js; in the next section, we are going to learn how to use a cascade classifier to detect faces.

Face detection using a Haar cascade classifier in your browser

To finish this chapter on OpenCV.js, we are going to learn how to create a face detector using Haar features in a cascade classifier algorithm. To get detailed information about face detector using Haar and Cascade classifier you can read it in Chapter 3, *Face Landmark and Pose with the Face Module*, in the *Facial Landmark Detection in OpenCV* section and Chapter 5, *Face Detection and Recognition with the DNN Module*, in the *Face detection* section that describe in detail how this two methods works.

Like the previous chapter, we are going to work with video input and canvas output, then we are going to reuse the same HTML structure to start our development:

```
<div class="row">
    <div class="col">
    <div id="status" class="alert alert-primary" role="alert"><img
src="img/ajax-loader.gif" /> Loading OpenCV...</div>
</div>
</div>
<a href="#" class="btn btn-primary" style="display: none;"
id="cv_start">Start</a>
<div class="row">
    <div class="col">
        <video id="videoInput" width="320" height="240"></video>
    </div>
    <div class="col">
        <canvas id="canvasOutput" class="small" height="300px"></canvas>
    </div>
</div>
</div>
```

First, we have to work on the Haar cascade face detector, which loads the required model file. We are going to use a util function that requests the file via HTMLRequest and saves it to memory using an OpenCV.js function called FS_createDataFile, which allows our algorithm to load as a system file:

```
function createFileFromUrl(path, url, callback) {
    let request = new XMLHttpRequest();
    request.open('GET', url, true);
    request.responseType = 'arraybuffer';
    request.onload = function(ev) {
    if (request.readyState === 4) {
        if (request.status === 200) {
            let data = new Uint8Array(request.response);
            cv.FS_createDataFile('/', path, data, true, false, false);
            callback();
```

```
            } else {
                self.printError('Failed to load ' + url + ' status: ' +
    request.status);
            }
        }
    };
    request.send();
};
```

Then, when OpenCV.js is loaded, we call this function to load our model and init the variables when it's done:

```
function start_cv(){
    createFileFromUrl("haarcascade_frontalface_default.xml",
                        "haarcascade_frontalface_default.xml", ()=>{
        init_cv();
        // schedule the first one.
        setTimeout(processVideo, 10);
    });
}
```

In this example, we only need to init the input and output images, the video capture, where save detected faces and the classifier:

```
function init_cv(){
    src = new cv.Mat(video.height, video.width, cv.CV_8UC4);
    dst = new cv.Mat(video.height, video.width, cv.CV_8UC4);
    cap = new cv.VideoCapture(video);
    gray = new cv.Mat(video.height, video.width, cv.CV_8UC1);
    faces = new cv.RectVector();
    classifier = new cv.CascadeClassifier();
    // load pre-trained classifiers
    classifier.load('haarcascade_frontalface_default.xml');
}
```

Now, we have to process each frame to detect the faces that appear in it. Then, in the processVideo method that we are going to reuse, we capture the actual frame, convert it to grayscale with the cvtColor function, and use the detectMultiScale2 function to detect all the faces in the frame, which we will save in the faces vector. Finally, we will draw a rectangle for each face detected. The code looks like this:

```
// start processing.
cap.read(src);
src.copyTo(dst);
cv.cvtColor(src, gray, cv.COLOR_RGBA2GRAY);
// detect faces.
let numDetections = new cv.IntVector();
```

```
classifier.detectMultiScale2(gray, faces, numDetections, 1.1, 3, 0);
// draw faces.
for (let i = 0; i < faces.size(); ++i) {
    let face = faces.get(i);
    let point1 = new cv.Point(face.x, face.y);
    let point2 = new cv.Point(face.x + face.width, face.y + face.height);
    cv.rectangle(dst, point1, point2, [255, 0, 0, 255]);
}
cv.imshow('canvasOutput', dst);
```

The final result on an HTML page is this:

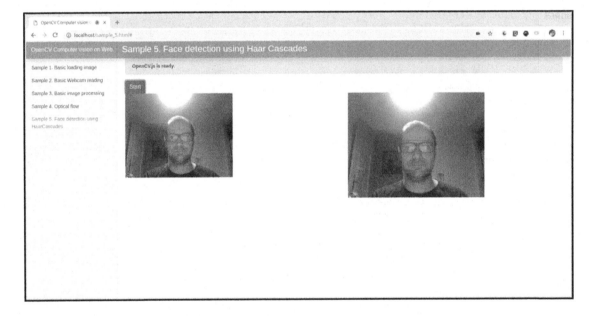

Summary

In this chapter, we learned how to use OpenCV.js in a web page, how to basically create a HTML structure, and how to access each HTML element in order to interact with them. We learned how to create a basic user interface and access image and video streaming through `video` HTML tags, using the newest HTML5 standards which most browsers implement.

We learned how to load OpenCV.js and check that it is ready to use in our JavaScript programs. We created a web application to apply multiple filters by applying to the input image.

We created an optical flow application that allows developers to create new possibilities of applications like augmented reality and so on.

Finally, we learned how to detect faces in real time using the webcam allowing us to extend it to create new applications for face identification, gestures, or emotion detection.

Now, OpenCV is on the web. Enjoy with these new possibilities of applications!

In the next chapter, we are going to learn how to use the ARUco module to create an awesome augmented reality application using OpenCV on our mobile devices.

7
Android Camera Calibration and AR Using the ArUco Module

Mobile devices running Google's Android outnumber all other mobile OSes and, in recent years, they have featured incredible computing power alongside high-quality cameras, which allows them to perform computer vision at the highest levels. One of the most sought after applications for mobile computer vision is **augmented reality (AR)**. Blending real and virtual worlds has applications in entertainment and gaming, medicinel and healthcare, industry and defense, and many more. The world of mobile AR is advancing quickly, with new compelling demos popping up daily, and it is undeniably an engine for mobile hardware and software development. In this chapter, we will learn how to implement an AR application from scratch in the Android ecosystem, by using OpenCV's ArUco `contrib` module, **Android's Camera2 APIs**, as well as the **jMonkeyEngine 3D game engine**. However, first we will begin with simply calibrating our Android device's camera using ArUco's ChArUco calibration board, which provides a more robust alternative to OpenCV's `calib3d` chessboards.

The following topics will be covered in this chapter:

- Introduction to light theory of camera intrinsic parameters and calibration process
- Implementing camera calibration in Android using Camera2 APIs and ArUco
- Implementing a *see-through* AR world with jMonkeyEngine and ArUco markers

Technical requirements

The technologies and softwares used in this chapter are the following:

- OpenCV v3 or v4 Android SDK compiled with the ArUco contrib module: `https://github.com/Mainvooid/opencv-android-sdk-with-contrib`
- Android Studio v3.2+
- Android device running Android OS v6.0+

Build instructions for these components, as well as the code to implement the concepts presented in this chapter, will be provided in the accompanying code repository.

To run the examples, a printed calibration board is required. The board image can be generated programmatically with the ArUco `cv::aruco::CharucoBoard::draw` function, and can then be printed using a home printer. The board works best if it is glued to a hard surface, such as a cardboard or plastic sheet. After printing the board, precise measurements of the board marker's size should be taken (with a ruler or caliper), to make the calibration results more accurate and true to the real world.

The code for this chapter can be accessed through GitHub: `https://github.com/PacktPublishing/Mastering-OpenCV-4-Third-Edition/tree/master/Chapter_07`.

Augmented reality and pose estimation

Augmented reality (AR) is a concept coined in the early 1990s by Tom Caudell. He proposed AR as a mix between real-world rendering from a camera and computer generated graphics that smoothly blend together to create the illusion of virtual objects existing in the real world. In the past few decades, AR has made great strides, from an eccentric technology with very few real applications, to a multi-billion industry in many verticals: defense, manufacturing, healthcare, entertainment, and more. However, the core concept remains the same (in camera-based AR): register graphics on top of 3D geometry in the scene. Thus, AR has ultimately been about 3D geometry reconstruction from images, tracking this geometry, and 3D graphics rendering registered to the geometry. Other types of augmented reality use different sensors than the camera. One of the most well known examples is AR performed with the gyroscope and compass on a mobile phone, such as in the Pokemon Go app.

In the past, AR was mostly based on using **fiducial markers**, clearly contrasting (mostly black and white), usually rectangular printed markers (see examples of such markers in the following section). The reason for using them was that they can be found easily in the image, for they are high contrast, and they have four (or more) clear corners by which we can calculate the plane of the marker with respect to the camera. This has been the practice since the very first AR applications of the 90s, and it is still a highly used method today in many AR technology prototypes. This type of AR detection will be used in this chapter, but, nowadays AR technology has shifted toward other 3D geometry reconstruction methods, such as **natural markers** (non-rectangular, mostly unstructured), **structure-from-motion (SfM)**, and **mapping-and-tracking** (also known as **simultaneous localization and mapping (SLAM)**).

One other reason for the meteoric rise of AR in recent years is the advent of mobile computing. While in the past, rendering 3D graphics and running complex computer vision algorithms required a powerful PC, today even low-end mobile devices can tackle both tasks with ease. Today's mobile GPUs and CPUs are powerful enough to process much more demanding tasks than fiducial-based AR. Major mobile OS developers, such as Google and Apple, already offer AR toolkits based on SfM and SLAM, with inertial sensors fusion that operate at speeds greater than real-time. AR is also being incorporated into other mobile devices, such as head-worn displays, cars, and even flying drones equipped with cameras.

Camera calibration

In our vision task at hand, recovering geometry in the scene, we will employ the **pinhole camera model**, which is a big simplification of the way images are acquired in our advanced digital cameras. The pinhole model essentially describes the transformation of world objects to pixels in the camera images. The following diagram illustrates this process:

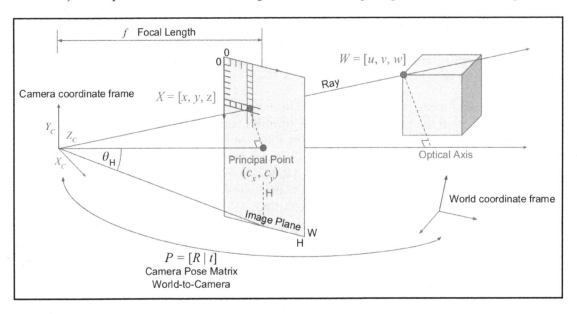

Camera images have a local 2D coordinate frame (in pixels), while the location of 3D objects in the world are described in arbitrary units of length, such as millimeters, meters, or inches. To reconcile these two coordinate frames, the pinhole camera model offers two transforms: **perspective projection** and **camera pose**. The camera pose transform (denoted P in the preceding diagram) aligns the coordinates of the objects with the local coordinate frame of the camera, for example, if an object is right in front of the camera's optical axis at 10 meters away, its coordinates become 0, 0, 10 at meters scale. The pose (a rigid transform) is composed of a rotation R and translation t components, and results in a new 3D position aligned with the camera's local coordinate frame as follows:

$$X = \begin{pmatrix} x \\ y \\ z \end{pmatrix} = R \begin{pmatrix} u \\ v \\ w \end{pmatrix} + t = \begin{pmatrix} r_1 & r_2 & r_3 & t_x \\ r_4 & r_5 & r_6 & t_y \\ r_7 & r_8 & r_9 & t_y \end{pmatrix} \begin{pmatrix} u \\ v \\ w \\ 1 \end{pmatrix} = PW'$$

Where W' are the **homogenous coordinates** of the 3D point W, obtained by adding a one to the end of the vector.

The next step is to project the aligned 3D points onto the image plane. Intuitively, in the preceding diagram we can see the aligned 3D point and the 2D pixel point exist on a ray from the camera center, which imposes an overlapping right triangles (90-degree) constraint. It therefore means if we know the z coordinate and the f coefficient, we can calculate the point on the image plane (x_I, y_I) by dividing by z; this is called the **perspective divide**. First, we divide by z to bring the point to normalized coordinates (distance one from the camera projection center), then we multiply it by a factor that correlates the real camera's focal length and the size of pixels on the image plane. Finally, we add the offset from the camera's center of projection (**principal point**) to end up at the pixel position:

$$x' = x/z$$
$$y' = y/z$$
$$x_I = f_x \cdot x' + c_x$$
$$y_I = f_y \cdot y' + c_y$$

In reality, there are more factors for determining the positions of objects in the image than simply the focal length, such as distortion from the lens (**radial, barrel distortion**), that involve non-linear calculations. This projection transformation is often expressed in a single matrix, known as the **camera intrinsic parameters matrix** and usually denoted by K:

$$s \begin{pmatrix} x_I \\ y_I \\ 1 \end{pmatrix} = KPW' = \begin{pmatrix} f_x & 0 & c_x \\ 0 & f_y & c_y \\ 0 & 0 & 1 \end{pmatrix} \begin{pmatrix} r_1 & r_2 & r_3 & t_x \\ r_4 & r_5 & r_6 & t_y \\ r_7 & r_8 & r_9 & t_y \end{pmatrix} \begin{pmatrix} u \\ v \\ w \\ 1 \end{pmatrix}$$

The process of **camera calibration** is the process of finding the coefficients of K (and the **distortion parameters**), which is a fundamental step for any precise work in computer vision. It is usually done by way of an optimization problem given measurements of correlated 3D and 2D points. Given enough corresponding image points (x_I, y_I) and 3D points (u, v, w), one can construct a **re-projection** cost functor such as the following:

$$L = \sum_i \left\| p_i^I - \hat{K} P W_i' \right\|_{L_2}$$

The re-projection cost function here looks to minimize the Euclidean distance between the original 2D image point P_i and the 3D image as re-projected on the scene using the projection and pose matrices: KPW_i.

Starting from approximate values for the K matrix (the principal point can be, for example, the exact center of the image), we can estimate the values of P in a direct linear fashion by setting up an over-constrained linear system, or an algorithm, such as **Point-n-Perspective (PnP)**. Then, we can proceed iteratively using the gradient over L with regards to to the parameters of K to slowly improve them until convergence, using a gradient descent algorithm such as **Levenberg-Marquardt**. The details of these algorithms are beyond the scope of this chapter; however, they are implemented in OpenCV for the purpose of camera calibration.

Augmented reality markers for planar reconstruction

AR fiducial markers are used for their convenience in finding the plane they lie on with regards to the camera. An AR marker usually has strong corners or other geometric features (for example, circles) that are clearly and quickly detectable. The 2D landmarks are arranged in a way that is pre-known to the detector, so we can easily establish 2D-3D point correspondence. The following are examples of AR fiducial markers:

In this example, there are several types of 2D landmarks. In the rectangular markers, these are the corners of the rectangles and the inner rectangles, while in the QR code (middle), these are the three big boxed rectangles. The non-rectangular markers are using the center of the circles as the 2D positions.

Given our 2D points on the marker and their paired 3D coordinates (in millimeters), we can write the following equation for each pair, using the principles we saw in the last section:

$$
\begin{pmatrix} x_i \\ y_i \\ 1 \end{pmatrix} = \underbrace{[R_{3\times3} \quad t]}_{P} W_i' = \begin{pmatrix} r_1 & r_2 & r_3 & t_x \\ r_4 & r_5 & r_6 & t_y \\ r_7 & r_8 & r_9 & t_y \end{pmatrix} \begin{pmatrix} u_i \\ v_i \\ 0 \\ 1 \end{pmatrix} = \begin{pmatrix} r_1 & r_2 & t_x \\ r_4 & r_5 & t_y \\ r_7 & r_8 & t_z \end{pmatrix} \begin{pmatrix} u_i \\ v_i \\ 1 \end{pmatrix}
$$

Notice that since the marker is flat and, without loss of generality, it exists on the ground plane, its z-coordinate is zero, and we can therefore omit the third column of the P matrix. We are left with a 3 x 3 matrix to find. Note we can still recover the entire rotation matrix; since it is orthonormal, we can use the first two columns to find the third by a cross product: $R^3 = R^1 \times R^2$. The remaining 3 x 3 matrix is a **homography**; it transforms between one plane (image plane) and another (marker plane). We can estimate the values of the matrix by constructing a system of homogeneous linear equations, as follows:

$$
\begin{pmatrix} x_i \\ y_i \\ 1 \end{pmatrix} - \begin{pmatrix} r_1 & r_2 & t_x \\ r_4 & r_5 & t_y \\ r_7 & r_8 & t_z \end{pmatrix} \begin{pmatrix} u_i \\ v_i \\ 1 \end{pmatrix} = \begin{pmatrix} 0 \\ 0 \\ 0 \end{pmatrix}
$$

Which can be worked into the following homogenous system of equations:

$$
\begin{pmatrix}
x_1 & -u_1 & -v_1 & -1 & 0 & 0 & 0 & 0 & 0 & 0 & 0 & 0 \\
0 & 0 & 0 & 0 & y_1 & -u_1 & -v_1 & -1 & 0 & 0 & 0 & 0 \\
0 & 0 & 0 & 0 & 0 & 0 & 0 & 0 & 1 & -u_1 & -v_1 & -1 \\
\vdots & \vdots & \vdots & \vdots & \vdots & \vdots & \vdots & \vdots & \vdots & \vdots & \vdots & \vdots \\
x_n & -u_n & -v_n & -1 & 0 & 0 & 0 & 0 & 0 & 0 & 0 & 0 \\
0 & 0 & 0 & 0 & y_n & -u_n & -v_n & -1 & 0 & 0 & 0 & 0 \\
0 & 0 & 0 & 0 & 0 & 0 & 0 & 0 & 1 & -u_n & -v_n & -1
\end{pmatrix}
\begin{pmatrix} 1 \\ r_1 \\ r_2 \\ t_x \\ 1 \\ r_4 \\ r_5 \\ t_y \\ 1 \\ r_8 \\ r_9 \\ t_z \end{pmatrix}
=
\begin{pmatrix} 0 \\ 0 \\ 0 \\ \vdots \\ 0 \\ 0 \\ 0 \end{pmatrix}
$$

We can solve this problem by taking the **singular value decomposition** of the A matrix, $A = U\Sigma V^t$, and the last column of V as the solution, and we can find P. This will only work with a planar marker, because of our flatness assumption from before. For calibration with 3D objects, more instrumentation of the linear system is needed in order to recover a valid orthonormal rotation. Other algorithms also exist, such as the **Perspective-n-Point (PnP)** algorithm we mentioned earlier. This concludes the theoretical underpinning we will need for creating an augmented reality effect. In the next chapter, we will begin constructing an application in Android to implement these ideas.

Camera access in Android OS

Most, if not all, mobile phone devices running Android are equipped with a video-capable camera, and the Android OS provides APIs to access the raw data stream from it. Up until Android version 5 (API level 21), Google recommended using the older Camera API; however, in recent versions, the API was deprecated in favor of the new Camera2 API, which we will use. A good example guide for using the Camera2 API is provided for Android developers by Google: `https://github.com/googlesamples/android-Camera2Basic`. In this section, we will only recount a few important elements, and the complete code can be viewed in the accompanying repository.

First, using the camera requires user permissions. In the `AndroidManifest.xml` file, we flag the following:

```
<uses-permission android:name="android.permission.CAMERA" />
<uses-permission
android:name="android.permission.WRITE_EXTERNAL_STORAGE" />
<uses-permission
android:name="android.permission.READ_EXTERNAL_STORAGE"/>
```

We also request file storage access for saving intermediate data or debugging images. The next step is to request permissions from the user, if not already granted earlier, with an on-screen dialog as soon as the application starts:

```
if (context.checkSelfPermission(Manifest.permission.CAMERA) !=
PackageManager.PERMISSION_GRANTED) {
    context.requestPermissions(new String[] { Manifest.permission.CAMERA },
REQUEST_PERMISSION_CODE);
    return; // break until next time, after user approves
}
```

Note that some further instrumentation is needed to handle the return from the permissions request.

Finding and opening the camera

Next, we try to find a suitable back-facing camera by scanning the list of available cameras on the device. A characteristics flag is given to the camera if it's back-facing, as follows:

```
CameraManager manager = (CameraManager)
context.getSystemService(Context.CAMERA_SERVICE);
try {
    String camList[] = manager.getCameraIdList();
    mCameraID = camList[0]; // save as a class member - mCameraID
    for (String cameraID : camList) {
        CameraCharacteristics characteristics =
manager.getCameraCharacteristics(cameraID);
        if(characteristics.get(CameraCharacteristics.LENS_FACING) ==
CameraCharacteristics.LENS_FACING_BACK) {
            mCameraID = cameraID;
            break;
        }
    }
    Log.i(LOGTAG, "Opening camera: " + mCameraID);
    CameraCharacteristics characteristics =
manager.getCameraCharacteristics(mCameraID);
    manager.openCamera(mCameraID, mStateCallback, mBackgroundHandler);
} catch (...) {
    /* ... */
}
```

When the camera is opened, we look through the list of available image resolutions and pick a good size. A good size will be something not too big, so calculation won't be lengthy, and a resolution that corresponds with the screen resolution, so it covers the entire screen:

```
final int width = 1280; // 1280x720 is a good wide-format size, but we can
query the
final int height = 720; // screen to see precisely what resolution it is.

CameraCharacteristics characteristics =
manager.getCameraCharacteristics(mCameraID);
StreamConfigurationMap map =
characteristics.get(CameraCharacteristics.SCALER_STREAM_CONFIGURATION_MAP);
int bestWidth = 0, bestHeight = 0;
final float aspect = (float)width / height;
for (Size psize : map.getOutputSizes(ImageFormat.YUV_420_888)) {
    final int w = psize.getWidth(), h = psize.getHeight();
    // accept the size if it's close to our target and has similar aspect
ratio
    if ( width >= w && height >= h &&
        bestWidth <= w && bestHeight <= h &&
```

```
        Math.abs(aspect - (float)w/h) < 0.2 )
    {
        bestWidth = w;
        bestHeight = h;
    }
}
```

We're now ready to request access to the video feed. We will be requesting access to the raw data coming from the camera. Almost all Android devices will provide a YUV 420 stream, so it's good practice to target that format; however, we will need a conversion step to get RGB data, as follows:

```
mImageReader = ImageReader.newInstance(mPreviewSize.getWidth(),
mPreviewSize.getHeight(), ImageFormat.YUV_420_888, 2);
// The ImageAvailableListener will get a function call with each frame
mImageReader.setOnImageAvailableListener(mHandler, mBackgroundHandler);

mPreviewRequestBuilder =
mCameraDevice.createCaptureRequest(CameraDevice.TEMPLATE_PREVIEW);
mPreviewRequestBuilder.addTarget(mImageReader.getSurface());

mCameraDevice.createCaptureSession(Arrays.asList(mImageReader.getSurface())
,
        new CameraCaptureSession.StateCallback() {
            @Override
            public void onConfigured( CameraCaptureSession
cameraCaptureSession) {
                mCaptureSession = cameraCaptureSession;
                // ... setup auto-focus here
                mHandler.onCameraSetup(mPreviewSize); // notify interested
parties
            }

            @Override
            public void onConfigureFailed(CameraCaptureSession
cameraCaptureSession) {
                Log.e(LOGTAG, "createCameraPreviewSession failed");
            }
        }, mBackgroundHandler);
```

From this point on, our class that implements `ImageReader.OnImageAvailableListener` will be called with each frame and we can access the pixels:

```
@Override
public void onImageAvailable(ImageReader imageReader) {
    android.media.Image image = imageReader.acquireLatestImage();
    //such as getting a grayscale image by taking just the Y component
(from YUV)
    mPreviewByteBufferGray.rewind();
    ByteBuffer buffer = image.getPlanes()[0].getBuffer();
    buffer.rewind();
    buffer.get(mPreviewByteBufferGray.array());
    image.close(); // release the image - Important!
}
```

At this point, we can send the byte buffer for processing in OpenCV. Next up, we will develop the camera calibration process with the `aruco` module.

Camera calibration with ArUco

To perform camera calibration as we discussed earlier, we must obtain corresponding 2D-3D point pairings. With ArUco marker detection, this task is made simple. ArUco provides a tool to create a **calibration board**, a grid of squares and AR markers, in which all the parameters are known: number, size, and position of markers. We can print such a board with our home or office printer, with the image for printing supplied by the ArUco API:

```
Ptr<aruco::Dictionary> dict =
aruco::Dictionary::get(aruco::DICT_ARUCO_ORIGINAL);
Ptr<aruco::GridBoard> board = aruco::GridBoard::create(
    10     /* N markers x */,
    7      /* M markers y */,
    14.0f  /* marker width (mm) */,
    9.2f   /* marker separation (mm) */,
    dict);
Mat boardImage;
board->draw({1000, 700}, boardImage, 25); // an image of 1000x700 pixels
cv::imwrite("ArucoBoard.png", boardImage);
```

Here is an example of such a board image, a result of the preceding code:

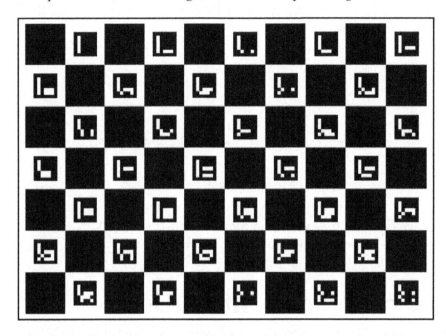

We need to obtain multiple views of the board by moving either the camera or the board. It is handy to paste the board on a piece of rigid cardboard or plastic to keep the paper flat while moving the board, or keep it flat on a table while moving the camera around it. We can implement a very simple Android UI for capturing the images with just three buttons, **CAPTURE**, **CALIBRATE**, and **DONE**:

The **CAPTURE** button simply grabs the grayscale image buffer, as we saw earlier, and calls a native C++ function to detect the ArUco markers and save them to memory:

```
extern "C"
JNIEXPORT jint JNICALL
Java_com_packt_masteringopencv4_opencvarucoar_CalibrationActivity_addCalibr
ation8UImage(
```

```
    JNIEnv *env,
    jclass type,
    jbyteArray data_, // java: byte[] , a 8 uchar grayscale image buffer
    jint w,
    jint h)
{
    jbyte *data = env->GetByteArrayElements(data_, NULL);
    Mat grayImage(h, w, CV_8UC1, data);

    vector< int > ids;
    vector< vector< Point2f > > corners, rejected;

    // detect markers
    aruco::detectMarkers(grayImage, dict, corners, ids, params, rejected);
    __android_log_print(ANDROID_LOG_DEBUG, LOGTAG, "found %d markers",
ids.size());

    allCorners.push_back(corners);
    allIds.push_back(ids);
    allImgs.push_back(grayImage.clone());
    imgSize = grayImage.size();

    __android_log_print(ANDROID_LOG_DEBUG, LOGTAG, "%d captures",
allImgs.size());

    env->ReleaseByteArrayElements(data_, data, 0);

    return allImgs.size(); // return the number of captured images so far
}
```

Here is an example of ArUco marker boards detected using the previous function. A visualization of the detected markers can be achieved with `cv::aruco::drawDetectedMarkers`. Points from the markers that were detected properly will be used for calibration:

After obtaining enough images (around 10 images from various viewpoints is usually sufficient), the **CALIBRATE** button calls another native function that runs the `aruco::calibrateCameraAruco` function, with the saved arrays of point correspondences as follows:

```
extern "C"
JNIEXPORT void JNICALL
Java_com_packt_masteringopencv4_opencvarucoar_CalibrationActivity_doCalibra
tion(
    JNIEnv *env,
    jclass type)
{
    vector< Mat > rvecs, tvecs;

    cameraMatrix = Mat::eye(3, 3, CV_64F);
    cameraMatrix.at< double >(0, 0) = 1.0;

    // prepare data for calibration: put all marker points in a single
array
    vector< vector< Point2f > > allCornersConcatenated;
    vector< int > allIdsConcatenated;
    vector< int > markerCounterPerFrame;
    markerCounterPerFrame.reserve(allCorners.size());
    for (unsigned int i = 0; i < allCorners.size(); i++) {
        markerCounterPerFrame.push_back((int)allCorners[i].size());
        for (unsigned int j = 0; j < allCorners[i].size(); j++) {
            allCornersConcatenated.push_back(allCorners[i][j]);
            allIdsConcatenated.push_back(allIds[i][j]);
        }
    }

    // calibrate camera using aruco markers
    double arucoRepErr;
    arucoRepErr = aruco::calibrateCameraAruco(allCornersConcatenated,
                                    allIdsConcatenated,
                                    markerCounterPerFrame,
                                    board, imgSize, cameraMatrix,
                                    distCoeffs, rvecs, tvecs,
CALIB_FIX_ASPECT_RATIO);

    __android_log_print(ANDROID_LOG_DEBUG, LOGTAG, "reprojection err:
%.3f", arucoRepErr);
    stringstream ss;
    ss << cameraMatrix << endl << distCoeffs;
    __android_log_print(ANDROID_LOG_DEBUG, LOGTAG, "calibration: %s",
ss.str().c_str());
```

```
    // save the calibration to file
    cv::FileStorage fs("/sdcard/calibration.yml", FileStorage::WRITE);
    fs.write("cameraMatrix", cameraMatrix);
    fs.write("distCoeffs", distCoeffs);
    fs.release();
}
```

The **DONE** button will advance the application to AR mode, where the calibration values are used for pose estimation.

Augmented reality with jMonkeyEngine

Having calibrated the camera, we can proceed with implementing our AR application. We will make a very simple application that only shows a plain 3D box on top of the marker, using the **jMonkeyEngine (JME)** 3D rendering suite. JME is very feature-rich, and full-blown games are implemented using it (such as Rising World); we could extend our AR application into a real AR game with additional work. When looking over this chapter, the code needed to create a JME application is much more extensive than what we will see here, and the full code is available in the book's code repository.

To start, we need to provision JME to show the view from the camera behind the overlaid 3D graphics. We will create a texture to store the RGB image pixels, and a quad to show the texture. The quad will be rendered by an **orthographic** camera (without perspective), since it's a simple 2D image without depth.

The following code will create a `Quad`, a simple, flat, four-vertex 3D object that will hold the camera view texture and stretch it to cover the whole screen. Then, a `Texture2D` object will be attached to the `Quad`, so we can replace it with new images as they arrive. Lastly, we will create a `Camera` with orthographic projection and attach the textured `Quad` to it:

```
// A quad to show the background texture
Quad videoBGQuad = new Quad(1, 1, true);
mBGQuad = new Geometry("quad", videoBGQuad);
final float newWidth = (float)screenWidth / (float)screenHeight;
final float sizeFactor = 0.825f;

// Center the Quad in the middle of the screen.
mBGQuad.setLocalTranslation(-sizeFactor / 2.0f * newWidth, -sizeFactor /
2.0f, 0.f);

// Scale (stretch) the width of the Quad to cover the wide screen.
mBGQuad.setLocalScale(sizeFactor * newWidth, sizeFactor, 1);

// Create a new texture which will hold the Android camera preview frame
```

```
pixels.
Material BGMat = new Material(assetManager,
"Common/MatDefs/Misc/Unshaded.j3md");
mCameraTexture = new Texture2D();
BGMat.setTexture("ColorMap", mCameraTexture);
mBGQuad.setMaterial(BGMat);

// Create a custom virtual camera with orthographic projection
Camera videoBGCam = cam.clone();
videoBGCam.setParallelProjection(true);
// Create a custom viewport and attach the quad
ViewPort videoBGVP = renderManager.createMainView("VideoBGView",
videoBGCam);
videoBGVP.attachScene(mBGQuad);
```

Next, we set up a virtual **perspective** `Camera` to show the graphic augmentation. It's important to use the calibration parameters we obtained earlier so that the virtual and real cameras align. We use the **focal length** parameter from the calibration to set the **frustum** (view trapezoid) of the new `Camera` object, by converting it to the **field-of-view (FOV)** angle in degrees:

```
Camera fgCam = new Camera(settings.getWidth(), settings.getHeight());
fgCam.setLocation(new Vector3f(0f, 0f, 0f));
fgCam.lookAtDirection(Vector3f.UNIT_Z.negateLocal(), Vector3f.UNIT_Y);

// intrinsic parameters
final float f = getCalibrationFocalLength();

// set up a perspective camera using the calibration parameter
final float fovy = (float)Math.toDegrees(2.0f *
(float)Math.atan2(mHeightPx, 2.0f * f));
final float aspect = (float) mWidthPx / (float) mHeightPx;
fgCam.setFrustumPerspective(fovy, aspect, fgCamNear, fgCamFar);
```

The camera is situated at the origin, facing the -z direction, and pointing up the y-axis, to match the coordinate frame from OpenCV's pose estimation algorithms.

Finally, the running demo shows the virtual cube over the background image, covering the AR marker preciesly:

Summary

This chapter introduced two key topics in computer vision: camera calibration and camera/object pose estimation. We saw the theoretical background for achieving these concepts in practice, as well as their implementation in OpenCV using the `aruco` contrib module. Finally, we built an Android application that runs the ArUco code in native functions to calibrate the camera and then detect the AR marker. We used the jMonkeyEngine 3D rendering engine to create a very simple augmented reality application using ArUco calibration and detection.

In the next chapter, we will see how to use OpenCV in an iOS app environment to build a panorama stitching application. Using OpenCV in a mobile environment is a very popular feature of OpenCV, as the library provides pre-built binaries and releases for both Android and iOS.

iOS Panoramas with the Stitching Module

8

Panoramic imaging has existed since the early days of photography. In those ancient times, roughly 150 years ago, it was called the art of **panography**, carefully putting together individual images using tape or glue to recreate a panoramic view. With the advancement of computer vision, panorama stitching became a handy tool in almost all digital cameras and mobile devices. Nowadays, creating panoramas is as simple as swiping the device or camera across the view, the stitching calculations happen immediately, and the final expanded scene is available for viewing. In this chapter, we will implement a modest panoramic image stitching application on the iPhone using OpenCV's precompiled library for iOS. We will first examine a little of the math and theory behind image stitching, choose the relevant OpenCV functions to implement it, and finally integrate it into an iOS app with a basic UI.

The following topics will be covered in this chapter:

- Introduction to the concept of image stitching and panorama building
- OpenCV's image stitching module and its functions
- Building a Swift iOS application UI for panorama capturing
- Integrating OpenCV component written in Objective C++ with the Swift application

Technical requirements

The following technologies and installations are required to recreate the contents of this chapter:

- macOSX machine (for example, MacBook, iMac) running macOS High Sierra v10.13+

- iPhone 6+ running iOS v11+
- Xcode v9+
- CocoaPods v1.5+: https://cocoapods.org/
- OpenCV v4.0 installed via CocoaPods

Build instructions for the preceding components, as well as the code to implement the concepts presented in this chapter, will be provided in the accompanying code repository.

The code for this chapter can be accessed via GitHub: https://github.com/PacktPublishing/Mastering-OpenCV-4-Third-Edition/tree/master/Chapter_08.

Panoramic image stitching methods

Panoramas are essentially multiple images fused together into a single image. The process of panorama creation from multiple images involves many steps; some are common to other computer vision tasks, such as the following:

- Extracting 2D features
- Matching pairs of images based on their features
- Transforming or warping images to a communal frame
- Using (blending) the seams between the images for the pleasing continuous effect of a larger image

Some of these basic operations are also commonplace in **Structure-from-Motion (SfM)**, **3D reconstruction**, **visual odometry**, and **simultaneous localization and mapping (SLAM)**. We've already discussed some of these in Chapter 2, *Explore Structure from Motion with the SfM Module* and Chapter 7, *Android Camera Calibration and AR Using the ArUco Module*. The following is a rough image of the panorama creation process:

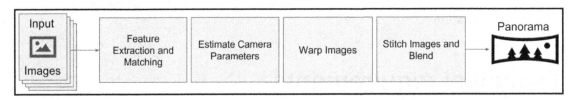

In this section, we will briefly review feature matching, camera pose estimation, and image warping. In reality, panorama stitching has multiple pathways and classes, depending on the type of input and required output. For example, if the camera has a fisheye lens (with an extremely high degree view angle) a special process is needed.

Feature extraction and robust matching for panoramas

We create panoramas from overlapping images. In the overlapping region, we look for common visual features that **register** (align) the two images together. In SfM or SLAM, we do this on a frame-by-frame basis, looking for matching features in a real-time video sequence where the overlap between frames is extremely high. However, in panoramas we get frames with a big motion component between them, where the overlap might be as low as just 10%-20% of the image. At first, we extract image features, such as the **scale invariant feature transform (SIFT)**, **speeded up robust features** (**SURF**), **oriented BRIEF** (**ORB**), or another kind of feature, and then match them between the images in the panorama. Note the SIFT and SURF features are protected by patents and cannot be used for commercial purposes. ORB is a considered a free alternative, but not as robust.

The following image shows extracted features and their matching:

Affine constraint

For a robust and meaningful pairwise matching, we often apply a geometric constraint. One such constraint can be an **affine transform**, a transform that allows only for scale, rotation, and translation. In 2D, an affine transform can be modeled in a 2 x 3 matrix:

$$\hat{X} = \begin{pmatrix} \hat{x} \\ \hat{y} \end{pmatrix} = \begin{pmatrix} r_1 & r_2 & t_x \\ r_3 & r_4 & t_y \end{pmatrix} \begin{pmatrix} x \\ y \\ 1 \end{pmatrix} = MX$$

$$\hat{M} = \underset{M}{\mathrm{argmin}} \sum_i \left\| X_i^{\mathrm{L}} - M X_i^{\mathrm{R}} \right\|_{\mathrm{L}_2}$$

To impose the constraint, we look for an affine transform $\hat{M}$ that minimizes the distance (error) between matching points from the left X_i^{L} and right X_i^{R} images.

Random sample consensus (RANSAC)

In the preceding image, we illustrate the fact that not all points conform to the affine constraint, and most of the matched pairs are discarded as incorrect. Therefore, in most cases we employ a voting-based estimation method, such as **random sample consensus (RANSAC)**, where a group of points is chosen at random to solve for a hypothesis of M directly (via a homogeneous linear system) and then a voting is cast between all points to support or reject this hypothesis.

The following is a pseudo-algorithm for RANSAC:

1. Find matches between points in image i and image j.
2. Initialize the hypothesis for the transform between image i and j, with minimal support.
3. While not converged:
    1. Pick a small random set of point-pairs. For an affine transform, three pairs will suffice.
    2. Calculate the affine transform T directly based on the pairs set, for instance with a linear equation set
    3. Calculate the support. For each point p in the entire i, j matching:
        - If the distance (the **error**) between the transformed point in image j and the matched point in image i is within a small threshold t: $\|p_i - Tp_j\| < t$,add 1 to the support counter.
    4. If the support count is bigger than the current hypothesis' support, take T as the new hypothesis.
    5. Optional: if the support is large enough (or a different breaking policy is true), break; otherwise, keep iterating.
4. Return the latest and best supported hypothesis transform.
5. Also, return the **support mask**: a binary variable stating whether a point in the matching was supporting the final hypothesis.

The output of the algorithm will provide the transform that has the highest support, and the support mask can be used to discard points that are not supportive. We can also reason about the number of supporting points, for example, if we observe less than 50% supporting points, we can deem this match as bad and not try to match the two images at all.

There are alternatives to RANSAC, such as the **least median squares (LMedS)** algorithm, which is not too different from RANSAC: instead of counting supporting points, it calculates the median of the square error for each transform hypothesis, and finally return the hypothesis with the least median square error.

Homography constraint

While affine transforms are useful for stitching scanned documents (for example, from a flatbed scanner), they cannot be used for stitching photo panoramas. For stitching photos, we can employ the same process to find a **homography**, a transform between one plane and another, instead of an affine transform, which has eight degrees of freedom, and is represented in a 3 x 3 matrix as follows:

$$\hat{X} = s \begin{pmatrix} \hat{x} \\ \hat{y} \\ 1 \end{pmatrix} = \begin{pmatrix} h_1 & h_2 & h_3 \\ h_4 & h_5 & h_6 \\ h_7 & h_8 & 1 \end{pmatrix} \begin{pmatrix} x \\ y \\ 1 \end{pmatrix} = HX$$

Once a proper matching has been found, we can find an ordering of the images to sequence them for the panorama, essentially to understand how the images relate to one another. In most cases, in panoramas the assumption is that the photographer (camera) is standing still and only rotating on its axis, sweeping from left to right, for example. Therefore, the goal is to recover the rotation component between the camera poses. Homographies can be decomposed to recover rotation, if we regard the input as purely rotational: $\hat{X} = HX = KRK^{-1}X$. If we assume the homography was originally composed from the camera intrinsic (calibration), matrix K, and a 3 x 3 rotation matrix R, we can recover R if we know K. The intrinsic matrix can be calculated by camera calibration ahead of time, or can be estimated during the panorama creation process.

Bundle Adjustment

When a transformation has been achieved *locally* between all photo *pairs*, we can further optimize our solution in a *global* step. This is called the process of **bundle adjustment**, and is widely constructed as a global optimization of all the reconstruction parameters (camera or image transforms). Global bundle adjustment is best performed if all the matched points between images are put in the same coordinate frame, for example, a 3D space, and there are constraints that span more than two images. For example, if a feature point appears in more than two images in the panorama, it can be useful for *global* optimization, since it involves registering three or more views.

The goal in most bundle adjustment methods is to minimize the **reconstruction error**. This means, looking to bring the approximate parameters of the views, for example, camera or image transforms, to values such that the re-projected 2D points back on the original views will align with minimal error. This can be expressed mathematically like so:

$$\{\hat{T}\}_{j=1}^{n_{\text{images}}} = \underset{\{T\}_{j=1}^{n_{\text{images}}}}{\arg\min} \sum_{i=1}^{n_{\text{points}}} v_{ij} \|X_i - \text{Proj}(T_j, X_i)\|^2$$

Where we look for the best camera or image transforms T, such that the distance between original point X_i and reprojected point $Proj(T_j, X_i)$ is minimal. The binary variable v_{ij} marks whether point i can be seen in image j, and can contribute to the error. These kinds of optimization problems can be solved with **iterative non-linear least squares** solvers, such as **Levenberg-Marquardt**, since the previous *Proj* function is usually non-linear.

Warping images for panorama creation

Given that we know the homographies between images, we can apply their inverse to project all the images on the same plane. However, a direct warping using the homography ends up with a stretched-out look if, for example, all the images are projected on the plane of the first image. In the following image, we can see a stitching of 4 images using *concatenated* homography (perspective) warping, meaning all the images are registered to the plane of the first image, which illustrates the ungainly stretching:

To cope with this problem, we think of the panorama as looking at the images from inside a cylinder, where the images are projected on the wall of the cylinder, and we rotate the camera at the center. To achieve this effect, we first need to warp the images to **cylindrical coordinates**, as if the round wall of the cylinder was undone and flattened to a rectangle. The following diagram explains the process of cylindrical warping:

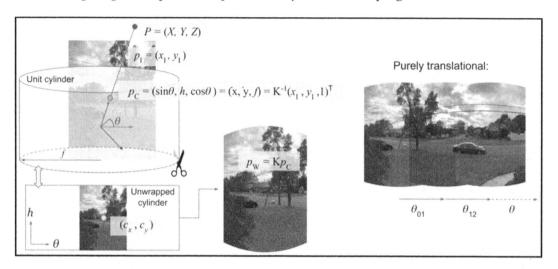

To wrap the image in cylindrical coordinates, we first apply the inverse of the intrinsic matrix to get the pixel in normalized coordinates. We now assume the pixel is a point on the surface of the cylinder, which is parameterized by the height h and the angle θ. Height h essentially corresponds to the y coordinate, while the x and z (which are perpendicular to one another with regards to y) exist on a unit circle and therefore correspond to $\sin\theta$ and $\cos\theta$, respectively. To get the warped image in the same pixel size as the original image, we can apply the intrinsic matrix K again; however, we can change the focal length parameter f, for example, to affect the output resolution of our panorama.

In the cylindrical warping model, the relationship between the images becomes purely translational, and in fact governed by a single parameter: θ. To stitch the images in the same plane, we simply need to find the θs, just a single degree of freedom, which is simple compared to finding eight parameters for the homography between every two consecutive images. One major drawback of the cylindrical method is that we assume the camera's rotational axis motion is perfectly aligned with its up axis, as well as static in its place, which is almost never the case with handheld cameras. Still, cylindrical panoramas produce highly pleasing results. Another option for warping is **spherical coordinates**, which allow for more options in stitching the images in both x and y axes.

Project overview

This project will include two major parts as follows:

- iOS application to support capturing the panorama
- OpenCV Objective-C++ code for creating the panorama from the images and integrating into the application

The iOS code will mostly be concerned with building the UI, accessing the camera, and capturing images. Then, we will focus on getting the images to OpenCV data structures and running the image stitching functions from the `stitch` module.

Setting up an iOS OpenCV project with CocoaPods

To start using OpenCV in iOS, we must import the library compiled for iOS devices. This is easily done with CocoaPods, which is a vast repository of external packages for iOS and macOS with a convenient command-line package manager utility called `pod`.

We begin by creating an empty Xcode project for iOS, with the "*Single View App*" template. Make sure to select a Swift project, and not an Objective-C one. The Objective-C++ code we will see will be added later.

After the project in initialized in a certain directory, we execute the `pod init` command in the terminal within that directory. This will create a new file called `Podfile` in the directory. We need to edit the file to look like the following:

```
# Uncomment the next line to define a global platform for your project
# platform :ios, '9.0'

target 'OpenCV Stitcher' do
  use_frameworks!
  # Pods for OpenCV Stitcher
  pod 'OpenCV2', '4.0.0.beta'
end
```

Essentially, just adding `pod 'OpenCV2', '4.0.0'` to the `target` tells CocoaPods to download and unpack the OpenCV framework in our project. Afterwards, we run `pod install` in the Terminal in the same directory, which will set up our project and Workspace to include all the Pods (just OpenCV v4 in our case). To start working on the project, we open the `$(PROJECT_NAME).xcworkspace` file, rather than the `.xcodeproject` file as usual with Xcode projects.

iOS UI for panorama capture

Before we delve into the OpenCV code for turning an image collection into a panorama, we will first build a UI to support the easy capture of a sequence of overlapping images. First, we must make sure we have access to the camera as well as saved images. Open the `Info.plist` file and add the following three rows:

Key		Type	Value
▼ Information Property List		Dictionary	(17 items)
Privacy - Photo Library Additions...	⌄	String	This app uses the photo library for saving images
Privacy - Photo Library Usage Des...	⌄	String	This app uses the photo library for saving images
Privacy - Camera Usage Description	⌄	String	This app uses the camera for creating panoramas
Localization native development re...	⌄	String	$(DEVELOPMENT_LANGUAGE)
Executable file	⌄	String	$(EXECUTABLE_NAME)
Bundle identifier	⌄	String	$(PRODUCT_BUNDLE_IDENTIFIER)
InfoDictionary version	⌄	String	6.0
Bundle name	⌄	String	$(PRODUCT_NAME)
Bundle OS Type code	⌄	String	APPL
Bundle versions string, short	⌄	String	1.0
Bundle version	⌄	String	1
Application requires iPhone enviro...	⌄	Boolean	YES
Launch screen interface file base...	⌄	String	LaunchScreen
Main storyboard file base name	⌄	String	Main
▼ Required device capabilities	⌄	Array	(1 item)
Item 0		String	armv7
▶ Supported interface orientations	⌄	Array	(3 items)
▶ Supported interface orientations (i...	⌄	Array	(4 items)

To start building the UI, we create a view with a `View` object for the camera preview on the right, and an overlapping `ImageView` on the left. `ImageView` should cover some area of the camera preview View, to help guide the user in capturing an image with enough overlap from the last. We can also add a few `ImageView` instances on top to show the previously captured images, and on the bottom a **Capture** button and a **Stitch** button to control the application flow:

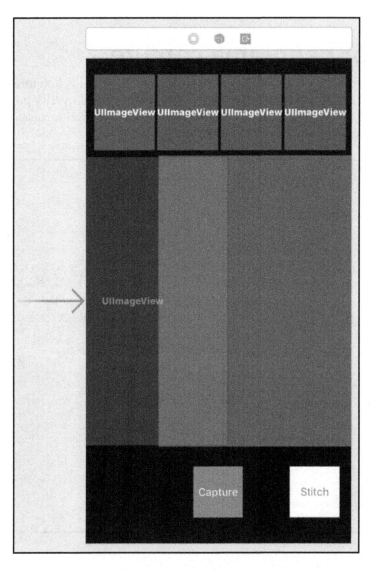

To connect the camera preview to the preview View, we must do the following:

1. Start a capture session (`AVCaptureSession`)
2. Select a device (`AVCaptureDevice`)
3. Set up the capture session with input from the device (`AVCaptureDeviceInput`)
4. Add an output for capturing photos (`AVCapturePhotoOutput`)

Most of these can be set up immediately when they are initialized as members of the ViewController class. The following code shows setting up the capture session, device, and output on the fly:

```
class ViewController: UIViewController, AVCapturePhotoCaptureDelegate {

    private lazy var captureSession: AVCaptureSession = {
        let s = AVCaptureSession()
        s.sessionPreset = .photo
        return s
    }()
    private let backCamera: AVCaptureDevice? =
AVCaptureDevice.default(.builtInWideAngleCamera, for: .video, position:
.back)

    private lazy var photoOutput: AVCapturePhotoOutput = {
        let o = AVCapturePhotoOutput()
        o.setPreparedPhotoSettingsArray([AVCapturePhotoSettings(format:
[AVVideoCodecKey: AVVideoCodecType.jpeg])], completionHandler: nil)
        return o
    }()
    var capturePreviewLayer: AVCaptureVideoPreviewLayer?
```

The rest of the initialization can be done from the `viewDidLoad` function, for example, adding the capture input to the session and creating a preview layer for showing the camera feed onscreen. The following code shows the rest of the initialization process, adding the input and output to the capture session, and setting up the preview layer.

```
    override func viewDidLoad() {
        super.viewDidLoad()

        let captureDeviceInput = try AVCaptureDeviceInput(device:
backCamera!)
        captureSession.addInput(captureDeviceInput)
        captureSession.addOutput(photoOutput)

        capturePreviewLayer = AVCaptureVideoPreviewLayer(session:
captureSession)
        capturePreviewLayer?.videoGravity =
```

```
AVLayerVideoGravity.resizeAspect
        capturePreviewLayer?.connection?.videoOrientation =
AVCaptureVideoOrientation.portrait
        // add the preview layer to the view we designated for preview
        let previewViewLayer = self.view.viewWithTag(1)!.layer
        capturePreviewLayer?.frame = previewViewLayer.bounds
        previewViewLayer.insertSublayer(capturePreviewLayer!, at: 0)
        previewViewLayer.masksToBounds = true
        captureSession.startRunning()
    }
```

With the preview set up, all that is left is to handle the photo capture on a click. The following code shows how a button click (`TouchUpInside`) will trigger the `photoOutput` function via `delegate`, and then simply add the new image to a list as well as save it to memory in the photo gallery.

```
@IBAction func captureButton_TouchUpInside(_ sender: UIButton) {
    photoOutput.capturePhoto(with: AVCapturePhotoSettings(), delegate:
self)
}

var capturedImages = [UIImage]()

func photoOutput(_ output: AVCapturePhotoOutput, didFinishProcessingPhoto
photo: AVCapturePhoto, error: Error?) {
    let cgImage = photo.cgImageRepresentation()!.takeRetainedValue()
    let image = UIImage(cgImage: cgImage)
    prevImageView.image = image // save the last photo, for the overlapping
ImageView
    capturedImages += [image] // add to array of captured photos
    // save to photo gallery on phone as well
    PHPhotoLibrary.shared().performChanges({
            PHAssetChangeRequest.creationRequestForAsset(from: image)
    }, completionHandler: nil)
}
```

This will allow us to capture multiple images in succession while helping the user align one image with the next. Here is an example of the UI running on the phone:

Next, we will see how to take the images to an Objective-C++ context, where we can work with the OpenCV C++ API for panorama stitching.

OpenCV stitching in an Objective-C++ wrapper

For working in iOS, OpenCV provides its usual C++ interface that can be invoked from Objective-C++. In recent years, however, Apple has encouraged iOS application developers to use the more versatile Swift language for building applications and forgo Objective-C. Luckily, a bridge between Swift and Objective-C (and Objective-C++) can be easily created, allowing us to invoke Objective-C functions from Swift. Xcode automates much of the process, and creates the necessary glue code.

To start, we create a new file (Command-N) in Xcode and select **Cocoa Touch Class**, as shown in the following screenshot:

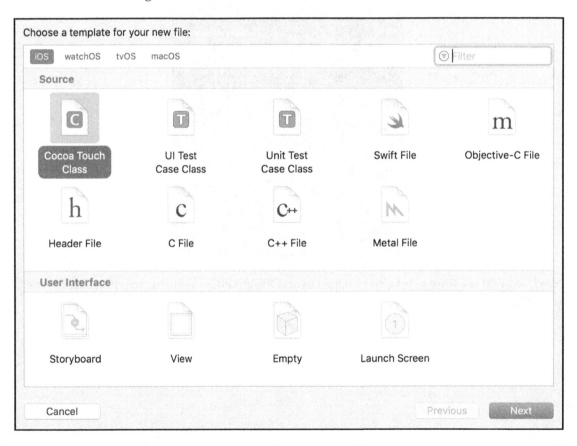

Choose a meaningful name for the file (for example, StitchingWrapper) and make sure to select **Objective-C** as the language, as shown in the following screenshot:

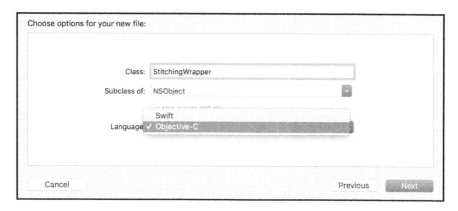

Next, as shown in the following screenshot, confirm that Xcode should create a **bridging header** for your Objective-C code:

This process will result in three files: StitchingWrapper.h, StitchingWrapper.m, and OpenCV Stitcher-Bridging-Header.h. We should manually rename StitchingWrapper.m to StitchingWrapper.mm, to enable Objective-**C++** over plain Objective-C. At this point, we are prepared to start using OpenCV in our Objective-C++ code.

In StitchingWrapper.h, we will define a new function that will accept an NSMutableArray* as the list of images captured by our earlier UI Swift code:

```
@interface StitchingWrapper : NSObject

+ (UIImage* _Nullable)stitch:(NSMutableArray*) images;

@end
```

And, in the Swift code for our ViewController, we can implement a function to handle a click on the **Stitch** button, where we create the NSMutableArray from the capturedImages Swift array of UIImages:

```
@IBAction func stitch_TouchUpInside(_ sender: Any) {
    let image = StitchingWrapper.stitch(NSMutableArray(array:
capturedImages, copyItems: true))
    if image != nil {
        PHPhotoLibrary.shared().performChanges({ // save stitching result
to gallery
                PHAssetChangeRequest.creationRequestForAsset(from: image!)
        }, completionHandler: nil)
    }
}
```

Back on the Objective-C++ side, firstly we need to get the OpenCV cv::Mat objects from the UIImage*s input, like so:

```
+ (UIImage* _Nullable)stitch:(NSMutableArray*) images {
    using namespace cv;
    std::vector<Mat> imgs;
    for (UIImage* img in images) {
        Mat mat;
        UIImageToMat(img, mat);
        if ([img imageOrientation] == UIImageOrientationRight) {
            rotate(mat, mat, cv::ROTATE_90_CLOCKWISE);
        }
        cvtColor(mat, mat, cv::COLOR_BGRA2BGR);
        imgs.push_back(mat);
    }
```

Finally, we're ready to call the stitching function on the array of images, like so:

```
    Mat pano;
    Stitcher::Mode mode = Stitcher::PANORAMA;
    Ptr<Stitcher> stitcher = Stitcher::create(mode, false);
    try {
        Stitcher::Status status = stitcher->stitch(imgs, pano);
        if (status != Stitcher::OK) {
            NSLog(@"Can't stitch images, error code = %d", status);
            return NULL;
        }
    } catch (const cv::Exception& e) {
        NSLog(@"Error %s", e.what());
        return NULL;
    }
```

An example of an output panorama created with this code (note the use of cylindrical warping) is shown as follows:

You may notice some changes in illumination between the four images, while the edges have been blended. Dealing with varying illumination can be addressed in the OpenCV image stitching API using the `cv::detail::ExposureCompensator` base API.

Summary

In this chapter, we've learned about panorama creation. We've seen some of the underlying theory and practice in panorama creation, implemented in OpenCV's `stitching` module. We then turned our focus to creating an iOS application that helps a user to capture images for panorama stitching with overlapping views. Lastly, we saw how to invoke OpenCV code from a Swift application to run the `stitching` functions on the captures images, resulting in a finished panorama.

The next chapter will focus on selection strategies for OpenCV algorithms given a problem at hand. We will see how to reason about a computer vision problem and its solution offering in OpenCV, as well as how to compare competing algorithms in order to make informed selections.

Further reading

Rick Szeliski's book on computer vision: `http://szeliski.org/Book/`

OpenCV's tutorial on image stitching: `https://docs.opencv.org/trunk/d8/d19/tutorial_stitcher.html`

OpenCV's tutorial on homography warping: `https://docs.opencv.org/3.4.1/d9/dab/tutorial_homography.html#tutorial_homography_Demo5`

Finding the Best OpenCV Algorithm for the Job

9

Any computer vision problem can be solved in different ways. Each way has its pros and cons and relative measures of success, depending on the data, resources, or goals. Working with OpenCV, a computer vision engineer has many algorithmic options on hand to solve a given task. Making the right choice in an informed way is extremely important since it can have a tremendous impact on the success of the entire solution, and prevent you from being boxed into a rigid implementation. This chapter will discuss some methods to follow when considering options in OpenCV. We will discuss the areas in computer vision that OpenCV covers, ways to select between competing algorithms if more than one exists, how to measure the success of an algorithm, and finally how to measure success in a robust way with a pipeline.

The following topics will be covered in this chapter:

- Is it covered in OpenCV? Computer vision topics with algorithms available in OpenCV.
- Which algorithm to pick? Topics with multiple available solutions in OpenCV.
- How to know which algorithm is best? Establishing metrics for measuring algorithm success.
- Using a pipeline to test different algorithms on the same data.

Technical requirements

The technologies and installations used in this chapter are the following:

- OpenCV v3 or v4 with Python bindings
- Jupyter Notebook server

Build instructions for the components listed above, as well as the code to implement the concepts presented in this chapter, will be provided in the accompanying code repository.

The code for this chapter can be accessed through GitHub: `https://github.com/PacktPublishing/Mastering-OpenCV-4-Third-Edition/tree/master/Chapter_09`.

Is it covered in OpenCV?

When first tackling a computer vision problem, any engineer should first asks: should I implement a solution from scratch, from a paper or known method, or use an existing solution and fit it to my needs?

This question goes hand-in-hand with the offering of implementations in OpenCV. Luckily, OpenCV has very wide and extensive coverage of both canonical and specific computer vision tasks. On the other hand, not all OpenCV implementations are easily applied to a given problem. For example, while OpenCV offers some object recognition and classification capabilities, it is by far inferior to the state-of-the-art computer vision one would see in conferences and the literature. Over the last few years, and certainly in OpenCV v4.0, there's an effort to easily integrate deep convolutional neural networks with OpenCV APIs (through the core `dnn` module) so engineers can enjoy all the latest and greatest work.

We made an effort to list the current offering of algorithms in OpenCV v4.0, along with a subjective estimation of the coverage they give of the grand computer vision subject. We also note whether OpenCV provides GPU implementation coverage, and whether the topic is covered in the core modules or in the contrib modules. Contrib modules vary; some modules are very mature and offer documentation and tutorials (for example, `tracking`), while others are a black box implementation with very poor documentation (for example, `xobjectdetect`). Having core module implementation is a good sign there is going to be adequate documentation, examples, and robustness.

The following is a list of topics in computer vision with their level of offering in OpenCV:

Topic	Coverage	OpenCV offering	Core?	GPU?
Image processing	Very good	Linear and non-linear filtering, transformations, colorspaces, histograms, shape analysis, edge detection	Yes	Good
Feature detection	Very good	Corner detection, key-point extraction, descriptor calculation	Yes + contrib	Poor

Segmentation	Mediocre	Watershed, contour and connected component analysis, binarization and thresholding, GrabCut, foreground-background segmentation, superpixels	Yes + contrib	Poor
Image alignment, stitching, Stabilization	Good	Panoramic stitching pipeline, Video stabilization pipeline, template matching, transform estimation, warping, seamless stitching	Yes + contrib	Poor
Structure from motion	Poor	Camera pose estimation, essential and fundamental matrix estimation, integration with external SfM library	Yes + contrib	None
Motion estimation, optical flow, tracking	Good	Optical flow algorithms, Kalman filter, object tracking framework, multi-target tracking	Mostly contrib	Poor
Stereo and 3D reconstruction	Good	Stereo matching framework, triangulation, structured light scanning	Yes + contrib	Good
Camera calibration	Very good	Calibration from several patterns, stereo rig calibration	Yes + contrib	None
Object detection	Mediocre	Cascade classifiers, QR code detector, face landmark detector, 3D object recognition, text detection	Yes + contrib	Poor
Object recognition, classification	Poor	Eigen and Fisher face recognition, bag-of-words	Mostly contrib	None
Computational photography	Mediocre	Denoising, HDR, superresolution	Yes + contrib	None

While OpenCV does a tremendous job with traditional computer vision algorithms, such as image processing, camera calibration, feature extraction, and other topics, it also has poor coverage of important topics such as SfM and object classification. In other topics, such as segmentation, it has a decent offering, but again falls short of state of the art, although that has moved almost exclusively to convolutional networks and can essentially be implemented with the dnn module.

In some topics, such as feature detection, extraction, and matching, as well as camera calibration, OpenCV is considered to be the most comprehensive, free, and usable library today, used in probably many thousands of applications. However, in the course of a computer vision project, engineers may consider decoupling from OpenCV after the prototyping phase since the library is heavy and adds significantly to the overhead in building and deploying (an acute problem for mobile applications). In those cases, OpenCV is a good crutch for prototyping, because of its wide offering, usefulness for testing, and choosing between different algorithms for the same task, for example, for calculating a 2D feature. Beyond prototyping, numerous other considerations become more important, such as the execution environment, stability and maintainability of the code, permissions and licensing, and more. At that stage, using OpenCV should satisfy the requirements of the product, including the considerations mentioned.

Algorithm options in OpenCV

OpenCV has many algorithms covering the same subject. When implementing a new processing pipeline, sometimes there is more than one choice for a step in the pipeline. For example, in Chapter 2, *Explore Structure from Motion with the SfM Module*, we made an arbitrary decision to use AKAZE features for finding landmarks between the images to estimate camera motion, and sparse 3D structure, however; there are many more kinds of 2D features available in OpenCV's features2D module. A more sensible mode of operation should have been to select the type of feature algorithm to use based on its performance, with respect to our needs. At the very least, we need to be aware of the different options.

Again, we looked to create a convenient way to see whether there are multiple options for the same task. We created a table where we list specific computer vision tasks that have multiple algorithm implementations in OpenCV. We also strived to mark whether algorithms have a common abstract API, and thus, easily and completely interchangeable within the code. While OpenCV offers the cv::Algorithm base class abstraction for most if not all of its algorithms, the abstraction is at a very high level and gives very little power to polymorphism and interchangeability. From our review, we exclude the machine learning algorithms (the ml module and the cv::StatsModel common API) since they are not proper computer vision algorithms, as well as low-level image processing algorithms, which do in fact have overlapping implementations (for example, the Hough detector family). We also exclude the GPU CUDA implementations that shadow several core topics such as object detection, background segmentation, 2D features, and more, since they are mostly replicas of the CPU implementations.

The following are topics with multiple implementations in OpenCV:

Topic	Implementations	Base API?
Optical flow	`video` module: `SparsePyrLKOpticalFlow`, `FarnebackOpticalFlow`, `DISOpticalFlow`, `VariationalRefinement` `optflow` contrib module: `DualTVL1OpticalFlow`, `OpticalFlowPCAFlow`	Yes
Object tracking	`track` contrib module: `TrackerBoosting`, `TrackerCSRT`, `TrackerGOTURN`, `TrackerKCF`, `TrackerMedianFlow`, `TrackerMIL`, `TrackerMOSSE`, `TrackerTLD` External: `DetectionBasedTracker`	Yes[1]

Object detection	`objdetect` module: `CascadeClassifier`, `HOGDescriptor`, `QRCodeDetector`,
	`linemod` contrib module: `Detector`
	`aruco` contrib module: `aruco::detectMarkers`
		No[2]

2D features	OpenCV's most established common API.
	`features2D` module: `AgastFeatureDetector`, `AKAZE`, `BRISK`, `FastFeatureDetector`, `GFTTDetector`, `KAZE`, `MSER`, `ORB`, `SimpleBlobDetector`
	`xfeatures2D` contrib module: `BoostDesc`, `BriefDescriptorExtractor`, `DAISY`, `FREAK`, `HarrisLaplaceFeatureDetector`, `LATCH`, `LUCID`, `MSDDetector`, `SIFT`, `StarDetector`, `SURF`, `VGG`
		Yes

Feature matching	`BFMatcher`, `FlannBasedMatcher`	Yes
Background subtraction	`video` module: `BackgroundSubtractorKNN`, `BackgroundSubtractorMOG2` `bgsegm` contrib module: `BackgroundSubtractorCNT`, `BackgroundSubtractorGMG`, `BackgroundSubtractorGSOC`, `BackgroundSubtractorLSBP`, `BackgroundSubtractorMOG`	Yes

Camera calibration	`calib3d` module: `calibrateCamera`, `calibrateCameraRO`, `stereoCalibrate`
	`aruco` contrib module: `calibrateCameraArcuo`, `calibrateCameraCharuco`
	`ccalib` contrib module: `omnidir::calibrate`, `omnidir::stereoCalibrate`
		No

Stereo reconstruction	calib3d **module:** `StereoBM, StereoSGBM`
	`stereo` **contrib module:** `StereoBinaryBM,`
	`StereoBinarySGBM`
	`ccalib` **contrib module:** `omnidir::stereoReconstruct`
		Partial[3]

Pose estimation	`solveP3P, solvePnP, solvePnPRansac`	No

[1] Only for the classes in the `track` contrib module.

[2] Some classes share functions with the same name, but no inherited abstract class.

[3] Each module has a base within itself, but not shared across modules.

When approaching a problem with a few algorithmic options, it's important not to commit too early to one execution path. We may use the preceding table above to see options exist, and then explore them. Next, we will discuss how to select from a pool of options.

Which algorithm is best?

Computer vision is a world of knowledge and a decades-long research pursuit. Unlike many other disciplines, computer vision is not strongly hierarchical or vertical, which means new solutions for given problems are not always better and may not be based on preceding work. Being an applied field, computer vision algorithms are created with attention to the following aspects, which may explain the non-vertical development:

- **Computation resources**: CPU, GPU, embedded system, memory footprint, network connectivity.
- **Data**: Size of images, number of images, number of image stream (cameras), data type, sequentiality, lighting conditions, types of scenes, and so on.
- **Performance requirements**: Real-time output or another timing constraint (for example, human perception), accuracy and precision.
- **Meta-algorithmic**: Algorithm simplicity (cross-reference Occam's Razor theorem), implementation system and external tools, availability of formal proof.

With every algorithm created in order to cater for perhaps a certain one of these considerations, one can never know for sure that it will outperform all others without properly testing some or all of them. Granted, testing all algorithms for a given problem is *unrealistic*, even if the implementations are indeed available, and OpenCV certainly has many implementations available, as we've seen in the last section. On the other hand, computer vision engineers will be remiss if they do not consider the possibility that their implementations are not optimal because of their algorithm choices. This in essence flows from the *no free lunch* theorem, which states, in broad strokes, that no single algorithm is the best one over the entire space of possible datasets.

It is, therefore, a very welcome practice to test a set of different algorithmic options before committing to the best one out of that set. But how do we find the *best one*? The word *best* implies that each one will be *better* (or *worse*) than the others, which in turn suggests there is an objective scale or measurement in which they are all scored and ranked in order. Obviously, there is not a single measure (**metric**) for all algorithms in all problems each problem will have its own. In many cases, the metric for success will form a measurement of **error**, deviation from a known **ground truth** value that was sourced from humans or other algorithms we can trust. In optimization, this is known as a **loss function** or cost function, a function that we wish to minimize (sometimes maximize) in order to find the best option that has the lowest score. Another prominent class of metrics cares less about the output performance (for example, error) and more about runtime timing, memory footprint, capacity and throughput, and so on.

The following is a partial list of metrics we may see in select computer vision problems:

Task	Example metrics
Reconstruction, registration, feature matching	**Mean absolute error (MAE), mean squared error (MSE), root mean squared error (RMSE), sum of squared distances (SSD)**
Object classification, recognition	Accuracy, precision, recall, f1-score, **false-positive rate (FPR)**
Segmentation, object detection	**Intersection-over-Union (IoU)**
Feature detection	Repeatability, precision recall

The why to find the best algorithm for a given task is either to set all the options at our disposal in a test scenario and measure their performance on the metrics of choice, or obtain someone else's measurements on a standard experiment or dataset. The highest ranking option should be picked, where the ranking is derived from a combination of the metrics (in the case of just a single metric, it's an easy task). Next, we will try our hand at such a task, and make an *informed* choice on the best algorithm.

Example comparative performance test of algorithms

As an example, we will set up a scenario where we are required to align overlapping images, like what is done in panorama or aerial photo stitching. One important feature that we need to measure performance is to have a **ground truth**, a precise measurement of the true condition that we are trying to recover with our approximation method. Ground truth data can be obtained from datasets made available for researchers to test and compare their algorithms; indeed, many of these datasets exist and computer vision researchers use them all the time. One good resource for finding computer vision datasets is **Yet Another Computer Vision Index To Datasets (YACVID)**, `https://riemenschneider.hayko.at/vision/dataset/`, which has been actively maintained for the past eight years and contains hundreds of links to datasets. The following is also a good resource for data: `https://github.com/jbhuang0604/awesome-computer-vision#datasets`.

We, however, will pick a different way to get ground truth, which is well practiced in computer vision literature. We will create a contrived situation within our parametric control, and create a benchmark that we can vary to test different aspects of our algorithms. For our example, we will take a single image and split it into two overlapping images, and apply some transformations to one of them. The fusing of the images with our algorithm will try to recreate the original fused image, but it will likely not do a perfect job. Choices we make in selecting the pieces in our system (for example, the type of 2D feature, the feature matching algorithm, and the transform recovery algorithm) will affect the final result, which we will measure and compare. Working with artificial ground truth data gives us a lot of control over the conditions and level in our trials.

Consider the following image and its two-way overlapping split:

Image: https://pixabay.com/en/forest-forests-tucholski-poland-1973952/

The left image we keep untouched, while we perform artificial transformations on the right image to see how well our algorithm will be able to undo them. To keep things simple, we will only rotate the right image at several brackets, like so:

We add a middle bracket for the *no rotation* case, in which the right image is only translated somewhat. This makes up our ground truth data, where we know exactly what transformation occurred and what the original input was.

Our goal is to measure the success of different 2D feature descriptor types in aligning images. One measure for our success can be the **Mean Squared Error (MSE)** over the pixels of the final re-stitched image. If the transformation recovery wasn't very well done, the pixels will not align perfectly, and thus we expect to see a high MSE. As the MSE approaches zero, we know the stitching was done well. We may also wish to know, for practical reasons, which feature is the most efficient, so we can also take a measurement of execution time. To this end, our algorithm can be very simple:

1. Split original image *left image* and *right image*.
2. For each of the feature types (SURF, SIFT, ORB, AKAZE, BRISK), do the following:
     1. Find keypoints and features in the left image.
     2. For each rotation angle [-90, -67, ..., 67, 90] do the following:
          1. Rotate the right image by the rotation angle.
          2. Find keypoints and features in the rotated right image.
          3. Match keypoints between the rotated right image and the left image.
          4. Estimate a rigid 2D transform.
          5. Transform according to the estimation.
          6. Measure the **MSE** of the final result with the original unsplit image.
          7. Measure the overall **time** it takes to extract, compute, and match features, and perform the alignment.

As a quick optimization, we can cache the rotated images, and not calculate them for each feature type. The rest of the algorithm remains untouched. Additionally, to keep things fair in terms of timing, we should take care to have a similar number of keypoints extracted for each feature type (for example, 2,500 keypoints), which can be done by setting the threshold for the keypoint extraction functions.

Note the alignment execution pipeline is oblivious of the feature type, and works exactly the same given the matched keypoints. This is a very important feature for testing many options. With OpenCV's `cv::Feature2D` and `cv::DescriptorMatcher` common base API, it is possible to achieve this, since all features and matchers implement them. However, if we take a look at the table in the *Is it covered in OpenCV?* section, we can see that this may not be possible for all vision problem in OpenCV, so we may need to add our own instrumentation code to make this comparison possible.

In the accompanying code, we can find the Python implementation of this routine, which provides the following results. To test rotation invariance, we vary the angle and measure the reconstruction MSE:

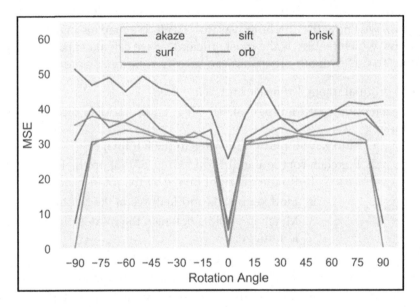

With the same experiments, we record the mean MSE across all experiments for a feature type, and also the mean execution time, shown as follows:

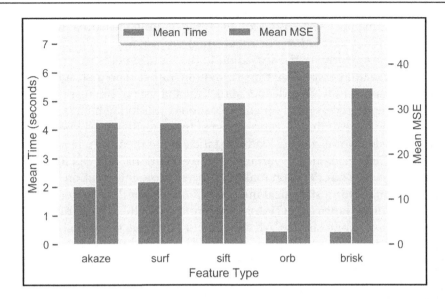

Results analysis, we can clearly see some features performing better than others in terms of MSE, with respect to both the different rotation angles and overall, and we can also see a big variance in the timing. It seems AKAZE and SURF are the highest performers in terms of alignment success across the rotation angle domain, with an advantage for AKAZE in higher rotations (~60°). However, at very small angular variation (rotation angle close to 0°), SIFT achieves practically perfect reconstruction with MSE around zero, and it also does as well as if not better then, the others with rotations below 30°. ORB does very badly throughout the domain, and BRISK, while not as bad, rarely was able to beat any of the forerunners.

Considering timing, ORB and BRISK (which are essentially the same algorithm) are the clear winners, but they both are far behind the others in terms of reconstruction accuracy. AKAZE and SURF are the leaders with neck-and-neck timing performance.

Now, it is up to us as the application developers to rank the features according to the requirements of the project. With the data from this test we performed, it should be easy to make a decision. If we are looking for speed, we would choose BRISK, since it's the fastest and performs better than ORB. If we are looking for accuracy, we would choose AKAZE, since it's the best performer and is faster than SURF. Using SURF in itself is a problem, since the algorithm is not free and it is protected by patent, so we are lucky to find AKAZE as a free and adequate alternative.

This was a very rudimentary test, only looking at two simple measures (MSE and time) and only one varied parameter (rotation). In a real situation, we may wish to insert more complexity into the transformations, according to the requirements of our system. For example, we may use full perspective transformation, rather than just rigid rotation. Additionally, we may want to do a deeper statistical analysis of the results. In this test, we only ran the alignment process once for each rotation condition, which is not good for capturing a good measure of timing, since some of the algorithms may benefit from executing in succession (for example, loading static data to memory). If we have multiple executions, we can reason about the variance in the executions, and calculate the standard deviation or error to give our decision making process more information. Lastly, given enough data, we can perform statistical inference processes and hypothesis testing, such as a **t-test** or **analysis of variance** (**ANOVA**), to determine whether the minute differences between the conditions (for example, AKAZE and SURF) have **statistical significance** or are too noisy to tell apart.

Summary

Choosing the best computer vision algorithm for the job is an illusive process, which is the reason many engineers do not perform it. While published survey work on different choices provides benchmark performance, in many situations it doesn't model the particular system requirements an engineer might encounter, and new tests must be implemented. The major problem in testing algorithmic options is instrumentation code, which is an added work for engineers, and not always simple. OpenCV provides base APIs for algorithms in several vision problem domains, but the cover age is not complete. On the other hand, OpenCV has very extensive coverage of problems in computer vision, and is one of the premier frameworks to perform such tests.

Making an informed decision when picking an algorithm is a very important aspect of vision engineering, with many elements to optimize for, for example, speed, accuracy, simplicity, memory footprint, and even availability. Each vision system project has particular requirements that affect the weight each of these elements receives, and thus the final decision. With relatively simple OpenCV code, we saw how to gather data, chart it, and make an informed decision about a toy problem.

In the next chapter we discuss the history of the OpenCV open source project, as well as some common pitfalls when using OpenCV with suggested solutions for them.

10
Avoiding Common Pitfalls in OpenCV

OpenCV has been around for more than 15 years now. It contains many implementations that are outdated or unoptimized and are relics of the past. An advanced OpenCV engineer should know how to avoid basic mistakes in navigating the OpenCV APIs, and see their project to algorithmic success.

In this chapter, we will review the historic development of OpenCV, and the gradual increase in the framework and algorithmic offering, alongside the development of computer vision at large. We will use this knowledge to see how to figure out whether a newer alternative exists within OpenCV for our algorithm of choice. Lastly, we will discuss how to identify and avoid common problems or sub-optimal choices while creating computer vision systems with OpenCV.

The following topics will be covered in this chapter:

- A historic review of OpenCV and the latest wave of computer vision research
- Checking the date at which an algorithm became available in OpenCV, and whether it's a sign that it is outdated
- Addressing pitfalls in building computer vision systems in OpenCV

History of OpenCV from v1 to v4

OpenCV started as the brainchild of **Gray Bradsky**, once a computer vision engineer at **Intel**, around the early 2000s. Bradsky and a team of engineers, mostly from Russia, developed the first versions of OpenCV internally at Intel before making v0.9 of it **open source software (OSS)** in 2002. Bradsky then transitioned to **Willow Garage**, with the former founding members of OpenCV. Among them were Viktor Eurkhimov, Sergey Molinov, Alexander Shishkov, and Vadim Pisarevsky (who eventually started the company **ItSeez**, which was acquired in 2016 by Intel), who began supporting the young library as an open source project.

Version 0.9 had a predominantly C API and already sported image data manipulation functions and pixel access, image processing, filtering, colorspace transformations, geometric and shape analysis (for example, morphologic functions, Hough transforms, contour finding), motion analysis, basic machine learning (K-means, HMM), camera pose estimation, basic linear algebra (SVD, Eigen decomposition), and more. Many of these functions lasted through the ages, even into today's versions of OpenCV. Version 1.0 was released in 2006, and it marked the beginning of the library as the dominant force in OSS computer vision. In late 2008, Bradsky and **Adrian Kaehler** published the best-selling *Learning OpenCV* book based on OpenCV v1.1pre1, which was a smashing worldwide success, and served for years to come as the definitive guide to OpenCV's C API.

For its completeness, OpenCV v1 became a very popular framework for vision work in both academic and industrial applications, especially in the robotics domain, although it was just a small departure from v0.9 in terms of feature offering. After the release of v1.0 (late 2006), the OpenCV project went into years of hibernation, as the founding team was occupied with other projects and the open source community wasn't as established as it became years later. The project released v1.1pre1 in late 2008 with minor additions; however, the foundation of OpenCV as the most well-known vision library came with version 2.x, which introduced the very successful **C++ API**. Versions 2.x lasted *6 years* (2009-2015) as the stable branch of OpenCV, and the branch was maintained even until very recently, in early 2018 (the last version, 2.4.13.6, was released in February 2018), almost *10 years* later. Version 2.4, released in mid-2012, had a very stable and successful API, lasted for three years, and also introduced a very wide offering of features.

Versions 2.x introduced the **CMake** build system, which was also used at the time by the **MySQL** project, to align with its goal to be completely **cross-platform**. Apart from the new C++ API, v2.x also brought the concept of **modules** (in v2.2, circa 2011), which can be built, included, and linked separately, based on the project assembly necessity, forsaking v1.x's `cv`, `cvaux`, `ml`, and so on. The 2D feature suit was extended, as well as the machine learning capabilities, built-in face recognition cascade models, 3D reconstruction functionality, and most importantly the coverage of **Python** bindings. Early investment in Python made OpenCV the best tool for vision prototyping available at that time, and probably still today. Version 2.4, released in mid-2012, continued development until 2018, with v2.5 never released due to fears of breaking API changes and simply rebranded as v3.0 (ca. mid-2013). Version 2.4.x continued to bring more important features such as **Android** and **iOS** support, **CUDA** and **OpenCL** implementations, CPU optimizations (for example, SSE and other SIMD architectures), and an incredible amount of new algorithms.

Version 3.0, first released out of beta in late 2015, was first received with lukewarm adoption from the community. They were looking for a stable API, since some APIs had breaking changes and a drop-in replacement was impossible. The header structure also changed (from `opencv2/<module>/<module>.hpp` to `opencv2/<module>.hpp`), making the transition even harder. Version 2.4.11+ (February 2015) had instrumentation to bridge the API gap between the versions, and documentation was installed to help developers transition to v3.0 (`https://docs.opencv.org/3.4/db/dfa/tutorial_transition_guide.html`). Version 2.x maintained a very strong hold, with many package management systems (for example, Ubuntu's `apt`) still serving it as the stable version of OpenCV, while version 3.x was advancing at a very fast pace.

After years of cohabitation and planning, version 2.4.x gave way to version 3.x, which boasted a revamped API (many abstractions and base classes introduced) and improved GPU support via the new **Transparent API (T-API)**, which allowed the use of GPU code interchangeably with regular CPU code. A separate repository for community-contributed code was established, `opencv-contrib`, removing it from the main code as a module in v2.4.x, with improved build stability and timing. Another big change was the machine learning support in OpenCV, which was greatly improved and revised from v2.4. Version 3.x was also pushed for better Android support and optimizations for CPU architectures beyond Intel x86 (for example, ARM, NEON) via the OpenCV **HAL (Hardware Acceleration Layer)**, which later merged into the core modules. The first emergence of deep neural networks in OpenCV was recorded in v3.1 (December 2015) as a `contrib` module, and almost two years later in v3.3 (August 2017) was upgraded to a core module, `opencv-dnn`. The 3.x versions brought tremendous improvements to optimization and compatibility with GPU and CPU architectures, with support from Intel, Nvidia, AMD, and Google, and became OpenCV's hallmark as the optimized computer vision library.

Version 4.0 marks the mature state of OpenCV as the major open source project it is today. The old C API (of which many functions date back to v0.9) was let go and instead **C++11** was made *mandatory*, which also rid the library of its `cv::String` and `cv::Ptr` hybrids. Version 4.0 keeps track of further optimization for CPUs and GPUs; however, the most interesting addition is the **Graph API (G-API) module**. G-API brings the spirit of the times to OpenCV, with support for building compute graphs for computer vision, with heterogeneous execution on CPU and GPU, following the very big success of Google's **TensorFlow** deep learning library and Facebook's **PyTorch**. With long-standing investment in deep learning and machine learning, Python and other languages, execution graphs, cross-compatibility, and a wide offering of optimized algorithms, OpenCV is established as a forward-looking project with very strong community support, which makes it fifteen years later the leading open computer vision library in existence.

The history of this book series, *Mastering OpenCV*, is intertwined with the development history of OpenCV as the major library for open source computer vision. The first edition, released in 2012, was based on the everlasting v2.4.x branch. This dominated the OpenCV scene in 2009-2016. The second edition, released in 2017, hailed the dominance of OpenCV v3.1+ in the community (started in mid-2016). The third edition, the one you are reading now, welcomes OpenCV v4.0.0 into the fold, released in late October 2018.

OpenCV and the data revolution in computer vision

OpenCV existed before the data revolution in computer vision. In the late 1990s, access to big amounts of data was not a simple task for computer vision researchers. Fast access to the internet was not common, and even universities and big research institutes were not strongly networked. The limited storage capacities of personal and bigger institutional computers did not allow researchers and students to work with big amounts of data, let alone having the computational power (memory and CPU) required to do so. Thus, the research on large-scale computer vision problems was restricted to a selected list of laboratories worldwide, among them MIT's **Computer Science and Artificial Intelligence Lab (CSAIL)**, the University of Oxford Robotics Research Group, **Carnegie Mellon (CMU)** Robotics Institute, and the **California Institute of Technology (CalTech)** Computational Vision Group. These laboratories also had the resources to curate big amounts of data on their own to serve the work of local scientists, and their compute clusters were powerful enough to work with that scale of data.

However, the beginning of the 2000s brought a change to this landscape. Fast internet connections enabled it to become a hub for research and data exchange, and in parallel, compute and storage power exponentially increased year over year. This democratization of large-scale computer vision work has brought the creation of seminal big datasets for computer vision work, such as **MNIST** (1998), **CMU PIE** (2000), **CalTech 101** (2003), and **MIT's LabelMe** (2005). The release of these datasets also spurred algorithm research around large-scale image classification, detection, and recognition. Some of the most seminal work in computer vision was enabled directly or indirectly by these datasets, for example, **LeCun's** handwriting recognition (circa 1990), **Viola and Jones'** cascaded boosting face detector (2001), **Lowe's** SIFT (1999, 2004), **Dalal's** HoG people classifier (2005), and many more.

The second half of the 2000s saw a sharp increase in data offerings, with many big datasets released, such as **CalTech 256** (2006), **ImageNet** (2009), **CIFAR-10** (2009), and **PASCAL VOC** (2010), all of which still play a vital role in today's research. With the advent of deep neural networks around 2010-2012, and the momentous winning of the ImageNet large-scale visual recognition (ILSVRC) competition by **Krizhevsky and Hinton's AlexNet** (2012), large datasets became the fashion, and the computer vision world had changed. ImageNet itself has grown to monstrous proportions (more than 14 million photos), and other big datasets did too, such as **Microsoft's COCO** (2015, with 2.5 million photos), **OpenImages V4** (2017, with less than nine million photos), and **MIT's ADE20K** (2017, with nearly 500,000 object segmentation instances). This recent trend pushed researchers to think on a larger scale, and today's machine learning that tackles such data will often have tens and hundreds of millions of parameters (in a deep neural network), compared to dozens of parameters ten years ago.

OpenCV's early claim to fame was its built-in implementation of the Viola and Jones face detection method, based on a cascade of boosted classifiers, which was a reason for many to select OpenCV in their research or practice. However, OpenCV did not target data-driven computer vision at first. In v1.0, the only machine learning algorithms were the cascaded boosting, hidden Markov model, and some unsupervised methods (such as K-means clustering and expectation maximization). Much of the focus was on image processing, geometric shape and morphological analysis, and so on. Versions 2.x and 3.x added a great deal of standard machine learning capabilities to OpenCV; among them were decision trees, randomized forests and gradient boosting trees, **support vector machines** (SVM), logistic regression, Naive Bayes classification, and more. As it stands, OpenCV is not a data-driven machine learning library, and in recent versions this becomes more obvious. The `opencv_dnn` core module lets developers use models learned with external tools (for example, TensorFlow) to run in an OpenCV environment, where OpenCV provides the image preprocessing and post-processing. Nevertheless, OpenCV plays a crucial role in data-driven pipelines, and plays a meaningful role in the scene.

Historic algorithms in OpenCV

When starting to work on an OpenCV project, one should be aware of its historical past. OpenCV has existed for more than 15 years as an open source project, and despite its very dedicated management team that aims to better the library and keep it relevant, some implementations are more outdated than others. Some APIs are left for backward compatibility with previous versions, and others are targeted at specific algorithmic circumstances, all while newer algorithms are added.

Any engineer looking to choose the best performing algorithm for his work should have the tools to inquire about a specific algorithm to see *when* it was added and what are its *origins* (for example, a research paper). That is not to suggest that anything *new* is necessarily *better*, as some basic and older algorithms are excellent performers, and in most cases there's a clear trade-off between various metrics. For example, a data-driven deep neural network to perform image binarization (turning a color, or grayscale image to black-and-white) will likely reach the highest *accuracy*. However, the **Otsu method** (1979) for adaptive binary thresholding is incredibly *fast* and performs quite well in many situations. The key is therefore to know the requirements, as well as the details of the algorithm.

How to check when an algorithm was added to OpenCV

One of the simplest things to do in order to learn more about an OpenCV algorithm is to see when it was added to the source tree. Luckily, OpenCV as an open source project has retained most of its code's history, and changes were logged in various released versions. There are several useful resources to access this information, as follows:

- The OpenCV source repository: `https://github.com/opencv/opencv`
- The OpenCV change logs: `https://github.com/opencv/opencv/wiki/ChangeLog`
- The OpenCV attic: `https://github.com/opencv/opencv_attic`
- The OpenCV documentation: `https://docs.opencv.org/master/index.html`

Let's examine, for example, the algorithm in the `cv::solvePnP(...)` function, which is one of the most useful functions for object (or camera) pose estimation. This function is heavily used in 3D reconstruction pipelines. We can locate `solvePnP` in the `opencv/modules/calib3d/src/solvepnp.cpp` file. Using the search feature in GitHub, we can trace `solvepnp.cpp` back to its initial commit (`https://github.com/opencv/opencv/commit/04461a53f1a484499ce81bcd4e25a714488cf600`) on April 4, 2011.

There, we can see the original `solvePnP` function originally resided in `calibrate3d.cpp`, so we can trace that function back as well. However, we soon discover that there is not much history for that file, as it originated from the initial commit to the new OpenCV repository in May 2010. A search in the attic repository doesn't reveal anything beyond what exists in the original repository. The oldest version of `solvePnP` we have is from May 11, 2010 (`https://github.com/opencv/opencv_attic/blob/ 8173f5ababf09218cc4838e5ac7a70328696a48d/opencv/modules/calib3d/src/ calibration.cpp`) and it looks like this:

```
void cv::solvePnP( const Mat& opoints, const Mat& ipoints,
                   const Mat& cameraMatrix, const Mat& distCoeffs,
                   Mat& rvec, Mat& tvec, bool useExtrinsicGuess )
{
    CV_Assert(opoints.isContinuous() && opoints.depth() == CV_32F &&
              ((opoints.rows == 1 && opoints.channels() == 3) ||
               opoints.cols*opoints.channels() == 3) &&
              ipoints.isContinuous() && ipoints.depth() == CV_32F &&
              ((ipoints.rows == 1 && ipoints.channels() == 2) ||
               ipoints.cols*ipoints.channels() == 2));
    rvec.create(3, 1, CV_64F);
    tvec.create(3, 1, CV_64F);
    CvMat _objectPoints = opoints, _imagePoints = ipoints;
    CvMat _cameraMatrix = cameraMatrix, _distCoeffs = distCoeffs;
    CvMat _rvec = rvec, _tvec = tvec;
    cvFindExtrinsicCameraParams2(&_objectPoints, &_imagePoints,
&_cameraMatrix,
                                 &_distCoeffs, &_rvec, &_tvec,
useExtrinsicGuess );
}
```

We can clearly see it is a simple wrapper around the old C API's `cvFindExtrinsicCameraParams2`. The code for this C API function exists in `calibration.cpp` (`https://github.com/opencv/opencv/blob/ 8f15a609afc3c08ea0a5561ca26f1cf182414ca2/modules/calib3d/src/calibration. cpp#L1043`), and we can verify it as it has not changed since May 2010. The newer version of `solvePnP` (latest commit in November 2018) adds much more functionality, adding another function (allowing the use of **RANdom SAmple Consensus (RANSAC)**) and several specialty PnP algorithms such as EPnP, P3P, AP3P, DLS, UPnP, and also retaining the old C API (`cvFindExtrinsicCameraParams2`) method when supplying the `SOLVEPNP_ITERATIVE` flag to the function. The old C function, upon inspection, seems to solve the pose estimation problem by either finding a **homography**, in the case of planar objects, or using the **DLT method**, and then performing an iterative refinement.

As per usual, it'd be a mistake to directly assume the old C method is inferior to the other methods. However, the newer methods are indeed methods suggested decades after the DLT method (which dates back to the 1970s). For example, the UPnP method was proposed in just *2013* by Penate-Sanchez et al. (2013). Again, without careful examination of the particular data at hand and a comparative study, we cannot conclude which algorithm performs best with respect to the requirements (speed, accuracy, memory, and so on), although we can conclude that computer vision research has certainly advanced in *40 years* from the 1970s to the 2010s. Penate-Sanchez et al. actually show in their paper that UPnP performs much better than DLT, in terms of both speed and accuracy, based on empirical studies they carried out with real and simulated data. Please refer to `Chapter 9`, *Finding the Best OpenCV Algorithm for the Job,* for tips on how to compare algorithm options.

In-depth inspection of the OpenCV code should be a routine job for serious computer vision engineers. It not only reveals potential optimizations and guides choices by focusing on newer methods, but it also may teach much about the algorithms themselves.

Common pitfalls and suggested solutions

OpenCV is very feature rich and provides multiple solutions and paths to resolve a visual-understanding problem. With this great power also comes hard work, choosing and crafting the best processing pipeline for the project requirements. Having multiple options means that probably finding the exact best performing solution is next to impossible, as many pieces are interchangeable and testing *all* the possible options is out of our reach. This problem's exponential complexity is compounded by the input data; more unknown variance in the incoming data will make our algorithm choices even more unstable. In other words, working with OpenCV, or any other computer vision library, is still a matter of experience and art. A priori intuition as to the success of one or another route to a solution is something computer vision engineers develop with years of experience, and for the most part there are no shortcuts.

There is, however, the option of learning from someone else's experience. If you've purchased this book, it likely means you are looking to do just so. In this section, we have prepared a partial list of problems that we encountered in our years of work as computer vision engineers. We also look to propose solutions for these problems, like we used in our own work. The list focuses on problems arising from computer vision engineering; however, any engineer should also be aware of common problems in *general purpose software and system engineering,* which we do not enumerate here. In practice, no system implementation is without some problems, bugs, or under-optimizations, and even after following our list, one will probably find there is much more left to do.

The primary common pitfall in any engineering field is **making assumptions instead of assertions**. For any engineer, if there's an option to measure something, it should be measured, even by approximation, establishment of lower and upper bounds, or measuring a different highly correlated phenomenon. For some examples on which metrics can be used for measurement in OpenCV, refer to `Chapter 9`, *Finding the Best OpenCV Algorithm for the Job*. The best made decisions are the informed ones, based on hard data and visibility; however, that is often not the privilege of an engineer. Some projects require a fast and cold start that forces an engineer to rapidly build up a solution from scratch, without much data or intuition. In such cases, the following advice can save a lot of grief:

- **Not comparing algorithm options**: One pitfall engineers often make is choosing algorithms categorically based on what they encounter first, something they've done in the past and seemed to work, or something that has a nice tutorial (someone else's experience). This is called the **anchoring** or **focalism cognitive bias**, a well-known problem in decision making theory. Reiterating the words from the last chapter, the choice of algorithm can have tremendous impact on the results of the entire pipeline and project, in terms of accuracy, speed, resources, and otherwise. Making uninformed decisions when selecting algorithms is not a good idea.

    - **Solution**: OpenCV has many ways to assist in testing different options seamlessly, through common base APIs (such as `Feature2D`, `DescriptorMatcher`, `SparseOpticalFlow`, and more) or common function signatures (such as `solvePnP` and `solvePnPRansac`). High-level programming languages, such as Python, have even more flexibility in interchanging algorithms; however, this is also possible in C++ beyond polymorphism, with some instrumentation code. After establishing a pipeline, see how you can interchange some of the algorithms (for example, feature type or matcher type, thresholding technique) or their parameters (for example, threshold values, algorithm flags) and measure the effect on the final result. Strictly changing parameters is often called **hyperparameter tuning**, which is standard practice in machine learning.

- **Not unit testing homegrown solutions or algorithms**: It is often a programmer's fallacy to believe their work is bug-free, and that they've covered all edge cases. It is far better to err on the side of caution when it comes to computer vision algorithms, since in many cases the input space is vastly unknown, as it is incredibly highly dimensional. Unit tests are excellent tools to make sure functionality doesn't break on unexpected input, invalid data, or edge cases (for example, an empty image) and has a graceful degradation.
  - **Solution**: Establish unit tests for any meaningful function in your code, and make sure to cover the important parts. For example, any function that either reads or writes image data is a good candidate for a unit test. The unit test is a simple piece of code that usually invokes the function a number of times with different arguments, testing the function's ability (or inability) to handle the input. Working in C++, there are many options for a test framework; one such framework is part of the Boost C++ package, **Boost.Test** (https://www.boost.org/doc/libs/1_66_0/libs/test/doc/html/index.html). Here is an example:

```
#define BOOST_TEST_MODULE binarization test
#include <boost/test/unit_test.hpp>

BOOST_AUTO_TEST_CASE( binarization_test )
{
    // On empty input should return empty output
BOOST_TEST(binarization_function(cv::Mat()).empty())
    // On 3-channel color input should return 1-
channel output
    cv::Mat input = cv::imread("test_image.png");
    BOOST_TEST(binarization_function(input).channels()
== 1)
}
```

After compiling this file, it creates an executable that will perform the tests and exit with a status of 0 if all tests passed or 1 if any of them failed. It is common to mix this approach with **CMake's CTest** (https://cmake.org/cmake/help/latest/manual/ctest.1.html) feature (via ADD_TEST in the CMakeLists.txt files), which facilitates building tests for many parts of the code and running them all upon command.

- **Not checking data ranges**: A common problem in computer vision programming is to assume a range for the data, for example a range of [0, 1] for floating-point pixels (`float`, `CV_32F`) or [0, 255] for byte pixels (`unsigned char`, `CV_8U`). There really are no guarantees that these assumptions hold in any situation, since the memory block can hold any value. The problems that arise from these errors are mostly value saturation, when trying to write a value bigger than the representation; for example, writing 325 into a byte that can hold [0, 255] will saturate to 255, losing a great deal of precision. Other potential problems are differences between expected and actual data, for example, expecting a depth image in the range of [0, 2048] (for example, two meters in millimeters) only to see the actual range is [0, 1], meaning it was normalized somehow. This can lead to underperformance in the algorithm, or a complete breakdown (imagine dividing the [0, 1] range by 2048 again).

  - **Solution**: Check the input data range and make sure it is what you expect. If the range is not within acceptable bounds, you may throw an `out_of_range` exception (a standard library class, visit `https://en.cppreference.com/w/cpp/error/out_of_range` for more details). You can also consider using `CV_ASSERT` to check the range, which will trigger a `cv::error` exception on failure.

- **Data types, channels, conversion, and rounding errors**: One of the most vexing problems in OpenCV's `cv::Mat` data structure is that it doesn't carry data type information on its variable type. A `cv::Mat` can hold any type of data (`float`, `uchar`, `int`, `short`, and so on) in any size, and a receiving function cannot know what data is inside the array without inspection or convention. The problem is also compounded by the number of channels, as an array can hold any number of them arbitrarily (for example, a `cv::Mat` can hold `CV_8UC1` or `CV_8UC3`). Failing to have a known data type can lead to runtime exceptions from OpenCV functions that don't expect such data, and therefore to potential crashing of the entire application. Problems with handling multiple data types on the same input `cv::Mat` may lead to other issues of conversion. For example, if we know an incoming array holds `CV_32F` (by checking `input.type() == CV_32F`), we may `input.convertTo(out, CV_8U)` to "normalize" it to a `uchar` character; however, if the `float` data is in the [0, 1] range, the output conversion will have all 0s and 1s in a [0, 255] image, which may be a problem.

- **Solution**: Prefer `cv::Mat_<>` types (for example, `cv::Mat_<float>`) over `cv::Mat` to also carry the data type, establish very clear conventions on variable naming (for example `cv::Mat image_8uc1`), test to make sure the types you expect are the types you get, or create a "normalization" scheme to turn any unexpected input type to the type you would like into work with in your function. Using `try .. catch` blocks is also a good practice when data type uncertainty is feared.

- **Colorspace-originating problems: RGB versus perceptual (HSV, L*a*b*) versus technical (YUV)**: Colorspaces are a way to encode color information in numeric values in a pixel array (image). However, there are a number of problems with this encoding. The foremost problem is that any colorspace eventually becomes a series of numbers stored in the array, and OpenCV does not keep track of colorspace information in `cv::Mat` (for example, an array may hold 3-byte RGB or 3-byte HSV, and the variable user cannot tell the difference). This is not a good thing, because we tend to think we can do any kind of numeric manipulation on numeric data and it will make sense. However, in some colorspaces, certain manipulations need to be cognizant of the colorspace. For example, in the very useful **HSV (Hue, Saturation, Value)** colorspace, one must remember the **H (Hue)** is in fact a measure of *degrees* [0,360] that usually is compressed to [0,180] to fit in a `uchar` character. There is, therefore, no sense in putting a value of 200 in the H channel, as it violates the colorspace definition and leads to unexpected problems. Same goes for linear operations. If for example, we wish to dim an image by 50%, in RGB we simply divide all channels by two; however, in HSV (or L*a*b*, Luv, and so on) one must only perform the division on the **V (Value)** or **L (Luminance)** channels.

The problem becomes much worse when working with non-byte images, such as YUV420 or RGB555 (16-bit colorspaces). These images store pixel values on the *bit* level, not the byte level, compounding data for more than one pixel or one channel in the same byte. For example, an RGB555 pixel is stored in two bytes (16 bits): one bit unused, then five bits for red, five bits for green, and five bits for blue. All kinds of numeric operations (for example, arithmetics) in that case fail, and may cause irreparable corruption to the data.

- **Solution**: Always know the colorspace of the data you process. When reading images from files using `cv::imread`, you may assume they are read in **BGR** order (standard OpenCV pixel data storage). When no colorspace information is available, you may rely on heuristics or test the input. In general, you should be wary of images with only two channels, as they are more than likely a bit-packed colorspace. Images with four channels are usually **ARGB** or **RGBA**, adding an **alpha channel**, and again introduce some uncertainty. Testing for perceptual colorspaces can be done visually, by displaying the channels to the screen. The worst of the bit-packing problem comes from working with image files, memory blocks from external libraries, or sources. Within OpenCV, most of the work is done on single-channel grayscale or BGR data, but when it comes to saving to the file, or preparing an image memory block for use in a different library, then it is important to keep track of colorspace conversions. Remember `cv::imwrite` expects *BGR* data, and not any other format.

- **Accuracy versus speed versus resources (CPU, memory) trade-offs and optimization**: Most of the problems in computer vision have trade-offs between their computation and resource efficiency. Some algorithms are fast because they cache in memory crucial data with a fast lookup efficiency; others may be fast because of a rough approximation they make on the input or output that reduces accuracy. In most cases, one fetching trait comes at the expense of another. Not paying attention to these trade-offs, or paying too much attention to them, can become a problem. A common pitfall for engineers is around matters of **optimization**. There is under-or **over-optimization**, **premature optimization**, unnecessary optimization, and more. When looking to optimize an algorithm, there's a tendency to treat all optimizations as equals, when in fact there is usually just one culprit (code line or method) causing most of the inefficiency. Dealing with algorithmic tradeoff or optimization is mostly a problem of research and development *time*, rather than *result*. Engineers may spend too much or not enough time in optimization, or optimize at the wrong time.

- **Solution**: Know the algorithms before or while employing them. If you choose an algorithm, make sure you have an understanding of its the complexity (runtime and resource) by testing it, or at least by looking at the OpenCV documentation pages. For example, when matching image features, one should know the brute-force matcher `BFMatcher` is often a few orders of magnitude slower than the approximate FLANN-based matcher `FlannBasedMatcher`, especially if preloading and caching the features is possible.

Summary

OpenCV is becoming a mature computer vision library, more than 15 years in the making. During that time, it saw many revolutions happen, both in the computer vision world and in the OpenCV community.

In this chapter, we reviewed OpenCV's past through a practical lens of understanding how to work with it better. We focused on one particular good practice, inspecting the historical OpenCV code to find the origins of an algorithm, in order to make better choices. To cope with the abundance of functionality and features, we also proposed solutions to some common pitfalls in developing computer vision applications with OpenCV.

Further reading

Refer to the following links for more information:

- **OpenCV Change Logs**: https://github.com/opencv/opencv/wiki/ChangeLog
- **OpenCV Meeting notes**: https://github.com/opencv/opencv/wiki/Meeting_notes
- **OpenCV Releases**: https://github.com/opencv/opencv/releases
- **OpenCV Attic Releases**: https://github.com/opencv/opencv_attic/releases
- **Interview with Gary Bradsky, 2011**: https://www.youtube.com/watch?v=bbnftjY-_lE

Other Books You May Enjoy

If you enjoyed this book, you may be interested in these other books by Packt:

Learn OpenCV 4 By Building Projects - Second Edition
David Millán Escrivá, Vinícius G. Mendonça, Prateek Joshi

ISBN: 9781789341225

- Install OpenCV 4 on your operating system
- Create CMake scripts to compile your C++ application
- Understand basic image matrix formats and filters
- Explore segmentation and feature extraction techniques
- Remove backgrounds from static scenes to identify moving objects for surveillance
- Employ various techniques to track objects in a live video
- Work with new OpenCV functions for text detection and recognition with Tesseract
- Get acquainted with important deep learning tools for image classification

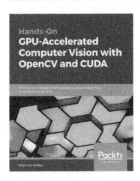

Hands-On GPU-Accelerated Computer Vision with OpenCV and CUDA
Bhaumik Vaidya

ISBN: 9781789348293

- Understand how to access GPU device properties and capabilities from CUDA programs
- Learn how to accelerate searching and sorting algorithms
- Detect shapes such as lines and circles in images
- Explore object tracking and detection with algorithms
- Process videos using different video analysis techniques in Jetson TX1
- Access GPU device properties from the PyCUDA program
- Understand how kernel execution works

Leave a review - let other readers know what you think

Please share your thoughts on this book with others by leaving a review on the site that you bought it from. If you purchased the book from Amazon, please leave us an honest review on this book's Amazon page. This is vital so that other potential readers can see and use your unbiased opinion to make purchasing decisions, we can understand what our customers think about our products, and our authors can see your feedback on the title that they have worked with Packt to create. It will only take a few minutes of your time, but is valuable to other potential customers, our authors, and Packt. Thank you!

Index

Made in the USA
Coppell, TX
10 March 2020